YOUR
LIFE
IN MY
HANDS

'From the very heart of the NHS comes this brilliant insight into the continuing crisis in the health service. Rachel Clarke writes as the accomplished journalist she once was and as the leading junior doctor she now is – writing with humanity and compassion that at times reduced me to tears.'

Jon Snow, *Channel 4 News*

'Eloquent and moving [...] There have been many books written by young doctors, but none comes close to Clarke's in describing the physical and emotional exhaustion, and the intense highs and lows, of working as a hospital doctor. Clarke's description of one of her consultants gently telling a young girl that no more treatment for her leukaemia is possible – that it is time for her to die – will reduce you to tears. [...] Anybody who wants to understand what is happening to the NHS should read this book.'

Henry Marsh, author of *Do No Harm and Admissions*

'A powerful account of life on the NHS frontline. If only Theresa May and Jeremy Hunt could see the passion behind the people in the NHS, they might stop treating them as the enemy, and understand that without them we don't have an NHS worth the name.'

Alastair Campbell

'I absolutely loved it this book. Such an elegant, moving and honest account of life on the frontline. This is mandatory reading for anyone who cares about the NHS. I am very often asked what it's like to be a junior doctor, and I can now direct people to this book. It's so refreshing to see someone tell it exactly as it is.'

Joanna Cannon, author of *The Trouble with Goats and Sheep*

RACHEL CLARKE

YOUR
LIFE
IN MY
HANDS

A JUNIOR DOCTOR'S STORY

metro

Published by Metro Books
an imprint of John Blake Publishing Ltd
3 Bramber Court, 2 Bramber Road,
London W14 9PB, England

www.johnblakebooks.com

www.facebook.com/johnblakebooks ▪
twitter.com/jblakebooks ▪

First published in hardback in 2017
This edition printed in 2017

ISBN: 978 1 78606 8651

British Library Cataloguing-in-Publication Data:

A catalogue record for this book is available from the British Library.

Design by www.envydesign.co.uk

Printed and bound in Great Britain by Clays Ltd, Elcograf S.p.A.

3 5 7 9 10 8 6 4

Papers used by John Blake Publishing are natural, recyclable products made
from wood grown in sustainable forests. The manufacturing processes conform
to the environmental regulations of the country of origin.

Every attempt has been made to contact the relevant copyright-holders,
but some were unobtainable. We would be grateful if the
appropriate people could contact us.

John Blake Publishing is an imprint of Bonnier Publishing
www.bonnierpublishing.com

*To my father – whose kindness and dedication
to his patients I try, every day, to live up to*

Author's note

A note on confidentiality. The stories told here are grounded in my clinical experience, but I have changed a great many of the details to ensure that individuals are so disguised as to be unrecognisable. Occasionally, a story may draw upon a composite of different experiences from different times, to ensure the confidentiality of any individual to whom it refers is protected.

CONTENTS

PROLOGUE ix

CHAPTER 1: WORDS 1

CHAPTER 2: DEEDS 17

CHAPTER 3: EXALTATION 31

CHAPTER 4: BRILLIANCE 45

CHAPTER 5: KINDNESS 61

CHAPTER 6: CALLOUSNESS 75

CHAPTER 7: HAEMORRHAGE 95

CHAPTER 8: MILITANCY 117

CHAPTER 9: OESTROGEN 133

CHAPTER 10: RESILIENCE 151

CHAPTER 11: INSURRECTION 169

CHAPTER 12: WONDER   189

CHAPTER 13: CHEER   207

CHAPTER 14: CANDOUR   217

CHAPTER 15: HAEMOSTASIS   237

CHAPTER 16: HOPE   253

EPILOGUE   273

ACKNOWLEDGEMENTS   279

REFERENCES   283

PROLOGUE

A red dirt road steeped in red dawn light and the faintest mutter of guns. The first refugees, hazy in the distance, slowly bearing down on the town. Women and children leading the retreat, bin bags and mattresses balanced upon heads, babies swaddled tight to adult hips. They crossed a façade of buildings peppered with bullet holes, impassive and mute, looking past us. My cameraman and I couldn't believe our luck. The juxtaposition of gentle morning light with the ugliness of war – it was television gold, and we knew it.

Before I became a doctor, I turned people's lives into films for a living. I was a journalist, producing and directing current-affairs documentaries like this one about the civil war in the Democratic Republic of Congo. It was 2003. The conflict, described by Prime Minister Tony Blair as 'a scar on the conscience of the world', had already claimed 5 million lives, most of which were civilian. Bunia, the battered town into which we'd flown a few days earlier, was widely regarded as the heart of the slaughter. Rape and brutalities were commonplace. Only a month before our arrival, five hundred townsfolk had been butchered by militiamen armed with machetes. The town's makeshift, tented hospital was still filled with amputees, the youngest of whom was seven.

Even as the pace of the displaced began to quicken, and the rumble of guns grew more insistent, I couldn't resist keeping the camera rolling. The crowd began to jog and then to scatter. Bedding and possessions were dumped in the dust, children started to wail. Defeated militiamen now joined the civilians, armed with AK-47s, yet in flight and disarray. As the army from which they fled finally burst through the trees, all at once we came under their incoming fire. The air hummed with bullets. We stampeded for the only safe place in town: the United Nations peacekeepers' compound with six thousand refugees already crammed behind its razor wire.

Inside the UN building, twenty or so journalists now cowered on a concrete floor as gunfire raged around us. Every grenade made the walls shake. We prayed they didn't have mortars. I was certain I'd be raped, then cut to pieces. I wished I knew nothing about Bunian militiamen's preferred modalities of killing. I wondered if the man from Agence France-Presse against whom I was crushed would mind if I held his hand for a moment. I longed to call my parents to tell them that I loved them. Our cameras never stopped rolling.

After four interminable hours, the gunfire finally abated. Casualties now besieged the town's rudimentary hospital. The UN's tented city had swollen by another few hundred refugees. We'd gratefully escaped our concrete bunker but, with night falling and distant guns still rumbling, we had absolutely nowhere safe to go. Every street in town was overrun with militia, so we begged the protection of UN peacekeepers' guns. I lay all night on a plastic sheet beneath the compound's walls, clutching my mosquito net, too scared to close my eyes. Years later, our footage would help successfully prosecute a Congolese warlord in the UN International Criminal Court. But, at the time, filming in Bunia felt less like an achievement than an act of monumental stupidity. I'd been out of my depth, flying blind.

At age twenty-nine, I left my career in television journalism to retrain as a doctor. On swapping current affairs for a caring profession, I imagined I'd put war zones behind me. Yet ironically – given that hospitals are meant to be citadels of healing – the most frightening experience of my professional life was not those hours spent under fire in Congo's killing fields but my first night on call in a UK teaching hospital. Had anyone predicted this at the time, I'd have laughed at their hyperbole. But nothing, it turned out, quite matched for me the terror of being spat out of medical school into a world of blood, pain, distress and dying that I believed I must expertly navigate, while feeling wholly ill-equipped to do so.

My first set of nights loomed like a prison sentence. As a newly minted doctor, I knew twenty-eight causes of pancreatitis, the names of all two hundred and six bones in the human body, the neurophysiology of stress and fear, but not – not even remotely – how to make the emergency decisions that, if I got them wrong, might end up being the death of someone. No one had taught me what to *do* with all my knowledge. I wasn't even sure I could correctly pick out the sick patients from the ones I didn't need to worry about. And yet, in dimly lit wards across the hospital at night, several hundred patients' lives were about to rest, at least initially, in my inexpert hands. I felt like a white-coated fraud.

In an effort to manage my imposter syndrome, I prepared for my nights like a military campaign. My Royal Air Force fighter-pilot husband – a man for whom aerial dogfights in a Tornado F3 barely even quickened the heart rate – advised me that the key, at all costs, was to 'stay frosty'. In a forlorn effort to acquire Dave's elusive inner frostiness, I retreated to what I knew: my textbooks, revising how to manage every life-or-death emergency I could possibly think of until – in my head at least – I was handling them all like George Clooney. I stocked up on Diet Coke, cashew nuts and morale-boosting chocolate bars. I snuck a pocket guide to emergency medicine into the bottom of my rucksack and chose sensible shoes for sprinting to crash calls. And, when I arrived at my first ever hospital handover at 9 p.m., I took custody of my on-call bleep – the electronic pager through which the nurses would spend the night contacting me – with what I hoped looked like battle-weary nonchalance, while secretly wanting to vomit.

The departing house officer handed me a barely legible list of jobs – patients needing cannulas placed in their veins, blood tests or urinary catheters – before fleeing into the night. The medical registrar, the senior doctor to whom I was meant to turn for help should I find myself out of my depth, told me in no uncertain terms that he'd be busy all night in A&E, but to bleep him if I absolutely had to. The other doctors dispersed, all looking grimly competent.

Bleep. It started. Nurses calling me about the patients on their wards with racing hearts, plummeting blood pressure or worryingly low levels of oxygen. Bleep. They all wanted me to come immediately to assess their patients. But, even as I tried to answer the first bleep, the second and third were lighting up my pager.

'For God's sake,' I wanted to tell them, 'will you please bleep somebody else, because I'm not a doctor, not even remotely?'

There was, of course, nobody else. I was alone at the start of my shift, wanting to cry, with a jobs list already covering two pages.

Mr Frith was one of the first patients I reviewed that night. All his numbers, rattled off by a nurse on the end of a phone, were bad. Heart too fast, blood pressure too low, oxygen levels barely compatible with consciousness. Even I knew enough to rush straight to his bedside. He lay alone in the semi-darkness – eyes rolling wildly, breaths coming in short fitful gasps, lips clearly blue – trying to communicate in fractured monosyllables. A retired linguist in his early seventies, he had been admitted to hospital some ten days previously with a mild heart attack that had been complicated by a pneumonia picked up in hospital. All this was eminently reversible. There was no reason why he should not be able to return safely home to his wife of forty years. But, right now, he looked deathly. His nurse was nowhere to be seen.

I was certain that something was terribly wrong, despite not being able to name it. The sounds in his chest, magnified by my stethoscope, were like nothing I had heard before. A grinding and rattling more mechanical than human, ugly and wrong. I guessed that Mr Frith's heart was failing, causing fluid to swamp and overwhelm his lungs. If I was right, he was drowning before my eyes.

Sick with dread, I fumbled to put an oxygen mask over his stubble and ran to the nurses' station to try to find his nurse.

'Who's looking after Mr Frith, please?' I asked the three nurses sitting behind the desk.

'Who?' said one of them. 'Frith? Oh, you mean Bed 4. Miriam. She's on a break.'

'Well – please could you help me?' I asked, far too hesitantly.

'No. He's not my patient.'

'I – I think I need help.'

'Well, you need to call your boss, then, don't you?'

So I did. I did not know what else to do. I bleeped the registrar once, twice, multiple times. But my calls to his bleep went unanswered. I had no nurse, no senior doctor to help me, and a patient on the brink of death. In sheer desperation, I ran down seven flights of stairs to the Emergency Department to try to physically manhandle my missing senior doctor up to my patient's bedside. It was precisely at that moment, while I was frantically scouring A&E for help, that Mr Frith's heart stopped beating.

Everything I did that night was wrong, starting with my pitiful meekness. There is a code no one teaches you at medical school, a certain way of getting things done. When you find a patient *in extremis*, for example, you shout as loudly as you can from the bedside, 'I need some help, please' and four of five staff will instantly materialise. Better yet – it is not rocket science – you simply press the red emergency button beside every patient's bed and a wardful of staff will rush to your aid. Most effectively, if you think your patient is 'peri-arrest' – on the brink of suffering a cardiac arrest – you put out a crash call via the hospital switchboard and in moments a crack squad of resuscitation experts should rally to the bedside.

I violated the code. I was timid and polite when I should have been assertive. I gave the nurses none of the right cues, and I lacked the practical knowledge that a crash call is appropriate for anyone you think is about to fall off a cliff, not only those who have already done so. Perhaps it is the fear of being seen to do the wrong thing – the embarrassment of mistaking a patient's minor unwellness for a full-blown emergency – that holds young doctors back from calling the cavalry. This reticence has the potential to cost patients their lives.

That night, when the crash call came, I was the most junior member of the crash team, and also the farthest away from Mr Frith's bedside. I was still in A&E, searching in vain for my registrar. The four shrill bleeps that herald an arrest call are deliberately designed to stop you in your tracks, focusing your attention on the crackling, barely audible telephonist's voice instructing you where to assemble.

'Adult arrest call. Adult arrest call. Adult crash team to Level 7. I repeat, Level 7.'

In this case, I already knew exactly where to head. With sick clarity, I confronted the fact that I had physically abandoned my patient just before his heart has stopped beating. Horrified, wishing it were anyone but him, I ran back up the seven flights of stairs just in time to hear the consultant leading the team ask, 'Who the hell is this "Clarke" who last saw the patient?'

'It was me,' I muttered, barely audibly, as all eyes turned on me.

My entry in the patient's notes, now in the hands of the consultant, was hastily scrawled and abruptly curtailed by my panicked departure. It must have looked woefully inadequate.

'I'm sorry,' I whispered, burning with shame. 'I didn't know what to do. I went to get help.'

The registrar who had failed to answer my bleeps stood silently beside the consultant, eyeballing me defiantly. I did not dare mention his involvement – or, rather, the lack of it.

Mr Frith had been submerged beneath wires, tubes and defibrillator leads. The team had already given intravenous drugs to take the pressure off the heart and lungs. The chest compressions were brutal but effective and the first electric shock brought his heart leaping back into a normal rhythm. He started to pink up and open his eyes, blooming back to life. I wanted to weep with relief and gratitude. It was slick, textbook, a rare perfect crash call – except for the fact, so it seemed to me, that, had a better doctor done a better job earlier, it might have been entirely preventable.

As the team busied themselves transferring Mr Frith to the intensive care unit, I had never felt more incompetent. The shame and guilt made me want to quit medicine, barely before I'd begun.

—/\ʅ—

Britain's junior doctors are often described by politicians as the 'backbone of the NHS', the workhorses whose slog – alongside that of the nurses, paramedics and all the other allied health professionals hard at work on the front line – keeps the NHS alive. But our first steps onto a hospital ward, heads typically crammed with facts but little life experience, can be steeped in isolation and hidden fears. In a profession that should be defined by compassion, growing a backbone can be brutal.

Perhaps in medicine there is no way to avoid toughening up the hard way, through repeated exposure to life-or-death situations until your skills, expertise and the thickness of your skin can finally, just about, handle them. But what if this process takes place in a health service so overstretched and understaffed that its doctors, along with everyone else, feel they are routinely scrabbling against impossible odds merely to keep their patients safe, let alone dispense compassion and exemplary care? So that – even if a young doctor has acquired the experience to handle anything medicine can throw at them – they feel increasingly paralysed as a practitioner by a system that is crumbling and being rationed around them?

In 2016, these questions were thrown into sharp relief by the dispute between junior doctors and the government over our terms and conditions of work. The conflict mobilised thousands of medics like me out on strike when we should have been looking after our patients. It ignited a war of words so toxic between government and doctors that their corrosive legacy will take years to repair. It drove many doctors, some of them my friends, to quit the NHS in unprecedented numbers. And ultimately, after months of conflict, it led to what were perhaps the saddest two days in NHS history: the country's first ever all-out doctors' strike, with complete withdrawal of junior doctor care. There were no winners during the junior doctor saga, yet no one lost as much as our patients.

Throughout the dispute, according to government press officers, the rage, upheaval and bitterness centred on one issue alone: junior doctors' refusal to give up their Saturday overtime. Our intractability made it impossible, they claimed, for former Prime Minister David Cameron to deliver on his general-election pledge to give the electorate a 'truly seven-day NHS'. And the stakes could not have been higher. According to the Secretary of State for Health, Jeremy Hunt, every year in the UK eleven thousand people were losing their lives unnecessarily because too few doctors worked at the weekend.

Hunt's line was powerful, emotive stuff. While the doctor in me flinched at each insinuation, my journalistic self recognised a shrewd and effective political strategy. I'd learned about spin from the best. Some eighteen years earlier, as a fresh-faced TV researcher on Jonathan Dimbleby's ITV politics show, I'd helped construct the interviews that Labour's shrewdest spin doctors, Alastair Campbell and Peter Mandelson, had done their utmost to control. We interviewed Tony Blair a week or so before his 1997 general election victory. I remember sitting hunched on the floor over a tiny screen, jotting down soundbites to use in our ad break, when a presence loomed above me. 'I wouldn't bother wasting time on that,' Campbell said, grinning mirthlessly. 'Your boy won't get anything from mine.' He was absolutely right. We didn't.

Using fear to build political capital is a tactic as old as politics. All that was new on this occasion was the target – not foreigners, immigrants, scroungers or Muslims, but the medical profession itself. In 2015, the new majority Conservative government, unshackled at last from its Liberal Democrat coalition partners, had the NHS medical wage bill in its sights. Junior doctors, consultants and general practitioners all faced a renegotiation of their contracts and

– perhaps assuming 'junior' meant weak – Jeremy Hunt had decided to press ahead initially with ours.

The strategy was simple. First, put the fear of God into people by claiming that eleven thousand patients will die annually at weekends because doctors are too lazy or greedy to work them. Next, allay the fears you've just stoked so meticulously by promising the solution: the seven-day services the country currently lacks. Finally – and most audaciously of all – insist that a 'cost-neutral' renegotiation of the junior doctor contract will deliver said seven-day NHS. The small matter of more staff and more funds being an obvious prerequisite for improved front-line services was conveniently omitted from the government's narrative. Junior doctors, not the Treasury, were the barrier to safe weekends.

When the dispute began, I had been a journalist for ten years and a hospital doctor for another six, long enough to evolve from nervous ward ingénue into an experienced and valued member of my hospital's front line. Year on year, I had witnessed the human impact of funding cuts: patients waiting longer and longer for treatment, doctors quietly disappearing from the rotas as recruitment became ever more problematic. Still, my spirits were high. With six years of medicine and numerous postgraduate exams under my belt, I was ready and eager to embark upon my chosen speciality of palliative care. The distressing, sometimes haunting, challenges of helping patients at the end of life to live as fully and richly as possible had touched something deep within me. Not once had I ever predicted junior doctors being targeted by the Number 10 spin machine, or how destructive and demoralising Downing Street's crosshairs would be.

Through the dual perspectives of doctor and journalist, I

would look on, aghast, as the government ran rings round the doctors' trade union, the British Medical Association (BMA). But what was it really about? Beneath the slews of accusation and recrimination, what actually drove a generation of young doctors to abandon their patients and go out on strike? Even Jeremy Hunt could not in all seriousness have believed we did it merely to preserve our Saturday pay rates. This was a complex, nuanced dispute in which concerns surrounding pay, patient safety, staffing levels and morale were inextricably linked. Even the phrase 'junior doctor' glossed over the huge variety of individuals who were doctors in training, ranging from single twenty-three-year-olds, fresh out of medical school, to mothers and fathers in their late thirties or forties, experienced doctors on the brink of becoming specialist consultants.

For me, the junior doctor dispute – a pivotal moment in NHS history – was deeply embedded in the wider health of the modern NHS. Strikes were drastic, a last resort. This was the first time that young doctors had abandoned their patients in over forty years, and we would do so on eight different days. Fundamentally, going on strike, for the majority of us, was an act of desperation born out of our lived experience of the NHS front line. Ours is a supremely under-doctored health service. There is simply not the money to employ enough doctors. Statistics from the Organisation for Economic Cooperation and Development (OECD) show we have only 2.8 practising doctors per 1,000 heads of population, fewer than almost any country in Europe, including Poland, Latvia and Lithuania. In Germany, by contrast, that figure is 4.1 doctors, and in Greece it is 6.3 doctors.[1]

What that translates into for a junior doctor is understaffing that is at best exhausting, at worst soul-destroying. I can't count the number of times I've been left to shoulder two doctors' jobs when there's a gap – a missing doctor – in my junior doctor rota. Those 'rota gap' shifts are grim, thankless exercises in firefighting, and they are becoming increasingly prevalent. When I first qualified in 2009, they were mercifully rare, but these days they feel like the norm. We dread them and, perhaps more pertinently, so should our patients. Because, no matter how finely honed a doctor's acute resuscitation skills, we cannot be in two places at once. When understaffing has forced one doctor to carry two doctors' crash bleeps, the risks of a patient slipping through the cracks have clearly just doubled: too few doctors threatens lives.

A further casualty of doctor overstretch is the one that compelled us into medicine in the first place – and the one we can least afford to lose – our kindness. People say the NHS runs only on the goodwill of its staff: the doctors, nurses and allied healthcare professionals who are willing to go the extra mile not for money, or thanks, or praise, or self-promotion, but for the intrinsic rewards of helping a patient. If that's right, then working conditions that grind away relentlessly at our capacity for kindness threaten the survival of the NHS itself. More immediately, they are the enemy of the doctor–patient relationship. When doctors are too few on the ground, when you haven't a chance of managing your workload in the time you are meant to be at work, then every precious second is spent scrabbling merely to keep your patients safe. Talking to patients and their relatives is inevitably left until last. The humanity of a conversation has become a luxury your conditions of work deny. Doctors are turned into hardened machines, patients are left in the dark. You know it's wrong, you hate what you've become, and now perhaps you consider quitting the profession you once loved with all your soul.

We've already reached this point. The question that led me, heavy-hearted, full of doubt, to the picket lines in 2016 was not 'How can I protect my Saturday overtime?' but, 'How can I continue to conduct myself with compassion and humanity in an NHS that is falling apart?' Like so many of my fellow junior doctors, I knew I had nothing more to give. A contract that stretched us even more sparsely across seven days, not five, would, I had no doubt, be the breaking of me.

This is a book about working within the institution in which I was born, gave birth and will probably die, provided it still exists then. An NHS doctor saved the life of my newborn son and, as I write, an NHS oncology team is attempting to prevent cancer from taking the life of my father. Like so many other families in Britain, the members of mine have experienced some of the most joyous, momentous, harrowing and moving moments of our lives within Britain's National Health Service. And, like so many other NHS doctors, nurses, midwives, porters, physiotherapists, radiographers, pharmacists and dieticians, when it comes to the institution I professionally serve, I am unashamedly partisan. That we are willing, collectively, to pay sufficient tax to ensure no one is denied the healthcare they need because they cannot afford it makes me feel genuinely proud to be British. And providing my patients with cradle-to-grave NHS care based on that clinical need, not ability to pay, is my absolute joy and privilege.

Every day, I bear witness to ordinary NHS staff going about

their extraordinary work – dressing the wounds, breaking the bad news, holding the hands, wiping the excrement, restarting the stalled hearts, smoothing the eyelids of the newly dead – with the utmost compassion and care. I love my job. I could not imagine a more rewarding and fulfilling career than medicine. But I am afraid we may have reached the point at which the NHS's greatest asset – its staff – has become terminally exhausted. The goodwill and kindness without which the NHS will not survive are being inexorably squeezed out by underfunding, understaffing and the ever more unrealistic demands placed upon a floundering workforce. This is the untold story of the challenges of trying to stay kind while practising on an overstretched NHS front line.

CHAPTER 1

WORDS

Four days before the 1997 general election that swept Tony Blair to a historic victory, the then Prime Minister, John Major, was trapped in a chauffeur-driven car in central London gridlock. At 1 p.m. precisely, he was meant to be interviewed on live national television. It was 12.50 p.m. and, under unseasonably warm April skies, temperatures in the TV studio were rising.

'I don't give a fuck how bad the traffic is. Get the fucking Prime Minister here now or we're not going to have a fucking programme, do you fucking understand?'

The question was directed at me, the most junior researcher on ITV's *Jonathan Dimbleby* programme. I stared aghast at my editor, feeling solely responsible for the capital's congested streets, wishing I could somehow pluck the Prime Minister from his immobilised vehicle and magic him into the studio. I was twenty-three, underconfident, convinced that everything was probably my fault, London traffic included.

The editor stared me down with contempt. 'Go and wait for him outside. And for fuck's sake get him here the second he arrives, do you fucking understand?'

At 12.58 p.m., a shiny black car hastily pulled up outside the entrance to the studios. I hustled John Major inside. As we weaved through the corridors to the back of the live studio, he asked me a pertinent question:

'Do you have a water closet?'

I suppose he'd been stuck in a traffic jam for God knows how long. His bladder was probably bursting. But, at the time, overwhelmed with stress and anxiety, I simply couldn't compute what this quaint phrase meant. Water closet? I had absolutely no idea what the Prime Minister was asking me. All I knew was that, if I didn't get him into the studio by 1 p.m., my short-lived career in television was over.

'W-water closet? I'm sorry, Prime Minister, I – I'm afraid we don't have one.'

With a thunderous look and a half-suppressed expletive, he allowed me nonetheless to lead him straight onto the set to begin his hour-long live interview. Seconds before one o'clock, the first few bars of our theme tune began. As I exhaled in relief, it suddenly dawned on me that all he'd wanted was an emergency stop at a WC, a urinal. Words. The power of an ill-chosen phrase. I wondered whether his straining bladder would put him off his interview.

—⁄\⁄—

On 16 July 2015, the Health Secretary went to war. For a former PR man turned politician, Jeremy Hunt's weapon of choice would always be words – deployed, on this occasion, with explosive aplomb. Whereas John Major came unstuck with a casual anachronism, the speech Hunt gave at a health think tank, the King's Fund, that morning appeared precisely calculated to infuriate doctors by casting aspersions on their sense of vocation.

Patients were dying unnecessarily in our hospitals, Hunt claimed, because consultants refused to work weekends, causing an excess of deaths at the weekend. There were six thousand avoidable fatalities a year, to be precise – death on a massive scale.[2] Later, he would adjust this figure upwards to eleven thousand weekend deaths a year, but even the more conservative estimate sounded wholly indefensible. 'When you turn medicine into a Monday-to-Friday profession,' he told BBC Radio 4's *Today* programme that morning, 'you end up with catastrophic consequences.'[3] Seven-day working, he insisted, should be 'part of the vocation of medicine – which is about being there for your patients'. The implication was clear. Doctors lacked the professionalism and dedication to their patients to give up their Saturdays and Sundays.

The speech had a midnight embargo, ensuring Hunt dominated most of the next day's front pages. I first learned of his attack at 4 o'clock that morning – the hazard of having a four-year old in the house with bladder issues of her own. Once I'd tucked up my daughter in her bed, I committed the nocturnal sin of glancing at the news on my smartphone. An error. Though Hunt had targeted on this occasion not junior doctors but our consultant colleagues, within moments I was incandescent.

The health secretary's speech implied that you were 15 per cent more likely to die at the weekend – the so-called 'weekend effect' – because consultants were exploiting a contractual loophole that enabled them to 'opt out' of weekend working in NHS hospitals. Instead, they would offer themselves back to their hospitals as locum doctors, private contractors whose extortionate weekend rates – up to £200 an hour – were crippling NHS finances. Hunt contrasted these avaricious consultants with their altruistic betters, the ones who every weekend would, 'go into the hospital to see their patients, driven by professionalism and goodwill, but in many cases with no thanks or recognition'.

Still groggy, initially I was unable to decipher these allegations. For six years as a junior doctor, I'd worked weekends in multiple specialities, across multiple hospitals, typically one a month. Accident and Emergency, General Surgery, Cardiology, Acute General Medicine, Gastroenterology – you name it, I'd done it. But one thing united my one in four weekends. During every one, a consultant had been there by my side to lead a morning ward round on both Saturday and Sunday. For the rest of the day, they were never more than a phone call away. And, when working nights, if required, I could call my consultant at any hour. Should their expertise be needed, they would come straight back to the hospital. Indeed, from what I'd observed, most consultants' weekends on call began on Friday evening and stretched a full sixty hours, without a break, all the way to Monday morning.

So on this, day one of the NHS strike year, just what was Hunt's game? The picture he painted of senior medics as opt-out dilettantes was so wildly at odds with my own experience, I stared nonplussed at the screen. Then it clicked. This was the classic politician's tack of conflating the actual with the hypothetical to construct a superficially watertight case. Consultants did indeed have a weekend opt-out in their contract – but for elective, not emergency care. They could choose to opt out of only non-essential work such as planned operations or extra weekend outpatient clinics. Their weekends 'on call' – those spent looking after their existing inpatients and any new admissions – were, in almost all cases, obligatory. Hunt had glossed over this crucial difference to convey a lurid depiction of mass avoidable death for which consultants were to blame. Yet the ones I'd worked with at weekends had been there not as locums, but as NHS employees, already providing seven-day care.

Having stoked our fears with his erroneous depiction of consultant weekend slackers, Hunt simultaneously set out to reassure us. As a result of contractual changes he would impose upon doctors – through brute force if necessary – he would cure the problem he'd just fabricated: 'by the end of the Parliament, I expect the majority of hospital doctors to be on seven-day contracts'. He issued the doctors' trade union, the BMA, with a six-week ultimatum: if it could not negotiate a new consultant contract with Hunt in that time, its members would face an imposed one.

It was a beautiful instance of political doctoring. Take some truth, sprinkle in some non-truths, insinuate, cast aspersions and manipulate the data to ensure your argument, however tenuously rooted in fact, guarantees the superficial headlines you seek.

For the rest of the night, I seethed in silent fury. The notion that any of us, junior or senior, exploited weekend opt-outs for financial gain was so deeply offensive it rendered sleep impossible. Doctors can be many things – pompous, opinionated, arrogant, self-righteous – but I've yet to meet a single one who joined the NHS because they planned to get rich quick. If it was megabucks that drove us, we'd have chosen the City, not medicine. Way more cash, way less bodily fluid – or so one would hope.

My rage was ignited only in part by the insinuations against my senior colleagues. Almost more infuriating was the brazen spinning – the cynical distortion of the facts to try to turn public opinion against doctors and their union. Could there be a more effective way to win an industrial dispute than to bathe it in avoidable bloodshed? In Hunt's narrative, the price of the BMA's refusal to capitulate was nothing less than six thousand lives a year. How could consultants live with the sheer quantity of blood on their hands? How could the public not turn against them? It was disingenuous, deceptive and utterly brilliant – a public-relations masterstroke.

The morning Hunt's speech went public, I arrived at my hospital's doctors' mess, groggy with sleeplessness and still fuming. Even at the best of times, doctors' messes invariably live up to their name. At any time their grotty sofas may be strewn with takeaway detritus, abandoned scrubs, grubby hospital blankets, long-lost stethoscopes, perhaps a random rotting trainer. I have encountered doctors' messes where cockroaches infest the floorboards, sidling out to keep you company on night shifts. Occasionally in the early hours I have seen a rat peep down from the vents in the ceiling. Glamorous the doctors' mess is not. But, on the morning of 16 July, the filthiness was primarily verbal. Five or six acute medical teams were hunched over their lists of inpatients, ostensibly discussing the day's issues and concerns before commencing their morning ward rounds. Except on this occasion the talk was all Jeremy. And, when I say 'talk', I mean four-letter, no-holds-barred obscenities. This was platinum-level vitriol, Old Testament-style ferocity, from consultants and juniors alike.

What struck me, as we lambasted the Health Secretary, was the unusual sense of unity between seniors and juniors, indivisible under fire. Hunt may have anticipated – even relished – the anger his speech would unleash, but the solidarity would later prove to have caught him unawares. Typically, doctors are notoriously tribal. Medics snipe at surgeons, seniors at juniors, and every medical speciality secretly believes that its is superior to the others. Today, though, we were all just doctors. An angry, aggrieved, cohesive whole. Something in me had shifted, a boundary had been breached, and I sensed I wasn't alone.

Some two years earlier, at four o'clock one Sunday morning, a weekend night shift got the better of me.

Amid the standard torrent of bleeps from the nurses summoning me from one patient's bedside to another, I'd answered a call from the cancer ward. Unusually, a patient had arrived by ambulance in the middle of the night, requiring admission for end-of-life care. Such admissions tend to be planned in advance, ensuring dying patients are not subjected to gruelling journeys during antisocial hours. No one was quite sure why this patient had turned up when she did.

'Of course,' I chirped brightly, 'I'll come right away,' while inwardly cursing the miserable luck of having to admit a patient for palliation during the early hours of the morning. It's not that I have no heart whatsoever, but that nocturnal firefighting for fourteen or fifteen hours straight leaves time and energy only for emergencies. When one doctor is on call for several hundred patients scattered up and down the hospital, reaching those with strokes, bleeds, heart attacks and life-threatening sepsis before they come to further harm requires ruthless, robotic efficiency. Tender loving care is all but ripped out of hospitals at night by the shoestring staffing. Now, in the midst of the usual mêlée, a patient had arrived who was actively dying. They'd need hospice-style care – limitless compassion, patience and time – that was simply not in my power to give, enslaved as I was to my incessant pager.

Before entering the patient's room, I asked the nurses to hold my bleep. 'Please only interrupt me for crash calls and emergencies,' I asked, anticipating finding someone in uncontrolled pain, potentially facing the end of her life with neither dignity nor solace.

Instead, the room was perfectly silent. Various family members obscured the patient, crouched like supplicants around the bedside, shoulders heaving with inaudible sobs. A mother, father, sister, brother and, as they drew back, the patient herself, a young woman in her early twenties. I felt more an intruder than a healer, invading collective grief as thick as blood. The family turned to me as one, eyes bright with tears and the expectation that I could give them something, anything. In one glance, I knew I could not. My patient had end-stage cervical cancer. Too young to be approaching death, she looked gaunt, defeated, as exhausted by the effort of remaining alive as it is possible to be while still living. Her eyes met mine. Not once before had I seen anyone so tired, so tenuously connected to life. Bleached and waxen, she was as insubstantial as air. I knew she knew as clearly as I did that she was dying. Words were superfluous; her look said it all.

Anticipating the effort it would take her to speak, I too crouched down low by her bedside, gently taking her hand.

'My name is Rachel,' I said. 'I'm your doctor and I'm here to help you. It's Sarah, isn't it? Please tell me, if you can, how you are. And how I can help you.'

Slowly, as if summoning all remaining strength, she shook her head imperceptibly. Then, a barely audible whisper. 'You can't.'

I felt redundant, incapable, too inept to make things better.

'Are you in any pain?' I asked quietly. Another faint shake of her head. 'Is there anything making you uncomfortable?' Another. 'Is there anything you need me to do?' Another.

She allowed me to conduct the briefest, most cursory version of an examination I felt I could safely manage. Cancer had stripped her to skin and bone and I knew any movement of her uncushioned frame might cause her unnecessary pain. Her breathing was shallow and rattled. Her heart murmured in between beats as it worked above the odds to keep her blood in motion. Her belly, though grossly swollen with fluid from the cancer, was not unbearably tense. Her skin was intact, her peripheries warm. I found nothing requiring immediate intervention.

As patients approach the end of life, the same symptoms tend to prevail. Pain, of course, often predominates but, in a great many cases, modern medicine has found ever more ingenious ways to control even the most intractable of pains. Breathlessness, too, is common, as lungs fill with fluid, tumour or infection. Managing agitation, anxiety and fear is the third great challenge in palliative care, since the so-called 'anxiolytics' – anxiety-lulling drugs – can also, in high doses, leave patients too drowsy to be fully aware of their surroundings.

My patient appeared neither anxious nor in pain. Still, I needed to make sure. I asked her directly, 'Sarah, are you frightened?' Another minuscule shake of the head. I wondered whether overwhelming fatigue had obliterated any feelings of fear. Perhaps she had come to see death as a release from the ordeal – the sheer slog – of still living. Though her death was clearly imminent, for now she appeared free from distressing symptoms. I asked her if she was willing for me to talk to her family and, with her murmured assent, we adjourned to a typically tiny NHS relatives' room.

My patient, at age twenty-four, had lived with her cancer for over a year. Radical, disfiguring surgery had failed to eradicate the tumour, which, it later transpired, had already infiltrated distant parts of her body. Though chemotherapy had given her extra time, it had offered no prospect of cure. Her mother, impassive, led the discussion, while her two siblings cried with heads bowed, and her father faced the wall, looking away from me. A third sibling was abroad in South America, and Sarah's mother said he would drop everything to come home immediately if there was any danger of Sarah dying.

Doctors try to avoid rash prognostication. If we cannot judge accurately someone's life expectancy – and all too often we can't – we are loath to offer what may prove to be misleading speculation. Junior doctors in particular, lacking the years of experience that hone our older colleagues' instincts for a patient's survival, are acutely conscious of our limitations. I was very junior, only four years into my training. But it was two or three in the morning, and Sarah's mother had asked a simple but important question. Should her son catch the first flight home?

I didn't have to give an honest answer. I could have fudged it, exploited my inexperience to defer a difficult conversation until my more erudite colleagues arrived in the morning. But that felt like the coward's option. Incapable though I was of giving any consolation, at least I could give them the truth. So, after important caveats about the challenges of making accurate prognoses, I said that, yes, Sarah's brother should catch the first plane he could, because his sister was very, very unwell. It was possible she could die very soon. Indeed, I would not be surprised if she failed to survive the next few days.

Time hung still for a moment, then the room reverberated with grief. Shrieking, sobbing, a family howled its despair. Sarah's father punched the wall over and over, moaning and shaking his head. I sat stricken with horror at the emotion I'd unleashed. He turned to face me, almost snarling with anger.

'You will not dope her up. You won't take her away from us. I will not allow you to drug her. I swear to God, I will kill you if you drug her.'

The rest of the family turned on him.

'Dad,' shouted the sister, 'the doctor's not going to drug her up. She just wants to make sure she's comfortable.'

The father responded by pounding fist against brick more aggressively. His wife screamed at him to stop. As accusations flew back and forth between family members, I felt like a crumb in a maelstrom. I knew it was cancer, not me, that had ripped their world to bits, but that didn't stop me feeling responsible. Trying to give them time to assimilate the prognosis, I retreated outside to write in the patient's notes. Perhaps I was trying to hide.

On returning, I found rage had subsided into slumped

resignation. Still Sarah's father wouldn't look me in the eye, but now he wept quiet tears with the rest of the family. I talked about the delicate balance between minimising distressing symptoms and ensuring a patient remained as alert as possible. How my overriding priority was Sarah's comfort. That I would strive, I promised, to ensure the end of her life was the best it could be. We discussed the manner in which the next hours and days might unfold. Finally, words ran dry.

On the brink of departing, I found my hand hovering uncertainly above the door handle. I had decimated this exceptionally devoted family and I wanted, I think, to atone for this.

'I – I hope you don't mind,' I said to Sarah's mother. 'I'd like to say something to you before I leave.'

She stood up and we confronted each other. As I spoke, slightly nervously, light-headed with the risk of it, her eyes never left mine.

'When I first arrived in Sarah's room tonight, I saw two things. First, I saw a patient who was as ill as it is possible for someone to be. You know I didn't need to be a doctor to see how unwell your daughter was. But I saw something else as well. I saw someone who was surrounded by love. You were all there, and you were giving her what she needed more than anything. You were surrounding her with love. I've seen many people die alone. But Sarah is not. She knows she is loved. Because of you.'

It could have been mawkish, crassly inappropriate. But it was, undeniably, true. I have held the hands of too many elderly, forgotten patients, sole witness to their final exhalation in the absence of family and friends. That an entire lifetime can be reduced to this – an end so inconsequential that not one person mourns or even notices – never fails to appal me. Sarah's mother, to my surprise, stepped forwards and embraced me, tears streaming as she thanked me.

I was spent. I left before I too started crying.

At the nurses' station, the list of new jobs I'd accrued since depositing my bleep covered most of an A4 sheet of paper. My heart sank. I'd be playing catch-up all night. As if on cue, my crash bleep crackled into life. 'Adult cardiac arrest team. Adult cardiac arrest team. Ward 6A. Crash call, ward 6A.' The Nights God had decided to play dirty. 'Aw, I was going to make you a cup of tea after that,' said the night sister kindly as I ran, cursing inwardly, down the corridor.

Around this time, the Medical Director of NHS England, a heart surgeon called Professor Sir Bruce Keogh, was starting to make waves in the media with his talk of an important new mission, a 'seven-day' NHS. Only that weekend, the papers were full of his quotes, each glaringly omitting to mention how anyone would actually pay for his visionary new seven-day service.

Several hours, the crash call and a small mountain of jobs after my encounter with Sarah, I paused for a few minutes to slurp caffeine in Diet Coke form, my drug of choice on night shifts. I glanced at one of the headlines about Keogh and something in me snapped. Only an NHS apparatchik singularly disconnected from the overstretched NHS front line could possibly push for seven-day services in the absence of seven-day funding. In five minutes, through a haze of rage, I found I'd hammered out a draft of a letter to a national newspaper. Over the coming weeks and months, I weighed carefully whether or not to submit the letter for publication.

On balance, I decided that highlighting my concerns about the potential costs to patients of an unfunded expansion of services was not only defensible but necessary, since my first duty as a doctor was always to act in the best interests of my patients. The letter read:

Dear Sir,

It is 4 a.m. and I am a junior doctor writing from a weekend night shift at a respected teaching hospital. I have run arrest calls, treated life-threatening bleeding and sepsis, held the hand of a young woman dying of cancer, tried to comfort her family, scuttled down miles of dim corridors occasionally wanting to sob with exhaustion, forgotten to eat, forgotten to drink, drawn on every fibre of strength I possess to keep dispensing compassion, kindness and, above all, good medicine to my patients this never-ending night.

And right now, huddled over a Diet Coke and a laptop, I am struck by the utter absurdity of the fantasy politics played by Professor Sir Bruce Keogh, government and opposition alike that a seven-day NHS is possible without an appropriate increase in funding.

Do they really not know how desperately thinly we are stretched? I don't think so. The maths is simple. Pretending that the NHS can provide a seven-day weekday service without funding it isn't just disingenuous, it is downright dangerous for patients.

Yours sincerely,

Dr Rachel Clarke

I wouldn't know it for many months, but this letter, when published – to the considerable ire of the hospital I worked in – framed the essence of many junior doctors' opposition to Jeremy Hunt's seven-day crusade. It certainly wasn't hostility to better weekend services *per se*. Although the evidence on the 'weekend effect' was debatable – some studies demonstrating an increase in deaths at the weekend, others showing no increase in weekend mortality – the fact remained for me that I would dearly love weekends to be better resourced in my hospital. Junior doctors know better than anyone that, while some parts of the hospital, such as Accident and Emergency, are equally staffed every day of the week, most hospital inpatients are looked after by a skeleton crew of doctors whose main objective is to attempt to keep their patients safe until Monday morning, when full routine services resume. Patients can sit in a two-day limbo, denied non-urgent scans and other investigations through lack of weekend capacity.

But where we differed from the politicians was in the knowledge that beefed-up weekend services could not be manufactured from spin alone. They needed resourcing, they needed staffing. From the front line, it was perfectly clear that the primary barrier to better weekends was not contractual change in our terms of employment but the finite number of NHS doctors, nurses and other allied health professionals. Without additional medics, there were only two ways to roster more of us at weekends: either take us away from our patients Monday to Friday, or force us to work longer overall hours. I failed to see how either option could possibly have patient safety at its core.

At ten o'clock that morning, punch-drunk with fatigue, I

finally set off home. Driving post-nights can be fraught. Several junior doctors in the UK have died in recent years after falling asleep at the wheel. Indeed, the journey home after my first ever Easter weekend on call was very nearly the death of me. In the split second during which my eyelids drooped, I crashed my car headlong into a stationary vehicle, somehow emerging unscathed from the wreckage. On the morning after meeting Sarah, however, I pulled over for a different reason. Not because my eyes were closing but because, without warning, I'd found myself blinded by tears. I hadn't cried all night but now, in a dual carriageway lay-by, still dressed in trainers and my stinking scrubs, I thought I'd never stop.

She was more than a decade younger than I was, with a cancer that had consumed her before her parents' eyes. Attempting to help them that night, while keeping all my other patients safe, had required enormous stamina, yet failing to do so had not been an option: it would have felt inhuman. And this was nothing special. This was routine, everyday stuff. This – in one night – was the NHS front line. Threadbare, scrappy, perilously understaffed, decent, bloody-minded, barely held together by the indefatigable legions of nurses, doctors and allied health professionals not asking for thanks or expecting recognition, but simply getting on with it, heads down. A thousand such scenarios played out across our hospitals day in, day out, up and down the country.

Against this backdrop, on 16 July 2015, Jeremy Hunt chose to take an axe to doctors' efforts at caring. He portrayed us, quite deliberately, as lazy and grasping. It was as calculated as it was aggressive.

Smarting, astonished, furious, the front line was about to fight back.

CHAPTER 2

DEEDS

Until the summer of 2015, I was the kind of social media ingénue who befriended only actual friends on Facebook, followed approximately three people on Twitter, regarded what teenagers got up to on Snapchat as apocalyptically terrifying (would my children really be sexting within the decade?) and certainly didn't know what a 'meme' was. Whenever a photo of a cute cat appeared on my Facebook timeline, inexplicably 'liked' by 2.3 million people, my overwhelming emotion was exasperation. As for WhatsApp, that sounded sinister – a bit too much like Snapchat for my taste.

But, the weekend immediately after Jeremy Hunt's opening salvo against doctors, even a crusty old Luddite like me would feel energised by the power of social media. An anonymous junior doctor devised a consummately modern response to Jeremy Hunt's claims about doctors not working weekends: a hashtag. Due to spend thirteen hours at work each day on the Friday, Saturday and Sunday immediately after Hunt gave his speech, the doctor in question coined the perfect slogan. It simply read: #ImInWorkJeremy.

The doctor launched his campaign on the Friday evening. Within hours, Twitter and Facebook were overwhelmed with #ImInWorkJeremy selfies from junior doctors, consultants, nurses and paramedics at work in hospitals and general practices all over the UK. An impromptu eruption of grass-roots defiance, this was NHS staff nationwide giving a collective two fingers to a Health Secretary who had presumed to scare the unsuspecting public with the erroneous notion that the NHS wasn't there to look after them seven days a week.

Thousands of health workers joined in as #ImInWorkJeremy became one of the top-trending hash-tags that weekend. Inevitably, the mainstream media picked up the trend, with the national press running stories throughout the weekend on how 'NHS staff turned to Twitter to condemn Jeremy Hunt', as the *Daily Mail* put it.[4] #ImInWorkJeremy had officially gone viral.

Hunt's PR team at the Department of Health, presumably rattled by the ferocity of the backlash against him, decided to attempt social media spontaneity themselves. And so, on the Saturday morning, Hunt set out to promote his own weekend working credentials by tweeting a picture of himself with a neurosurgical team at University College London Hospital. The accompanying text enthused: 'Fascinating visit 2 see brain surgery at UCLH and inspirational leadership of Neil Kitchen. Thx 4 making me welcome [*sic*]'.[5] Alas, in an unfortunate own goal, the photograph he posted included a whiteboard listing the full names of the patients on the neurosurgical ward he attended. Hunt had just tweeted them to his then seventy thousand followers, an eye-watering breach of patient confidentiality. Though the picture was swiftly edited to take out the compromising information, enraged doctors – for whom protecting patients' confidence is a deeply ingrained imperative – clamoured *en masse* for an apology. As one, Lauren Nicole Jones, put it on Twitter: 'If I tweeted a photo with patient identifiable information to over 70,000 people I would deserve to lose my job as NHS worker.'[6] Perhaps Hunt apologised privately to all the patients concerned, but in public no such apology was forthcoming.

I too was at work that weekend, assessing acutely unwell patients in my hospital's Emergency Assessment Unit. As usual, the EAU was bursting with demand and my consultant and fellow junior doctors were wrestling with the challenges of racing against the clock to manage each patient while ensuring we were sufficiently safe and thorough. But even I – social media sceptic as I was – took ten seconds to snap a smartphone selfie and post it on my new, devoid-of-followers Twitter account. Like everyone else, the #ImInWorkJeremy phenomenon had captured my imagination and the Tweet felt like taking a stand, albeit a minuscule one, against government-level misinformation.

With hindsight, the weekend's social-media furore encapsulated some of the defining characteristics of the year-long dispute between doctors and the government. First, it revealed that, no matter how carefully the Department of Health laboured to control the message, social media possessed the verve and agility to subvert, on occasion, the intended narrative. The government had taken unusual lengths to manage their 'weekend effect' story, going so far as to issue Hunt's infamous speech to the media on a 'no approach' basis, meaning it released the details in advance to journalists only on the condition that they did not approach those it involved. This controversial and infrequently used tactic ensured that doctors' side of the story did not appear in any of the initial press coverage, giving the Department free rein to try to control its slant.

The mercurial whims of the Internet, on the other hand, lay beyond the reach of departmental spin doctors. As with the cute cat with its inexplicable 2.3 million fans, who could have predicted that a random doctor's improvised hashtag would so galvanise the 1.4 million individuals who staff the NHS? Or that it would shift the media message – at least temporarily – away from the allegedly workshy NHS consultants onto the Health Secretary's sharp practice of implying hospitals at weekends were doctor-free zones. For the Department of Health press office, it must have been infuriating.

The second salient feature of the weekend's initiative was the BMA's role in it: far from leading the #ImInWorkJeremy campaign, the union latched onto it only retrospectively. A single junior doctor had just done more to challenge Jeremy Hunt's rhetoric than anything the BMA had produced in the last seventy-two hours. The stage was therefore set for a peculiarly modern industrial dispute, one in which the trade union's activity would regularly be eclipsed by the efforts of its grassroots members – and the smartphone would prove mightier than the sword.

At the time, none of this was apparent to me. All I knew was that, contrary to Jeremy Hunt's rhetoric, I had a consultant working alongside me that Saturday and Sunday, with his presence – his deeds – belying the government spin.

He had – as always – arrived an hour before his juniors to help shoulder the workload of an acute medical 'take' – assessing and admitting all the non-surgical patients to the hospital. 'Mad Dog', as we called him, though never to his face, was something of a hospital legend. Close to retirement, he commanded universal respect by combining pragmatism, compassion and encyclopedic knowledge with straight talking, profuse swearing and not giving a damn about bogus authority. Four decades previously, while he was a medical student on an elective placement in a remote Kenyan hospital, local staff had nicknamed him 'mbwa kali', the Swahili for 'mad dog', on account of his fearsome outbursts whenever he felt a patient had received substandard care, in spite of not yet being a qualified doctor.

That morning, Mad Dog was desperately needed. Despite it being only 10 a.m. – and a full six months prior to the NHS's annual winter crisis – a lack of hospital beds was already jamming up our EAU.

'Good God!' we teased him. 'What are you doing here? It's Saturday. Surely you should have parked your Porsche near the eighteenth hole by now.'

He muttered something unrepeatable involving golf clubs and the Health Secretary and we turned to face July's eternal winter.

Unless a hospital has empty inpatient beds into which new arrivals can be admitted, those patients end up marooned in the temporary holding bays of the Accident and Emergency Department and its offshoot, the EAU. Queuing ambulances may now be forced to sit idly on the hospital forecourt, unable to deliver their occupants since all A&E beds are already filled with patients who are themselves unknowingly queuing for the inpatient beds their illnesses warrant. Paramedics, eager to be responding to more 999 calls, must languish in their vehicles, sometimes for hours on end, until someone ekes out a space within the hospital into which the patient – trapped inside the ambulance – can be transferred. Small wonder A&E managers sometimes resort to deploying trolleys in corridors as *de facto* beds, or attempt to disguise the areas they've temporarily stuffed with trolleys with fancy-sounding names (the 'Hub', the 'Atrium' – and certainly not the 'Trolley Park of Last Resort Because the Hospital's Imploding'). Anything to try to stop the crippling stasis in the flow of patients through the hospital.

A nasty little phrase – 'bed blockers' – beloved of the British press, implies that patients themselves are somehow to blame for this logjam. But of course no one gets in unless someone goes out, and, when the social services – required to discharge frail patients safely – are themselves tightly rationed, the hapless patients don't stand a chance. Nor, frankly, do the hospital CEOs. No matter how ingeniously hospital management grapples with the challenges of freeing up capacity, when lack of social services can keep medically fit patients trapped in acute hospital beds for weeks or even months at a time, a CEO's hands are tied.

Early on in my medical career, when I first saw the stranded ambulances outside my A&E, I found myself wishing I were still a journalist. The system was clearly broken and I believed the public had a right to know this. It was entirely possible in this gridlocked world that, thanks to insufficient funds to fit a stair lift in one elderly patient's home, somewhere on the other side of the county another patient could be left lying on the floor, post-cardiac-arrest, because the ambulance they urgently needed was pointlessly pinned down on a hospital forecourt. And if the limiting factor was funds, I reasoned, then no amount of paramedics, nurses, doctors or hospital managers could prevent this from happening. The onus was on those controlling the purse strings: the politicians who assured us our NHS was thriving while starving social services of sufficient funds to enable the safe discharge of patients from NHS hospitals. Avoidable deaths, Jeremy Hunt had assured us, mattered to him deeply. Yet some deaths clearly mattered more than others.

Back in my EAU, patients were piling up in the waiting room. Any one of them could have a potentially life-threatening stroke, blood clot, infection, the works – we just wouldn't know until we had somewhere to assess them. In every sense, temperatures were rising. Patients and relatives were beginning to look as irate as they were anxious (reassuringly, in one sense: the really sick don't care enough to get angry). Thwarted and embarrassed, I averted my eyes each time I walked past them, hoping to avoid being targeted by an enraged family member who needed someone upon whom to vent their spleen. My secret assessment room of last resort – essentially a store cupboard with a couch squeezed inside – had already been occupied by a canny fellow junior. There was literally nowhere to see the patients who continued to flood through the doors.

Respite, unusually, came from my crash bleep. Sometimes, the only effective antidote to the hospital being so swamped with patients that it is impossible to do one's job properly is the perfect focus of a cardiac arrest. In the tumult of endeavouring to restart a heart at least lies the solace of being able to feel like a functioning doctor.

With crash calls, you never quite know what you'll find. By the time you've rushed to the bedside, the patient may have already come round from their innocent faint and your presence is entirely superfluous. On other occasions, what confronts you from the pillow is the sickly grey of a face already distorted by lifelessness. Heart stopped, the flow of blood at a standstill, these patients are already dead – it is your job to bring them back again. There may be uncertainty, even panic among the staff at the bedside, the defibrillator unattached, the chest compressions not yet started. Once – on her first ever crash call – my fellow house officer arrived out of breath at the bedside only to be told by the nurses to stand down since the patient was 'DNACPR': their notes apparently contained the distinctive purple form bearing the instruction, 'Do not attempt cardiopulmonary resuscitation.' Except – after precious minutes of inactivity while someone hunted down the patient's missing notes – it transpired that the nurses had mixed up two different patients. The dead patient, the one for whom my colleague had done nothing – and who is haunted still by that knowledge – had been for full resuscitation all along.

The best arrests are the ones devoid of panic and muddle because someone has taken charge with quiet authority, assigned discreet tasks to each member of the crash team, given a clear running commentary that unifies their efforts, and inspired calm through their own unflappability. This particular arrest was a textbook example. By the time I reached the bedside, a large team of doctors and nurses, led by a senior medical registrar, the grade of doctor just beneath consultant, were already on their second cycle of chest compressions. The initial electric shock from the defibrillator had failed to restart the patient's heart, but that didn't mean the next wouldn't. The team – relaxed, unruffled – appeared to have all the time in the world. It was perfect.

The patient herself, Mrs Bridges, a married woman in her late seventies with a known history of an irregular heartbeat, had been admitted that morning for treatment of an aggressive pneumonia with intravenous antibiotics. No one seemed to know much about her general health or her home life and, when a second shock failed to kick-start the heart, a heated discussion broke out between the two most senior doctors present: the registrar running the arrest and another registrar from Intensive Care. Were we really, the ICU registrar asked, intending to keep going when an ICU bed was clearly inappropriate for this patient? It was time to call time, to stop this well-meaning but futile activity that served only, at this point, to degrade the patient.

'We're not achieving anything here,' he asserted. 'This is completely pointless.'

'But – who knows the patient?' I asked. 'Does anyone here actually know the patient?'

No one answered. The admitting doctor's entry in Mrs Bridges's notes was too sketchy to provide any meaningful insight into her 'pre-morbid level of function' – our shorthand for what you used to be capable of before illness struck you down. Amid chest compressions so brutal we all clocked the unmistakable crunch of breaking ribs, the two most senior doctors present continued to argue for and against giving up. Blood slowly seeped across the thin cotton sheets from the artery I'd just stabbed to obtain an urgent blood sample. We looked as if we were committing an assault.

In an ideal world, the doctors and nurses hovering above

what may or may not prove to be your deathbed would weigh the pros and cons of calling off CPR with the utmost poise and gravity. We'd take time, judiciously exploring the risks and benefits of continuing, and with family members, ideally, at the heart of the discussion. But time, of course, is precisely what a crash team lacks. Only a quarter of patients who suffer a cardiac arrest while in hospital survive to discharge and, for those whose hearts stop in the community, the survival rate is less than 10 per cent. Every second's delay decreases the odds of successfully restarting a heart. And so, *in extremis*, sometimes dripping with sweat through the effort of pounding the heart, we frantically assess you against the clock, trying to decide if you are worth persevering with.

This isn't a matter of egocentric doctors playing God. There are fates worse than death. One, perhaps, is a catastrophic brain injury caused by hypoxia, the brain being starved of oxygen. During cardiac 'down time' – when the heart has stopped beating and blood reaches the brain only via the brute force of a set of human fists bearing down on a breastbone – hypoxic brain damage can leave patients in a twilight existence of minimal consciousness in which memory and personality have been lost for good. At any time on my Coronary Care Unit, a kind of intensive care unit reserved for patients with cardiac disease, there are often one or two such patients – saved by well-intended efforts from death, but at what enduring human cost?

The ICU registrar had marshalled his consultant to the bedside. Both argued in unison that resuscitation must stop. While nurses and doctors deftly swapped in and out of the manual labour on Mrs Bridges's chest, I could sense the medical registrar leading the arrest starting to defer to the senior presence, the consultant gatekeeper to the beds on ICU. If there was to be no bed for the patient anyway, why continue to strip a human being's final moments of their last vestiges of dignity? Beyond the flimsy nylon curtains that nominally separated us from the rest of the ward, the conversation was being broadcast to a further twenty-five patients and their assembled families. The matter of whether this particular patient lived or died, it seemed, was about to be determined by which of the doctors at her bedside had the strongest personality, the loudest voice. Rank was now calling the shots.

I was far too junior to influence anything, but my instincts screamed that we should try a little longer. None of us knew Mrs Bridges. We hadn't met her, hadn't appraised her physical robustness for ourselves. Ordinarily, for all we knew, she was fitter than we were. A presumption that her frailty would doom our efforts to failure might be right – but it might not. I felt sick at my impotence. I needed this patient to be given more of a chance. As the daughter of a woman in her seventies who until very recently has liked to relax by climbing mountains and holidaying in the Arctic circle, perhaps I was inherently biased, compromised by sentiment. But I knew a man who wasn't.

'Run,' I whispered to the house officer. 'Get Mad Dog. Get him here now. Tell him it's an emergency.'

Meanwhile, I pulled a form of rank of my own. In the rigidly hierarchical world of medicine, the one thing that can trump seniority is territory. Turf, as well as title, matters. The person with whom the buck ultimately stops is the consultant under whom a patient is admitted to hospital, which on this occasion meant Mad Dog.

'I'm afraid we can't stop CPR until my consultant is here. He's on his way right now,' I piped up with as much authority as I could muster. No one liked it, but compressions went on.

Just as Mad Dog reached the bedside, Mrs Bridges confounded us all. At the next shock from the defibrillator, her heart jolted back into a weak but steady rhythm. We stared incredulously at the ECG trace as a tense conversation between the consultants ensued.

'In the absence of any known evidence to the contrary, I think we probably have to assume a degree of baseline fitness, don't we?' asked Mad Dog with all the gentle menace of a medical Vito Corleone. 'And, given that her pneumonia may respond very quickly to antibiotics, might an ICU bed perhaps be appropriate in this case?'

It was an offer the ICU boss could not refuse.

At moments like these – as a junior doctor with neither rank nor experience, feeling out of your depth and overwhelmed by your own ineffectuality – what you crave more than anything is consultant backup. The big guns, fighting your corner on your patient's behalf. So, in essence, one might argue, events in my EAU that Saturday morning encapsulated precisely why Jeremy Hunt was right: a consultant presence at weekends potentially saved lives. The argument was inconvenienced, of course, by the fact that, rather than teeing up with his mates on the golf course, Mad Dog *was* here, spending his Saturday in the hospital with me. My entire medical firm was already – undeniably – delivering a seven-day NHS. Something didn't add up.

Even in these earliest days of the showdown between the government and junior doctors, I had the sense we were at loggerheads over something far more profound than the terms and conditions of our contract alone. The ferocity of the reaction against Jeremy Hunt felt like an eruption of something deep-rooted and toxic, as though, in challenging doctors' professionalism, he had inadvertently unleashed years of festering discontent and rage.

The question that mattered most immediately for me was not whether junior doctors should go on strike, but why we were considering such drastic action in the first place. How had we gone from being enthusiastic ingénues, arriving on the wards brimming with big dreams of healing and making a difference, to angry, defiant, newly vocal campaigners who were damned if they were going to take a perceived degradation in their working conditions from a Health Secretary who had just insulted them? And what, most fundamentally of all, did this explosion of anger tell us about the current health of the NHS?

CHAPTER 3

EXALTATION

As measures of success in medicine go, being offered a gram of heroin by a raving, delirious, intravenous drug user is an unconventional plaudit. But that offer – a semiconscious promise of a Class A drug – made me feel like the queen of the world.

Mickey was a well-known face in the Emergency Department. Years of shooting up had ravaged most of the veins in his body, leaving only a weeping wound in his groin through which he could permanently inject heroin with ease. Periodically, an infected needle or something unspeakable with which his heroin had been cut would send showers of bacteria careering through his bloodstream, invariably wreaking havoc in whatever part of his anatomy they lodged. At age twenty-nine, one hip had already been ravaged by osteomyelitis – infection deep within the bone – and he'd previously required open-heart surgery to replace a rotting, infected heart valve. Now, the metallic click of his replacement valve could be heard from the end of his hospital bed.

Today, picked up off the street by the police, he'd been brought in by ambulance with a high fever and racing pulse, rambling semi-coherently. I assessed him quickly – time was of the essence – establishing that what Mickey needed more than anything was intravenous access, a cannula through which I could take urgent blood samples and give potentially life-saving antibiotics and fluids. He was filthy, flailing and laughing at my plan.

'You'll never stand a chance of getting a needle in me, love. Not a hope in hell.'

'Oh, yeah? You'll let me have a go, though? I'm pretty sure I can.'

Mickey found my confidence hilarious. Years of injecting had scarred his veins until accessing them with a needle was almost impossible.

'I'll give you one chance,' he said. 'Only one. And I bet you a gram of heroin you'll never do it.'

'A gram, you say? Right then, Mickey. You're on.'

If you had told me in my first weeks as a doctor that I'd come to relish the challenge of attempting to cannulate septic, trashed, sclerotic veins, I'd have dismissed your wishful thinking. New doctors are invariably inept at practical procedures, and I was no exception. Usually, we've practised only on plastic dummies and each other. I was lucky: I had my own *live* dummy to practise on. My poor, long-suffering husband, on return from our honeymoon, gamely endured his new medical student wife cajoling him into letting her stab his veins with needles. Frankly, I needed the practice. The first person from whom I'd ever taken blood, another newbie medical student, had neglected to tell me he was profoundly needle-phobic. A group of us were practising our blood-taking. As I plunged a needle into his arm, he fainted into the chair in which he was seated, becoming wedged bolt upright between its arms. Now he was thus immobilised, his plummeting blood pressure deprived his brain of its normal oxygen supply, precipitating – to my horror – a seizure. The more senior students who were gamely supervising our first efforts at blood-taking dragged him, foaming at the mouth, to the ground, where slowly he regained colour and consciousness, blood trickling down his arm from where my needle, I noted grimly, had hit its mark.

Fast-forward a year or two and I had somehow improbably evolved into a cannula junkie who liked her veins as challenging as possible. As I scrutinised Mickey's arms, legs, hands and feet, I could find nothing that felt as if it would yield to a needle. But there was, I discovered, one possibility. Snaking over the top of his right thumb was a tortuous yet springy vein I doubted he'd ever used before. This was my one shot. I tied my tourniquet as tightly as I could physically manage and gently nudged the needle into his thumb. A moment's hesitation and then – flashback – blood filled the end of my needle. I was in.

While I swiftly drew off blood and taped down the cannula, Mickey loudly extolled my virtues to the entire department.

'Fuck me, she's gone and done it! Fuck me! First time, too.'

But I was not to be distracted.

'Where's my heroin, Mickey?' I asked, deadpan. 'We had a deal, remember? I want my gram.'

As he flung back his head with laughter, exposing his rotting teeth to the ceiling lights, I wanted to dance a victory jig. I wanted the whole world to come and inspect the needle

I'd precariously lodged, against all the odds, in – of all places – a drug addict's thumb. I knew it was nothing really, that it certainly wasn't going to survive the volumes of fluids and drugs we would need to give him, but the tiny achievement of cannulating impossible-to-cannulate Mickey made me want to punch the air with joy.

Those first weeks and months as a floundering new doctor are peppered with moments of unexpected delight as you find within yourself new skills whose acquisition has caught you unawares. But nothing quite matches the sheer exaltation of knowing, without any doubt, that for the very first time you have just saved somebody's life.

A couple of months after believing I had failed my patient, Mr Frith, as he teetered on the brink of death during my first ever night on call, I was given what in hindsight felt like a chance of redemption. It was the end of a gruelling weekend on call. Sunday night, approaching nine o'clock, the start of evening handover and liberty. Tessa, my fellow house officer, and I had just spent forty-five of the preceding seventy-two hours responsible for the clinical needs of several hundred medical inpatients. We were exhausted, run ragged and desperate for it to end.

As I worked my way through my last few jobs on the ward, twitchy and impatient to be free, Tessa bleeped me from another ward upstairs.

'Rach, can you just come and have a look at this guy? He's got pneumonia and I've started him on antibiotics but – I don't know – there's something about him that doesn't look right. I just want a second pair of eyes on him.'

Tessa was my friend and fellow foot soldier on the lowest rung of the medical ladder. Equally inexperienced, we were loyal comrades, united in battle – as much of our job felt like in those early days – and we would drop everything to help each other as a matter of course. But the particular words she used about her patient 'not looking right' sent a flicker of anxiety down my spine. I'd already learned the hard way that even the most junior doctor's instinctive unease that something is wrong – though they may lack the knowledge or experience to delineate precisely why – can herald impending catastrophe. I rushed upstairs to find her.

Tessa had been asked to review Mr Brewer, a man in his sixties with a new diagnosis of bowel cancer, on account of his fever and mildly low oxygen levels. When she listened to his chest, the telltale crackles at the base of one lung clinched a clinical diagnosis of pneumonia, for which she had prescribed antibiotics. Quietly writing up her entry in his notes and already looking forward to her post-on-call beer, she had noticed a change in the sound of his breathing. Mr Brewer had just returned to his bed from the toilet. Previously comfortable and chatty, he now looked distressed and pale. He denied any pain in his chest and, when she listened with her stethoscope, nothing had changed. He just looked . . . wrong.

With the benefit of not having seen Mr Brewer when well, I confronted with fresh eyes a man who was obviously and horribly unwell. Tessa's instincts were right. This was clearly no ordinary pneumonia. Something had abruptly changed. While she ran to find a nurse to bring equipment for real-time monitoring of his vital signs, I worked my way through the 'A, B, C' protocol that should frame every doctor's emergency assessment.

I knew that 'A', his airway, was not blocked since he could whisper, albeit almost inaudibly. I ignored, for now, the poignancy of his words, coming from a man who looked as if he was dying and worse, wore the dread of someone who knew it: 'Please ... tell my ... wife ... not ... to worry ... about me.' I had to stay hard. There was no time to be distracted by sentiment.

'B', his breathing, was horrendous. This time, I knew the sounds all too well. Like that of Mr Frith before him, Mr Brewer's chest had the horrible wet rasp of a patient who is drowning in his own bodily fluid. His lungs, I knew, were flooded.

'C', circulation, was no better. His hands were clammy, cold and sweaty. Where the pulse in his wrist should be, I could feel nothing at all. His blood pressure must have crashed.

It all pointed to one diagnosis. In spite of his feeling no pain in his chest, I was certain he had suffered a massive heart attack while he had been away in the toilet. As the nurses arrived, applying wires and monitoring, I asked one of them to run for intravenous morphine and diuretics that would take the fluid off his lungs and heart. Without them, his heart would remain unable to beat properly and a cardiac arrest was inevitable. The nurse refused.

'Sorry?' I asked.

'He's got no blood pressure. If you give him those drugs, you're going to kill him. You're incompetent. There's no way I'm giving them.'

There was no time to debate the physiology, nor even to summon a crash team. Mr Brewer's lungs were now so overloaded with fluid that blood-tinged foam had started frothing from his lips and he was slipping into unconsciousness. I – or, rather, he – had only seconds. Self-doubt couldn't come into it. And so, almost snarling – the pressure felt so fierce – I shouted, 'Get me the drugs! Now. I'll give them myself.'

It wasn't professional, it certainly wasn't polite, but every intuition I possessed as a doctor screamed at me to give the drugs. The nurse was absolutely right, though. If my call was wrong, my actions were probably going to kill him.

Without hesitation, acting purely on instinct, I pushed ten milligrams of morphine straight into Mr Brewer's vein. For a second, nothing. Then, as we all stared, aghast, the blue-grey mask of imminent death started to blossom into normal, healthy, pink flesh as blood began to suffuse his oxygen-starved tissues. It felt as if we had raised the dead, brought about a resurrection.

As Mr Brewer's observations started to normalise, we recorded an electrocardiogram. The ECG trace showed he had indeed suffered a catastrophic heart attack. It was only after the cardiologists had whisked him away to the Coronary Care Unit that I started to think about what I had done. It had been a risky call, based on something more intangible than a neat protocol like my 'A, B, C': a subtle blend of burgeoning gut instinct, pattern recognition and an understanding of the physiology of heart failure acquired in lecture rooms and libraries. Good doctoring, I'd just discovered, relied upon instinct and experience at least as much as checklists and guidelines. I felt shaky, overwhelmed by the odds I'd just naïvely managed, stricken by the what-ifs and maybes.

The fact remained that Tessa and I had just saved a life. Had we not acted upon newly informed instinct, Mr Brewer would have almost certainly arrested. I'd love to pretend that we reflected deeply and wisely on this clinical experience, but

I'm afraid we couldn't stop beaming. We walked out into the night feeling like real doctors at last – decisive, brave, going with our guts, just like the white-coated heroes on television. Later, drunk on euphoria and vodka, we sat up half the night, compulsively reliving the case in minute, obsessive detail. We felt – in our naïveté – temporarily invincible. For one night only, in our minds, we ruled the hospital.

In medicine, needless to say, the moment you feel as if you've mastered something is invariably the point at which your next experience will knock you straight back down to earth. But during the ups and downs of my first year as a doctor – the mercurial lurching from disappointment to fulfilment, elation to despair – I started to assemble within me a collection of faces that gave me ballast and solidity, whatever the day threw my way. These were the patients with whom, as our paths briefly crossed, I had formed a human connection that proved quietly to endure.

It didn't take much to make a difference. During a gruelling stint on the Surgical Emergency Unit – a wild west of pre-operative and post-operative surgical patients whose house officers were largely left to fend for ourselves while our seniors got to work cutting in theatre – a nineteen-year-old on our early-morning ward round caught my eye. Ellie had been rushed to theatre the day before to remove a grossly inflamed appendix. Now, despite the good news that she could go home later that day, she looked anxious and uncertain. As my consultant swept imperiously to the next patient's bedside, I whispered, 'I'll come back and have a chat with you.'

Later, when we spoke, I discovered Ellie was distraught at not being able to pass urine since her catheter had been removed earlier in the morning. Though her bladder was increasingly tense and painful, still she was unable to empty it. All it took was a five-minute chat. I taught her the tricks that can sometimes help – running a tap, putting a hand in hot water – and described my own mounting distress, after a Caesarean section for my first child, when I thought my newborn and I were never going to leave hospital simply because I couldn't get my bladder working. With a little encouragement from the nurses, Ellie left for home by lunchtime. Some weeks later, a handwritten card arrived at the nurses' station in which she thanked me for my kindness. It had been nothing, a five-minute attempt at empathy, but it had meant something important to her.

Occasionally, I found myself drawing on qualities honed not in medical school but during my old life as a journalist. In the hunt for the story, tenacity, doggedness and a stubborn refusal to take no for an answer were essential tools of the trade. I never anticipated how integral they would prove to be in navigating effectively the creaking, dysfunctional hospital bureaucracy. Only rarely was a patient's outcome in my control. Usually, getting something done meant managing and sometimes deliberately circumventing arcane systems that often seemed designed to waste our time and thwart good patient care. Hospital computer systems that were unfit for purpose; scan results that were accessible only to the team that performed the scan and not you, the doctor who requested it; a switchboard so desperately understaffed you could have whipped out an appendix in the time it took someone to answer. Sometimes, I felt less like a doctor than a paper-pushing, clipboard-carrying, largely ineffectual secretary.

With one patient, my persistence became an obsession. While I was still on the Surgical Emergency Unit, someone arrived whose military precision was the antithesis of the chaos, stench and racket of the ward. Major Robert Ashdown was a recently retired army officer who, in a week's time, was due to climb Mount Kilimanjaro with his daughter. He had awoken that morning in crippling abdominal pain and been rushed by ambulance to the unit. Now, my examination revealed a classic 'acute abdomen' – exquisitely tender to touch and protected by utterly rigid abdominal muscles, a clue that blood or infection was irritating his abdominal cavity. Through gritted teeth, he exhaled quietly as I pressed gently down on his belly. Anyone else would have screamed. It felt like palpating hardwood.

'I'm so sorry,' I told him. 'I have to do this to help make a diagnosis.'

'You do exactly what you need to,' he ordered. 'Carry on.'

Immaculately dressed, with the kind of posture that made standing to attention look like slouching, he was experiencing his first ever hospital admission. An urgent CT scan revealed a large amount of fluid around his stomach and the profound anaemia on his blood tests indicated the fluid was almost certainly blood. We put in a tube that drained litres of the stuff away; however, slowly but surely, it kept on coming. Every time the bleeding appeared to have finally settled, it would start to ooze, then flood again and I'd be straight back on the phone to the blood bank.

Throughout it all, Major Ashdown's wife and three daughters kept a restrained vigil at his bedside, equally immaculate and reserved. Not one of them expressed distress or fear. Eventually, with a diagnosis still eluding us, my consultant had no choice but to take him to theatre. The surgery revealed a gastric cancer, hidden beneath the huge blood clot, that had invaded the local blood vessels, causing bleeding too widespread and diffuse to fix. There was nothing to do but pack the abdomen tightly with gauze and stitch it back up again, temporarily staunching the bleeding, then keep Major Ashdown comfortable until it inevitably restarted.

'How long do I have?' he asked the surgeon that evening.

'I can't say for certain, but I would estimate at most a handful of days. It's only pressure that's stopping the bleeding. I'm afraid there is nothing we can do.'

There was something uniquely horrible about the situation. Perfectly lucid and composed, in only mild discomfort from his abdominal incision, Major Ashdown confronted the fact that, at an unspecified time in the next two or three days, he would begin to bleed from his tumour and, when it started, he would haemorrhage to death.

Late that night, just before setting off home, I called in to see him. His family had gone to eat dinner and we chatted about what was to come.

'Where would you like to be?' I asked him. 'Would you like to get home or prefer to stay here?'

'I don't think my wife would be able to bear the bleeding happening at home,' he said, 'but there is one place I think I'd like to be.'

Our local hospice was renowned for the excellence of its drinks trolley. If there's one thing the terminally ill deserve, it's a fine vintage with their lunch or dinner. Major Ashdown was currently trapped on a frenetic, raucous surgical ward with its relentless soundtrack of bleeping, clattering, moaning and shouting. What he longed for, in his final days, was somewhere peaceful and calm where he could be with his family and be expertly looked after when the bleeding began. There was one problem. Beds in the hospice were like gold dust. To earn one, you needed symptoms that were too difficult and distressing for GPs or ordinary hospital wards to manage. Major Ashdown was entirely asymptomatic. Yet he faced, albeit with apparently total stoicism, certain death in just a day or so. I couldn't pretend to imagine the psychology of that.

'I can't promise anything,' I told him, 'but I'm going to do my best.'

The next morning, in between the thousand and one other jobs I was juggling, I started making calls to the hospice. Initially, I explained the situation to a ward nurse. She sympathised, but said he wouldn't meet the criteria. After some shameless cajoling and begging, she agreed to pass me on to the ward doctor. Same conversation, same scepticism, but a reluctant agreement to let me speak to her senior registrar.

By now it was late afternoon. I wished I had never said anything to Major Ashdown. His family were ecstatic at the idea of the hospice bed it was not in my power to give. 'We know you can do it, Rachel,' they told me. I knew I almost certainly could not. A tense conversation with the hospice registrar ensued. It was a no. I lobbied and argued and finally, reluctantly, she agreed to let me speak to her consultant. Few phone calls had mattered to me more.

'I know that on one level he meets none of the criteria,' I said. 'His symptoms are not intractable; in fact, he has no physical symptoms at all. But he's living with the knowledge that, at any moment, torrential bleeding will begin that will be the certain death of him. And he's in the worst possible place to spend what little time he has left – you know what a Surgical Emergency Unit's like. Please give him his last few days with his family in a place that's peaceful.'

There was a long pause. I held my breath. Then the consultant told me a bed had unexpectedly become available in the hospice that evening, and the bed was Major Ashdown's. I put down the phone and slowly exhaled. I went to tell him and his family.

'You can go to the hospice tonight, Robert,' I told him. 'There's a bed there, and it's yours.'

Sometimes when a man – in particular a military man whose whole being radiates strength and composure – breaks down and cries it can feel awkward, embarrassing, as though he's let himself go. But, on this occasion, we all wept freely: the major, who would now enjoy fine wine with his last meals; the family, who would sit with him in tranquillity and comfort, sharing their precious final hours together; and the house officer, who had been enough of a bloody-minded irritant to be an effective advocate on her patient's behalf.

I later learned he had died two days later, surrounded by his family, in a private room overlooking the hospice garden, where pheasants liked to peck at the grass. That weekend in the supermarket I selected the most expensive bottle of single malt whisky I could find on the shelves, my small contribution to the drinks trolley.

Saving lives is seductive. In my earliest days as a doctor, I loved discovering that I could *do* things. That I was no longer the floundering bookworm but a competent, capable doctor. I soon found, however, that the adrenaline highs of those early days, though intoxicating, were short-lived. The quiet moments of connection with patients were what I began to cherish. A hand held in mine, a darkest fear calmly heard, the tiniest acts that infused each day with meaning and fulfilment. What had started as an ordeal was beginning to feel like a privilege.

CHAPTER 4

BRILLIANCE

My earliest memories of Christmas involve timorous footsteps down hospital corridors. Every year, my siblings and I would rip open the contents of our stockings in an orgy of excitement, devour our special festive breakfast, then set off for the local cottage hospital in the car with my mother and father. This was the 1970s – before Margaret Thatcher had done away with the vast majority of these small, rural hospitals, some of them barely bigger than a townhouse, that enabled villagers to avoid huge treks to a county hospital and to be treated close to home by the one doctor, their local general practitioner, who was familiar with their lives and illnesses. I dare say that, financially, they were inefficient and that economies of scale mandated their closure. Nevertheless, as the NHS was centralised under Thatcher, rural patients lost something of incalculable value: the intimacy, and thus humanity, of their medical care of old.

My father, having travelled the world as a Royal Naval anaesthetist, had chosen to alight as a GP in a village near a small market town in the West Country within whose cottage hospital he still practised anaesthetics. Babies were born there, great-grandparents died there. My father knew every one of them. Each year, five or six of his patients, invariably men and women in their eighties or their nineties, would spend Christmas stranded in the cottage hospital. Without fail, he would visit them all with his young family in tow. I remember smiling nurses thrusting Quality Street upon us and wondering how many I could stuff away before Mum and Dad cottoned on. At barely five or six years old, what really frightened me was leaving the nurses to meet my father's patients. We would move as a family unit from bedside to bedside, and I would hover uncertainly at a strange person's side while Dad chatted away with them warmly and easily. Sometimes, his patients were so ancient and frail I thought they must be about to die. Iodine and bodily fluids, the staple smells of the hospital, made me feel light-headed. Rarely do I remember the patient's own family being present at these elderly patients' bedsides. Often it seemed as though the visit from their family doctor was the highlight, so far, of their Christmas Day.

For all my anxieties about what to say, how to behave and whether someone was about to gasp their terminal breath in front of me, one thing was perfectly clear. These faces, so wizened and haggard, would light up with sheer delight at my father's arrival. I could see that a Christmas visit from their family doctor meant the world to them. And, when my siblings and I crept closer to their sides, often they would beam with joy at the chance to chat with a small child. Somehow I knew that, in spite of my awkwardness and fears, what we gave of our Christmas mornings was vastly eclipsed by what this meant to my father's bedbound patients. Eventually, as I approached my teens, I'd look forward to our annual visitations. Like my father and mother, I appreciated the pleasure of making a difference, however small.

Like so many children of doctors and nurses, I discovered early the unadorned realities of medicine. When I broke my arm trying to swing on a rope across a river in the highlands of Scotland, landing shoulder first on the riverbed, my father reassuringly mentioned as he drove me to the hospital that the doctors there would probably cut into my arm and fix the broken bones with a metal pin. Coughs and colds never warranted a day off school. With medical parents, we had to be moribund to earn a sick day, and even then would invariably be dragged to my mother's family planning clinic, to lie sweaty and miserable on an NHS couch while she advised the county's youth on contraception.

No one had a mother with stories like mine. A former ophthalmic nurse at London's Moorfields Eye Hospital, she would describe to our appalled delight the jars of medicinal leeches that sat tucked away out of sight. If a patient had bashed or inflamed their eyeball, how better to remove the blood trapped inside than to apply a creature honed by thousands of years of evolution to do one thing superlatively well: the imperceptible extraction of blood? Sometimes I'd lie awake at night, imagining a patient tucked up in their white cotton sheets, trying to sleep with a fat black bloodsucking slug squatting on their eyeball. Tellingly, far from being horrified, I only wished I could see it for myself.

Today, I observe this slightly skewed relationship with our bodies and their functions evolving in my own children. When he was four, my son was asked by his nursery teacher what happens if you do not drink enough water. Instead of replying that you become thirsty, he explained that you become dehydrated and this was very dangerous for your kidneys. Around the same time, he earned his first ever pocket money every few weeks by being a mock patient in my medical school's paediatrics exams. Nervous students, often with minimal experience of children, would attempt to win him over into allowing himself to be examined. Everything hinged on whether or not he warmed to them. Once, a particularly awkward candidate adopted that slow, loud voice people sometimes think will endear them to tiny children, as though they were mentally incapacitated.

'Hey, there, little guy, do you know what these are?' he asked over-brightly, making the ends of his stethoscope perform a little jig around his neck. 'These are my magic ears! Let's use these cool magic ears, shall we?'

My son stared up at him balefully. 'It is a stethoscope,' he stated bluntly. 'You use it to listen to my heart.'

Crushed by a four-year-old, the poor man was on the brink of tears. He never quite recovered.

As a child, I was torn between science and the arts. Once, when my mother had laboriously combed the nits from my long hair, I carefully preserved one on a specimen slide to inspect it closely under my microscope. At weekends, I liked to hunt for owl pellets while walking our dog in the countryside, then spend hours dissecting out the tiny rodent bones, obsessively mounting and labelling them on cardboard before writing melodramatic poems about the untimely demise of mice. One day, I found an entire cow's skull in the undergrowth, half hidden under ferns and brambles, almost too heavy to lift. I managed to haul it several miles back home and, when my parents refused to allow me to keep a cow's skull in my bedroom permanently, I donated it to the school art room so that generations of children hence would have the chance to map its contours.

Sharing with Jeremy Hunt a degree in Philosophy, Politics and Economics (PPE) – though we were not student contemporaries – I came to journalism full of lofty ideals about changing the world through the power of human stories. But even while making films about subjects such as Al-Qaeda's rise in the UK, Tony Blair's 'sexed-up' Iraq war dossier, the Monica Lewinsky scandal and the state of policing and the NHS in Britain, I kept hankering after medicine. Visiting home, I'd hang on my father's every word as he told me stories from his practice that captured all the gore, ugliness and beauty of doctoring. Like him, I wanted to be able to read a human body like a book and apply hard science to fixing its frailties. Above all, I had a sneaking suspicion that in the cutthroat world of political and current affairs television – with all its ego, ambition and frequent ruthlessness – I wasn't, and never would be, myself. The tough carapace I thought I wore to work fooled no one, least of all me. I was so busy trying to fake being Bob Woodward, I feared I might be missing out on the job I was born for.

'What?' asked my incredulous boss when I told him I was thinking of retraining. 'Why on earth would you give up television just to end up being some kind of lowly, part-time GP? You'll be bored out of your mind. You must be mad.'

He had a point. There is glamour, money and clout in

television, even at the current-affairs end of the spectrum. I had travelled all over the world for work, interviewed cabinet ministers, rubbed shoulders with heads of state, enjoyed affluence and agenda-setting power far greater than any I would know again. Giving it all up to go back to school as a first-year medical student was either brave or crazy. But, though my metropolitan media life was superficially seductive, I wanted to do the thing you are never allowed to mention in your medical school interviews. I wanted to help people. Not indirectly, via media influence, but as a hands-on, everyday experience.

There is a vogue these days among some doctors to dismiss the notion of medical vocation as self-aggrandising claptrap. As one American doctor and writer, Louis Profeta, puts it, medicine 'is just a job', no more special and important than any other. He despises doctors who want 'to be fawned over and congratulated on how compassionate they [are], and how they have the hardest jobs in the world, and that no one could possibly understand the work or appreciate how hard their jobs [are].'[7] Clearly having one particular job or another makes no one better or more hardworking than their peers, and there are undoubtedly some doctors out there with superiority complexes the size of small planets, though personally I have met very few of these. But that misses the point. Medicine is 'just a job' only in the same way that birth, death, disability and bereavement are all just everyday stuff. Run-of-the-mill is losing one's house key or being booked for speeding, not losing a limb or receiving a diagnosis of terminal cancer. Immersing oneself professionally in the world of human illness – other people's suffering, pain, hopes and fears – has always seemed to me to be an honour and a privilege, be it as a nurse, doctor, dietician, midwife or hospital porter. And I am not ashamed to say that for me – perhaps inevitably, given all the doctors and nurses in my family – it felt like a calling.

I started moonlighting in the evenings to pass my science A levels and finally, just before my thirtieth birthday, I self-funded my way for five years through medical school by working as a freelance typist during term times and as an ad hoc documentary maker in the long summer holidays. It was hard to stay afloat financially while keeping up with my studies, but from day one I felt liberated, as though finally I was doing what I was meant to. I loved every single bit of it. The complicated science, the dissection room, the conversations with patients, the sense of steeping myself in the knowledge and rigour that would underpin my future practice, the sheer luxury of learning again.

—∿—

Two years into my medical degree, my old and new lives collided happily when, during the long university summer holiday, I travelled to Phoenix, Arizona, to make a documentary about a remarkable feat of neurosurgery.

Brett Kehrer, a young farmer in his twenties from deepest rural Pennsylvania, had been plagued for years by excruciating headaches. Eventually, his insurance company had agreed to fund an MRI scan. What it revealed was devastating. Ballooning out from the side of one of the most important arteries in the human body – the basilar artery – was an aneurysm. Aneurysms typically start life as a small patch of weakness in the arterial wall against which blood pulsates relentlessly until the artery begins to billow outwards into a fragile, blood-filled sac. Its walls stretch ever more thinly until one day, inevitably, they cannot withstand the high pressures any longer. When an aneurysm bursts inside the brain, the haemorrhage unleashed is often catastrophic. Brett's aneurysm was one of the largest ever found on MRI. Its sheer dimensions led several neurosurgeons to conclude it was simply inoperable. Brett was given no choice but to wait for the blow-out that would certainly kill him.

But his family refused to give up, their tenacity leading them to Robert Spetzler, one of America's leading neuro-surgeons. Spetz, as he was known in his hospital in Phoenix, gave a remarkable second opinion. He was willing to operate, indeed was confident of success, but only after he had halted Brett's heartbeat and drained his body of blood in order to deflate the enormous aneurysm, creating a space in which to operate safely. The technique, one Spetz had pioneered twenty years previously, was known as hypothermic cardiac standstill. It relied on the principle that the colder the human brain becomes, the more sluggish its metabolic activity and so the lower its demands for oxygen. In the same way that a child can be submerged under ice for hours, yet miraculously wake up again afterwards, Spetz's cardiac-standstill patients could be cooled on ice into a state of suspended animation, able to survive intact for up to an hour without a functioning heart, brain, blood or oxygen. The price of Brett's one chance at life, in essence, was to experience death on a temporary basis.

I landed in Pennsylvania three days before Brett's surgery. The Kehrer family's whitewashed wooden farmhouses was nestled deep within fields of thigh-high wheat and barley. Brett towered a good foot above me, a gentle giant, all brawn and civility. Like his family and Ann, his childhood sweetheart turned fiancée, he exuded kindness and old-school Christian values. Without his faith, he told me, he would not have been able to bear the wait before his surgery. The day before he flew to Phoenix, his entire community came together in a Sunday afternoon open-air party, thrown for the benefit of their local boy. There were fiddlers, country dancing, hog roasts, barbecued corn cobs, haybale mountains for the children to scramble on, beer on tap for the adults. The celebration spanned four generations of locals, several hundred of whom had gathered to send Brett off in style, an extraordinary expression of community spirit. None of them knew if they would see him again. It was a scene saturated with poignancy and midsummer sunshine.

'I'm lucky I have God to put my trust in,' Brett told me as the night drew in. 'I believe I am destined to marry Ann this fall. And I believe in Dr Spetzler.'

In the high-stakes world of neurosurgery, Spetz had a reputation for doing operations that others dared not attempt. When the outcomes of major brain surgery include disability so devastating it is potentially a fate worse than death, this was controversial. Spetz thrived on risk, hurling his surgeon's hands down Arizona's rocky peaks on his mountain bike and out of helicopters to ski the most extreme slopes in Alaska. Tall and thin, he had the rangy appearance of a mountaineer. He attributed his skill in the operating theatre in no small part to his physical stamina, being able to endure eight or more hours of surgery without a flicker of fatigue undermining the precision of his hand movements.

Aneurysms are the heli-skiing of neurosurgery. Their repair demands the kind of calm under pressure that would make most of us quake in our boots. The heart pumps a quarter of our blood through the brain – a litre of blood every minute – and, if the neurosurgeon accidentally tears an aneurysm's paper-thin walls, their operating field will turn in seconds into a bloodbath. Handling a cerebral aneurysm must, I imagine, feel like bomb-disposal work – except that, in this case, one false move triggers not your own death, but your patient's.

The basilar artery, Spetz explained on camera, supplied blood to the all-important brain stem, the portion of the brain responsible for controlling a person's breathing, heartbeat, blood pressure, speech, swallowing, hearing and balance. If, during surgery, Spetz inadvertently interrupted this blood supply, Brett might awake to find himself a victim of the notoriously horrifying 'locked-in syndrome'. Fully alert and conscious, locked-in patients cannot voluntarily move any part of their body apart from their eyes, the closest thing I could imagine to purgatory. The extraordinary lengths of hypothermic cardiac standstill were an attempt to minimise the chances of such catastrophic damage as the surgeon wielded his scalpel.

Filming Spetz and Brett discussing his operation the day before surgery, I witnessed a very different kind of skill. Somehow, even while candidly describing the most terrifying of worst-case scenarios, Spetz managed to convey both implacable confidence and kindness. I observed Brett and his parents almost visibly relaxing as Spetz answered their questions with quiet authority. He seemed entirely at ease with the risks. Even had they not had their faith in God, Spetz came across as the next best thing. He made you rush to place your trust in him.

I embraced Brett as we said goodbye, acutely aware that these might be the last words we would say to each other. The next morning, reunited beneath the glare of the theatre lights, I found him lying beneath green surgical drapes, eyes taped shut, head shaved and fastened to the operating table by metal pins drilled into his skull. The first phase of the surgery was under way. Spetz and his assistant had peeled back Brett's scalp and were now cutting a window into his skull. As in all big surgeries, excitement and expectation crackled round the room. A crowd of doctors had gathered to watch. The case, in its own way as epic as *King Lear*, promised all the drama and suspense of every good theatre production. The electric saw hummed like a dentist's drill as a scrub nurse sprayed water to keep the skull cool and catch the bone dust as it rose from the freshly sawn edge. My cameraman began to feel queasy as Spetz finally held aloft to the lens a large, intact piece of cranium before placing it, with a clink of porcelain on metal, into the waiting kidney dish.

Now Brett's brain was exposed. A hush descended as the huge operating chair from which Spetz would cut was manhandled into position. Modern binocular operating microscopes are spectacular feats of engineering that weigh around a quarter of a tonne, yet allow the surgeon to work with infinitesimal precision. He or she sits behind the microscope, peering down through tens of thousands of pounds' worth of state-of-the-art lenses at vastly magnified vistas of brain. From here, they can manipulate an array of microscopic instruments that in time come to feel, so Spetz told me, like an extension of the surgeon's own hands.

Brett's brain, illuminated by brilliant xenon light from within the microscope, was projected onto big screens around the operating theatre. Its tightly coiled terrain looked almost too sharp and bright to be real. Spetz sat hunched like a hawk over its prey, slowly but surely prising the brain away from the floor of the skull without tearing any of the minute veins and arteries that traversed every inch of its surface. Finally, he reached the basilar artery and the aneurysm itself, huge and menacing in widescreen, pulsating darkly in time with the heartbeat.

'OK,' said Spetz, leaning back in his chair. 'That is a truly exceptional aneurysm. It's over to you now, team.'

So far, so good. The cardiac standstill team could now get to work. The most effective way to cool Brett down was to connect one large vein and one large artery to sterile tubing that ran through a huge vat of ice. His blood would be diverted via the tubes out of his body, through the ice and back again, becoming ever colder with each cycle. Spellbound, we watched on the anaesthetist's monitor as, over the course of the next hour, Brett's temperature crept inexorably downwards. His heart began to slow and beat more erratically. At around fifteen degrees, the cardiac muscle was too cold to contract properly, and his heart began to fibrillate, quivering uncontrollably. For a few moments, the ECG trace flailed wildly before silently flatlining: the heart had come to a standstill.

At this point, but for the fact that he was cold, Brett was technically dead. All brain activity had ceased on the monitor. He no longer breathed or moved for himself. His heart was an inert lump of muscle. The anaesthetist started a stopwatch, counting down the minutes in which Spetz could safely operate before Brett's brain would begin to be damaged irreparably from the prolonged lack of oxygen.

As his blood was decanted out of his body, the aneurysm shrivelled from bulging monstrosity to empty husk. Spetz now had the space in which to manipulate its frail walls with slightly better odds of avoiding death or brain damage. As he wrestled with positioning a metal clip across the neck of the aneurysm, the theatre held its collective breath. We could only watch and hope. Finally, at around forty-two minutes, Spetz again leaned back in his chair. He had successfully clipped the aneurysm and it was time to warm up the patient.

Hypothermic cardiac standstills combine hi-tech science with some pretty basic plumbing. In the absence of a beating heart, Brett's blood was mechanically pumped through hot water to warm him up gradually. We watched with baited breath as his core body temperature slowly rose. For around half an hour, nothing happened. The ECG trace remained a flatline. Then, in a mirror image of what had gone before, the heart began to fibrillate, jittering chaotically on the cardiac monitor. From there, in a triumph of order over chaos that made me wonder at the physical tenacity of the human species, a normal heartbeat emerged. The heart's inbuilt pacemaker had found its rhythm. Brett's heart was back. At no point did the clip across the neck of the aneurysm dislodge, in spite of the high pressure, newly pumping arterial blood. Spetz had successfully dealt with the aneurysm. It was a neurosurgical triumph. We just had no way of knowing if the person Brett had survived intact.

After major neurosurgery, anaesthetists are eager to wake up the patient as quickly as possible. Everyone is on tenterhooks to know whether he or she has escaped significant brain damage. With Brett, it was no exception. Barely an hour after he left the operating theatre, sutured, stapled and bandaged, his anaesthetic was halted and he began to come round. Spetz allowed his family to visit. Then, we too were permitted to join them at the bedside. To our astonishment, Brett's eyes were open. He was alert and talking. It was almost impossible to believe.

'Hey,' he said when he saw me, still slurring from his anaesthetic. 'You think the folk in Great Britain will be pleased if I say hi?'

Journalists, like doctors, are not meant to cry on the job. But how could I not? Thanks to the extraordinary surgical skills of Spetz, his otherworldly calm under pressure, the exquisite engineering of the operating microscope, the pioneering doctors and scientists who had honed the technique of cardiac standstill, the seamless teamwork inside the operating theatre, the technology behind the heart-lung machine and, of course, a bloody great vat of ice, Brett had been killed and brought back from the dead, reborn as a man with a future. The husband he dreamed of being, the children he longed to father, the old age he hoped to enjoy – Spetz had given him a shot at them all. Tears of delight and wonder streamed down most of the faces in the room as Brett grinned at us sleepily. It was medicine at its most dazzling. Still years away from qualifying as a doctor, I could not imagine doing anything more humbling or fulfilling.

—∿—

A decade or so later, at the height of the junior doctors' dispute, the president of the Royal College of Physicians, Jane Dacre, would strive to reach out to disenchanted junior doctors with a social media campaign that used the hashtag #medicineisbrilliant. Like many leading figures in the medical establishment, she was distraught at the disillusionment and anger unleashed by the dispute among young medics. At the time, I dismissed her initiative as out-of-touch wishful thinking. The brilliance of medicine, like the love of my job I had once taken for granted, had long since been tarnished by the barrage of attacks from the media and political spin from the Health Secretary. Being reminded of how deeply rewarding our work had used to be felt faintly like adding insult to injury. In fact, I now think she was right. From the moment I set foot inside my medical school, I was overawed by the potential of medicine – the extraordinary capacity of the human body to endure and survive serious illness, of doctors and scientists to discover new cures and, above all, of the human spirit to rise above adversity with the kind of dignity and strength at which so often I could only marvel. Medicine felt like a belated love of my life. Intoxicating, dazzling, it was indeed brilliant and I was a woman obsessed.

CHAPTER 5

KINDNESS

The fourth year of my medical degree was mildly compromised by frequent dashes from the bedside to the toilet – the unfortunate consequence of mixing the smells of the ward with first-trimester morning sickness. Week by week, as my firstborn grew, all my painstakingly drawn diagrams of foetal development from past classes in embryology acquired a thrilling weight and substance. I watched with grim satisfaction as my body did exactly what my physiology textbooks predicted – ankles swelling with excess fluid, joints acquiring disconcerting flexibility as my due date fast approached. I was the first student in my medical school to become pregnant and, towards the end, continued to waddle defiantly on the morning ward rounds, daring any consultant to make a disparaging comment.

The birth itself, though traumatic, was eclipsed by what happened afterwards. The day after my Caesarean section,

61

still unhinged by love and bliss, helplessly besotted with my newborn son, I noticed his swaddle starting to twitch and jerk. Unwrapping the blanket revealed tiny arms and legs moving in rhythmic spasms. He was fitting – in our jargon, a tonic clonic seizure – though my treacly brain couldn't quite compute what was happening. Somehow, while my husband ran for a nurse, I had the presence of mind to record the seizure on my smartphone. By the time the on-call paediatrician arrived, the seizure had already ended but, after he'd watched the footage, his advice was not to worry unduly but to keep a close eye in case it happened again.

A seizure in a newborn can herald all manner of horrors – epilepsy, meningitis, a hypoxic brain injury sustained during childbirth, an intracranial bleed or tumour – far too many a medical student mother's worst nightmares. Even entertaining them made me feel queasy with rising panic. So I didn't. I surrendered myself willingly to the paediatrician's instructions. Don't worry. Don't fear the worst. It may be a one-off, it may mean nothing at all. Doctor, in this situation, simply had to know best because the alternative was unthinkable.

A day of observation passed without incident. He slept, snuffled, sighed, suckled and lulled me back into a lovestruck swoon. Perhaps, on reflection, the paediatricians now wondered, the fit hadn't been a real fit at all. A false alarm, a misdiagnosis. It felt like a reprieve – by the skin of our teeth, we'd got away with it and our son was deemed safe to go home. We started packing our bags, incredulous – as perhaps all new parents are – that the hospital could possibly be so blasé as to allow two rank amateurs who knew nothing about babies to waltz away with an actual child. Dave had just brought our pristine car seat onto the ward when, without warning, it happened again. The twitching was unmistakeable, even beneath blankets. A second seizure playing out before an audience of the three other new mothers in my bay and their three perfectly healthy newborns.

This time, every fact, every statistic I had ever learned melted away as our infant son, head arched back, jerked and bucked before me. I couldn't move. There was a sound in the distance, faint and ugly, that slowly coalesced into a scream. It took some time for me to understand that I was the person screaming.

A paediatric crash team were suddenly everywhere, wresting control, stripping blankets away, pressing an oxygen mask over blue-tinged lips, applying electrodes and tubes until our son was lost beneath the paraphernalia that might hold his life in the balance. They swept him away at a sprint to the NICU, the Neonatal Intensive Care Unit, as I clung for dear life to an empty cot-side. Just as nothing had prepared me for the ferocity of maternal love, so my body's response to the terror that my child might be dying was overwhelming and brutal. I recall not a touch or a word from anyone. Someone, a doctor, midwife or nurse must have tried to reassure me, but their words were obliterated by fear.

We were left alone to trace the crash team's steps through winding corridors until we found the NICU. The ward was almost too short-staffed to cope with the births, let alone spare someone to guide us. My scar was burning and I could only shuffle slowly, doubled over in pain. By the time we reached Intensive Care, a paediatrician was daubing disinfectant on our son's exposed spine, about to perform the lumbar puncture that would rule in or out bacterial meningitis. Our baby was screaming uncontrollably, though his lungs were too small to generate much noise above the machinery, bleeping and frenetic activity.

'You'd better not see this,' someone stated in tone that invited no argument, and escorted us briskly away. Alone in a relatives room, bewildered and fearful, we waited and waited for news. I felt diminished to the point of irrelevance. For twenty-four hours, I had provided my son with everything, and now I could do nothing to help him. Other hands, other humans were tending and deciding. Cut out of the loop, we sat in silence on NHS plastic chairs, green-tinged under hospital strip lights.

Finally, a nurse took us to the clear Perspex cot in which our son now lay, expertly swaddled, antibiotics dripping into one bandaged wrist. He was sleeping peacefully. The paediatricians were systematically working their way through my list of worst nightmares: treating for meningitis in case he was infected, scanning his skull in case he had a brain tumour, running a battery of tests on blood and spinal fluid in the hope of identifying another possible cause. He was, we were assured, in safe hands, but our world had tilted away from the sun.

Visiting hours were long over. Dave helped me back to the ward, then drove home to an empty house. I can only imagine the night he spent there, having believed he would be home with his wife and newborn child. Myself, I lay in the darkness, shrouded by curtains, listening to three other babies that cried so lustily, fed so greedily and were cradled so lovingly in their mothers' arms that morning couldn't come too soon. NICU called up to the ward. Our son had had no further fits, was awake and hungry, and would I like to feed him? I made the long trek to the NICU as quickly as hobbling allowed, and held my baby at last as, with a gusto that made my inner hopes soar, he loudly demanded to be fed.

The morning ward round was in full swing and, seeing no one to consult about where I should breastfeed, I sat in a plastic chair on the edge of the unit and awkwardly began to nurse my baby. Suddenly, I seemed to be overshadowed by men.

'What do you think you're doing?' barked one of them. 'You can't do that here. What are you doing? Someone sort this out.'

The consultant at the helm of the ward round wore a look of disgust on his face. Too shocked to respond, feeling as though I'd just committed a crime by semi-baring a breast in, of all places, a hospital, I stayed mute as a nurse swiftly erected a portable screen around me, this offensive presence in the NICU. She drew up a chair beside mine. There was something intolerable about this act of minor humiliation, coming as it did after such a brutal twenty-four hours. I felt crushed and small. And, somehow, the nurse, whose name, appropriately enough, was Precious, seemed intuitively to feel and understand everything. Tenderly, she helped adjust my son's position on my breast and wiped away my tears. Smiling, she squeezed my hand and crooned with genuine delight, 'Oh, my God, he is beautiful. He is perfect. He is beautiful.'

I don't think I have ever felt such gratitude.

'Do you think so? Is he really?'

'Oh, God! This boy is beautiful.'

In fact, as even I would later concede, my son started life looking not dissimilar to Andrew Lloyd Webber, but that was entirely irrelevant. He was perfect. He was beautiful. In my eyes and now in those of Precious. She will never know what her kindness brought me. She gave me the one thing she didn't have – her time – when her jobs must have been stacking up, piling one upon the another. Yet still she sat, stroking my hand, beaming at my newborn. We stayed that way for far too long. I'm sure it made her morning hellish. And to this day I wish I had had the presence of mind to tell her what this had meant to me. That through her kindness – freely dispensed, yet priceless – I had found cause to believe that whatever happened next, however this would end, I wouldn't be in it alone.

Our son left the NICU after a couple of days, a diagnosis eluding the exhaustive testing. A few days after that, he was deemed fit for discharge and finally, gingerly, we carried our car seat and baby across the hospital grounds and into our car. I remember raising an eyebrow at Dave as he drove us home.

'How could they possibly have let us out with him?' I asked. The old joke, spoken only half in jest. 'Are they insane? Don't they know we have absolutely no idea what we're doing?'

We smiled at each other, elated and terrified. We were officially a family. Ten years later my son, mercifully, remains perfectly healthy. But, a decade after we faced the abyss, the compassion and humanity of one NICU nurse remain indelibly etched in my memory.

—∿—

Until I faced the prospect of losing a child, I didn't know what grief was. I regarded myself as reasonably empathetic and thought I could imagine what grieving must feel like. But that presumption, it turned out, was a glib one – itself a failure of imagination. I didn't know how it could suck the air from your lungs or cause your legs to buckle or have you feverishly doing deals with a God you didn't believe in to take you, not your child – anything in order to spare him. I'd had no idea.

Two experiences during my five years of medical school did more to shape how I would subsequently practise medicine than anything acquired from a textbook. This was the first. It took a brush with disaster to taste how disaster really feels. I now knew how little I really grasped about the impact upon patients and relatives of the diagnoses of cancer I would one day deliver, of the news I would break that a loved one had died, of the destruction I would come to unleash as I went about my daily work as a doctor. There were whole realms of pain and fear about which I knew almost nothing and never would, unless I lived something like them. I vowed never to forget that.

More prosaically, but equally important, my brief experience as a maternity-ward inpatient had taught me how profoundly disempowering hospital could be. The quasi-knowledge I'd acquired as a medical student offered no protection against the name tags, the anonymous hospital gowns, the patient notes that everyone reads bar the patient themselves, the subtle stripping of one's power and sense of identity. I'd hated it. It had made me feel so small and vulnerable.

Even as I continued to amass facts at a rate that made my brain ache, I could no longer shake the conviction that something fundamental was missing from medical school. Perhaps what every aspiring empathetic doctor needs is a compulsory stint as a patient. Instead, we acquire 'communication skills' through workshops with actors and, if we're lucky, opportunistic observation of real doctors having those difficult conversations with their patients.

What I discovered only through first-hand experience was that throughout all the toil of a degree in medicine – the painstaking acquisition of the knowledge and skills that would one day be the bedrock of my practice – I already possessed the quality that, above all others, could make my patients feel cared for: my ordinary, everyday humanity. The transformative power of a kind word or caring gesture was even now within my gift and I could use it, as Precious had, to ensure my patients felt neither abandoned nor alone. Kindness has always meant more than generosity and affection, with 'kind' finding its origins in the Old English noun 'cynd', meaning family, lineage or kin. For me, the core meaning of kindness resides in this sense of connectedness to – kinship with – others. In the alien, disorienting world of a hospital, I had experienced for myself that an act of reaching out to a patient as a fellow human being, a kindred spirit, no matter how small, could be invaluable. Their absence, on the other hand, made hospital a bleak and lonely place.

It seemed to me that, until now, medical school had largely taught us distance: how to separate from, not connect with, our patients. And nor, arguably, could it be otherwise. How else can a doctor effectively function amid the daily decay, stench and indignities of disease, all the pain and distress that infuses a hospital? Unlike the majority of medical students, I had already seen dead bodies close up during my time documenting the civil war in the Democratic Republic of Congo, and my instincts then were to flinch and recoil. At times I'd had to avert my eyes to stop myself weeping, at others to stop myself retching. I remember one young girl's leg being cleaned by a nurse as we filmed inside a Médecins Sans Frontièrs makeshift canvas hospital. As so often in Congo, most of the children were machete victims, double, triple or even quadruple amputees after a militia group had overrun their village. But, in this case, it was a bullet wound that gaped like a crater in the child's thigh and, even to my inexpert eyes, was horribly infected. Perhaps she was ten or eleven. Her screams of pain and pleas in Congolese for the torture to stop went unheeded as, with gentle words but relentless professionalism, the nurse continued the wound care without which her young patient might not survive. The smell of rotting flesh was overpowering and the nurse's ability to continue working while causing such suffering was beyond anything I could imagine.

Perhaps, in order to deliver a workforce of doctors capable of immersion in the brutality of illness, an essential role of medical school is to build up, not break down, barriers between doctors and the young people they used to be. After all, no one wants their doctor immobilised by sentiment. The acquisition of detachment, the blunting of 'normal' human responses to disfigurement and death, might just be what gives doctors the ability to get on and do their job.

More than anywhere else, medical students' innate taboos are confronted and overcome in the dissection room. Even after I'd witnessed death and dying, nothing prepared me for the act of supreme violation that dissecting a human corpse would feel like.

—/\\/—

Over a hundred of us crowded outside the heavy Victorian doors of the anatomy room, waiting to cross the threshold for the first time. A faint scent of formaldehyde hung in the air. That slightly too loud, bravado-driven chatter of people who want you to know they aren't remotely anxious flooded the corridor. We were first-year medical students, a few weeks into our course. Everyone seemed very young and jittery. Indeed, most of us were still teenagers. Appreciably older, at twenty nine, I was preoccupied with whether I could handle a morning spent precision-flaying a human corpse. My father had regaled me with stories of dissection from his day. Back then, in the sixties, some wisecracking wit would inevitably borrow a human hand from the dissection room and proffer it in greeting to a stranger in the pub, to be met with predictable horror – and the delight and amusement of the assembled medics. Did that kind of thing still happen? I was worried about being too prudish, out of kilter with my fellow students.

In fact, when the professor of anatomy ushered us inside, he did so with the utmost solemnity. Things had changed for the better. We gathered around him, feigning nonchalance, surrounded by a couple of dozen stainless-steel tables, each bearing a body shrouded in white muslin. Out of the corners of their eyes, everyone surreptitiously glanced at the contours of the corpses. The formaldehyde stung my nostrils. I could almost feel it permeating my skin. The walls were lined with shelves upon which jar after jar of anatomical specimen sat, suspended in preservative. Body parts, splayed and pinned, in various stages of dissection. Hands, hearts, torsos, heads. I found myself transfixed by a series of jars in which were marooned human foetuses, graded according to size, from the tiny to the almost full-term. Miniature fists, fiercely poised to leap at life, eyes closed for eternity. I was as prepared as I could be for a wizened old corpse, but I hadn't anticipated confronting dead babies.

The professor spoke of who the corpses we were about to start dissecting had been. Somebody's grandmother, somebody's grandfather. Someone who had chosen, before they died, to subject their future self to our inept blades that we might learn, in clumsy steps, to delay others, undead, from this room and its jars and silver slabs.

'Each body in this room today is that of a person who chose deliberately to give their body to you. They wanted you to learn. They believed that giving you their body might make you better doctors.' He paused to survey the room. 'It is your honour and privilege to dissect these bodies. Imagine someone close to death thinking of how they could help others after dying, choosing to sign the forms that would hand over their body to you.'

As he talked, gently yet authoritatively, like a father to his children, he deftly unfurled a sheet of plastic until there, before a hundred pairs of eyes, lay the body of a man who had chosen to offer up his withered limbs to us and to this peculiar afterlife, measured out in weekly doses of our scalpels' scrutiny. I couldn't shake the thought from my head that not even this man's dearest love had known his body as we would.

During our months of dissection, the professor went on, every scrap of embalmed flesh would be carefully collected and stored. At the end of the year, a church service would be held in which the relatives of the individuals who had so graciously donated their bodies to us would assemble to say goodbye to their loved ones. We were welcome, indeed encouraged, to attend. He knew exactly how to impress upon us the enormity of what we were about to undertake. These were human beings, our kindred who had bequeathed us their bodies, and he expected our respect. Long gone, to my relief, were the levity and japes of old.

We dispersed into small groups around a pre-allotted table and prepared to dissect a human thorax. First, we donned thin plastic gloves and unwrapped the body from its shroud, releasing a concentrated wave of formaldehyde. This would be 'our' body for the next six months. Skin grey, eyes closed, mouth open in a perpetual grimace – I found it easier to think of the corpse as an 'it' than as a human and hastily volunteered to make the first incision. I think I wanted to break that taboo as quickly as possible. I cut. Embalmed flesh has the consistency of cold wax. There is no elasticity. It slices like refrigerated parmesan. What in any other circumstances would have been a crime, the defilement of a corpse, was now our twice weekly ritual.

In those early days, so long as I didn't look at the face and refused to think of the corpse as he once might have lived, I found I could suspend my instinct to recoil. Swiftly, though, no mental effort was required. Familiarity bred detachment and, after only a couple of sessions, I came to love dissection. The physical craft was only the start of it. Learning anatomy, it turned out, was part linguistics, part cartography. Slowly but surely, I began to label in Latin every bone, nerve and muscle of the human body, lovingly mapping what had once, for me, been uncharted territory. Anconeus. Brachialis. Lunate. Triquetrum. The new language in which I was gaining proficiency seemed as exotic as it was beautiful.

Sometimes, lying on the sofa late at night revising my anatomy, I'd make a small movement – turning my hand inwards or flexing my thumb – and rehearse the Latin that described the intricate engineering underlying the action. The mere act of raising my little finger, for example, involved extensor digit minimi, the lateral epicondyle of humerus, the fifth metacarpophalangeal joint, the posterior interosseous nerve. Being able to visualise and whisper every part felt like earning exclusive membership of a secret society. The excluded, in this case, were the general public. More than once, my boyfriend caught me staring intently at the sinews of his arm or the veins of his neck, knowing full well the look wasn't lust but merely my latest attempt at reading his flesh. At the time, this didn't strike me as odd, although, with hindsight, I must concede amazement that he married me.

Like the formaldehyde that seeped into our skin and clothes, lingering long after we had left the department for the day, my relationship with the human body was enduringly altered by the experience of dissecting it. Before, the bodies of others had been, among other things, objects of desire, beauty and limitless comfort, when I considered the potency of a simple human embrace. But now they were also texts to interpret, with inner meanings to lay bare. Behind a spontaneous smile of greeting I saw risorius and zygomaticus major and minor elevating the corners of the lips into their upturned welcome. The classical lopsided facial 'droop' of a stroke, on the other hand, told me that the seventh cranial nerve controlling these muscles had been impaired by a mishap in the brain.

The price of six months in the dissection room was undoubtedly a loss of innocence. Bodies hadn't shed their beauty or desirability, but in death they no longer held the power to disturb. More than anything, what dissection taught me was the vital skill of distancing myself from my patients. Rather than worry about my newfound toughness, I'd been hardened in a way I approved of. I couldn't imagine a place for squeamishness in the doctors' mess.

CHAPTER 6

CALLOUSNESS

The first few years of a degree in medicine used to be devoted to giving students an exhaustive grounding in anatomy, biochemistry and physiology before letting them loose on the wards. The preferred model these days is for the students to encounter patients from day one, alongside the acquisition of theoretical knowledge, with the intended benefits of helping students feel comfortable around patients and of embedding all that theory in a meaningful context. A few universities still prefer the old style and, being something of a single-minded purist, I chose one of the few remaining traditional medical schools: total immersion in theory for two years followed by another three of living and breathing the hospital. I wanted the academic knowledge under my belt before surrounding myself with patients. Consequently, just before commencing my three years of clinical medicine, I knew next to nothing about its practice.

At this time, my grandfather, himself a retired doctor, was rushed one day to hospital, having collapsed from an irregular heartbeat. At ninety-two, he had been a doctor before the NHS even existed, spending the Second World War on a Royal Naval destroyer in the North Atlantic, protecting Britain's lifeline of food and supplies from America. His military officer's bearing never left him until his final days in hospital. After the war, he had become a general practitioner in the days when GPs were often the rocks of their local communities. My younger self thrilled at the story of him carrying one of his elderly patients from the flames of her burning home, after the fire brigade had deemed it too dangerous to enter. As a child, I hung on his every word.

Of the scores of stories I never tired of hearing, my favourite took place in his local greengrocer's, just after the end of the war. The grocer, whose children my grandfather had delivered in a downstairs bedroom, ushered him into a room at the back of the store.

'I've got something for you, Doctor,' he said, conspiratorially. 'I want you to take this home and give it to your family. They're the first ones we've seen since 1939. Give them to your children.'

He produced a large cardboard box, wrapped in brown paper and tied with string.

'Don't open it now. Take it home.'

As my grandfather carefully unwrapped the paper in the seat of his car, the concentrated aroma of a couple of dozen oranges flooded the vehicle. Almost garishly bright, the fruit looked impossibly exotic after years of wartime rationing. He sat for a while, contemplating his gift, then set off decisively, not on the route back home but up the hill to the local sanatorium for children with tuberculosis. In those days, with antibiotics still in their infancy, the only widely used treatments for tuberculosis were rest and fresh air, each as ineffectual as the other. Most of the young patients in the sanatorium were pale and skeletal, inexorably wasting away. My grandfather was well known to the staff.

'Dr Rendall!' welcomed the sister. 'Come in, come in.'

'Can't stay, Sister,' he said, handing over the package. 'Just called by to drop off something for the children. Here. I hope they enjoy them.'

Now my grandfather was himself in an institution, one of the acute medical wards of his local hospital. We had left him there earlier that day, frail but comfortable, on a cocktail of medications for his heart. That night, like most men in their nineties, he awoke with the need to pass urine. It was three in the morning. Though his hospital bed was only yards from the toilet, he was well aware that, at age ninety-two, deconditioned by illness, attempting to reach it unaided was fraught with jeopardy. He risked a fall he was too debilitated to survive. My grandfather was not a man for whom asking for help came naturally. Nonetheless, he pressed the button at his bedside to summon a nurse's assistance. Once, twice, multiple times. But, in the eternal twilight of a hospital at night – the incessant bleeping of blocked intravenous drips, the whining of the automated blood-pressure cuffs – flesh-and-blood nurses are thin on the ground. An old man needing to urinate commanded no one's attention. Time crawled by.

By 5 a.m., the choice he faced was stark. He could give in to the burning pressure in his overstretched bladder, soiling himself in his hospital bed, or he could attempt to stagger unaided to the bathroom. Possible calamity versus certain indignity. Falling onto hospital linoleum or spending what remained of the night lying soaked in cold urine. I imagine my granddad, this larger-than-life former NHS doctor, gingerly shuffling his six-foot frame to the edge of the mattress in the semidarkness. Gripping the bed for support, steadying himself for a moment, then clumsily rising to standing. A foot extended, a first attempted step. And then the fall, the smack of cranium on floor, the drip stand collapsing on top of him. How long he lay semiconscious is unclear. But, when his son, my father, arrived the next day at his bedside, he found his own father battered and bruised, in considerable pain, with a newly paralysed left arm hanging by his side.

The medical registrar on the morning ward round faced a doctor's worst nightmare: a relative who was himself a doctor, brimming with terse questions about his loved one's apparent mistreatment.

'Who examined my father's neurology after the fall and what were the findings?'

No one, it seemed, had bothered.

'Well, my examination just now indicates left-upper-limb paralysis and a large cervical haematoma. I suspect my father has had a broken neck since yesterday morning.'

There was a pause, a painfully long one.

'Did no one on your team consider examining him or imaging his neck? Not even your consultant?'

The hastily organised CT scan confirmed that my grandfather had indeed fractured a vertebra in his neck. He lasted two more days, awkwardly trussed up in a foam collar, before dying at night in a hospital side room.

—∿—

At the time of my grandfather's death, my father's bedside advocacy on behalf of his own father barely made clinical sense to me, still steeped, as I was, in only the theory of medicine. All I knew was that the manner in which he had died was terribly, inexcusably wrong. And, even now, I find that imagining anyone – let alone someone I love – reduced to such indignity causes me to recoil inside.

No one, I was certain, had set out to treat my grandfather unkindly. Nonetheless, through their failure to answer his buzzes for help – their seeming indifference – the night staff on his ward had indirectly caused him to suffer torment, humiliation and an ultimately fatal fall. It never occurred to me, as yet unexposed to how precariously staffed a hospital at night can be, that the nurses may have had no choice, too few of them stretched too thinly across too many patients. I struggled, perhaps naïvely, to see how this could have happened in any hospital, let alone in what was ostensibly a centre of NHS excellence. Something must be rotten, I reasoned, if staff who had chosen to devote their professional lives to caring for others were somehow, through inaction, so degrading their patients. Haunted by the gulf between the man I had loved and the shadow to which the hospital had reduced him, I felt that the NHS on this occasion had lost its humanity entirely.

Unbeknown to me, at exactly this time – in 2005 – patients in another UK hospital were being subjected to casual cruelty *en masse*. For years, the hospital in question, the Stafford, part of the Mid Staffordshire NHS Foundation Trust, treated patients with such shocking brutality that 'Mid Staffs' has since become a shorthand for the most barbaric failings of NHS care imaginable. While concerns about mistreatment and excessive mortality rates started to emerge in 2007, it took another two years before these were properly investigated. Hundreds of patients were estimated to have died unnecessarily in Stafford Hospital, now renamed the County Hospital and administered by University Hospitals of North Midlands NHS Trust. After increasing pressure from bereaved families, the government commissioned Sir Robert Francis QC to conduct two inquiries, one of which was a full public inquiry, into what became one of the biggest scandals in NHS history. His reports paint an extraordinarily detailed picture of routine neglect, humiliation and brutality at the hands of NHS staff:

> This is a story of appalling and unnecessary suffering of hundreds of people. They were failed by a system which ignored the warning signs and put corporate self-interest and cost control ahead of patients and their safety.
>
> There was a lack of care, compassion, humanity and leadership. The most basic standards of care were not observed, and fundamental rights to dignity were not respected. Elderly and vulnerable patients were left unwashed, unfed and without fluids. They were deprived of dignity and respect. Some patients had to relieve themselves in their beds when they were offered no help to get to the bathroom. Some were left in excrement stained sheets and beds. They had to endure filthy conditions in their wards. There were incidents of callous treatment by ward staff. Patients who could not eat or drink without help did not receive it. Medicines were prescribed but not

given. The accident and emergency department as well as some wards had insufficient staff to deliver safe and effective care. Patients were discharged without proper regard for their welfare.[8]

The first Francis report was published in 2010, my inaugural year as a qualified doctor. Like many other doctors in my hospital, I felt deeply ashamed of the press coverage, tainted by association, and keen to distance myself from the findings as far as possible. The more fervently we condemned what had gone on, the more clearly we signalled – or so we hoped – that we were a different, better breed of clinician.

'This could never happen here,' our consultant stated emphatically to us. 'It's inconceivable. This is a classic example of poor leadership. A culture was allowed to flourish when it should have been stamped out immediately.'

Barely six months a doctor, feeling uncharacteristically timid on this occasion about speaking up, I reluctantly kept quiet. I imagined similar pronouncements being made in doctors' messes up and down the country. The defensiveness was understandable, but the truth wasn't so simple. I knew, for example, that what my grandfather had endured in an entirely different hospital echoed the testimony provided by relatives of the patients who had died in Mid Staffs. That meant the inhumanity was not an isolated incident. In at least one other NHS hospital, the one in which my grandfather had died, staff were also failing – albeit perhaps on this one occasion alone – in their basic duty of providing safe, humane care. My consultant may have dismissed as inconceivable a repeat of Mid Staffs in our hospital, but conceivability, one could argue, reflects the mind of the conceiver as much as the world around them. Indeed, Sir Robert Francis singled out denial among the workforce at Mid Staffs as one of the drivers of the unchecked cruelty: staff had closed their eyes and ears to what was unfolding around them.

Arriving home from the hospital that night, I planted myself on the sofa with a large glass of wine and read the full report cover to cover. After a while, the cumulative effect of reading account after account of relentless mistreatment started to feel sickening. Invariably, it was the most vulnerable patients, the frail and elderly, who had been robbed of their dignity. The sister-in-law of a retired academic who could have been my grandfather described his deep humiliation at being left in soiled squalor in Mid Staffs:

> The nurses there weren't unkind to him, but they were overworked. We often felt that if we asked them if they would clean him up ... it would be hours before they came back to clean him up, and in that time he was just lying in a dirty bed with dirty nightwear on, and he didn't want me to go in the room, even. He would say: don't come near me, don't come near me, I smell; and he was a very fastidious man and he really was left lying in his own excrement.[9]

Late at night now, with most of the bottle of wine gone, I ruminated on how it is that good staff turn bad, though still skirting the obvious question: could this, one day, be me? Even if not quite yet, was I capable of becoming the kind of doctor who, at best, turns a blind eye to suffering and, at worst, behaves in ways that cause it? Francis had identified a large number of different causes of the scandal, not least a bullying culture in which many staff were too afraid to speak out and those who did felt their concerns were ignored. My own timidity earlier in the day – too compliant to disagree in public with my boss's declamations – hardly reflected well in that context. Suppose that day in, day out, my ward were an environment devoid of humanity. Would I put myself on the line by taking a stand, or would I quietly conform, following the lead of my colleagues?

The testimony given by one junior doctor to Francis nagged away at me. He described his shock, on arriving at Mid Staffs from another hospital, at the woefully inadequate care that his fellow doctors and nurses in the Emergency Department seemed to accept as normal:

> I think it had been an incremental thing where things had become harder and harder and harder and [the other staff] didn't actually realise just how far off acceptable standards things had slipped to, and I don't think that any of them would have let that happen if it had happened overnight. I think they would have been up in arms, but I think it was just so gradual that they didn't recognise it.[9]

I thought back to an incident on my own ward a few weeks earlier. The SEU, or Surgical Emergency Unit, had a reputation for being something of a patient-crunching factory. If you didn't earn yourself an operation pretty damn quickly, it often seemed, you were spat out as swiftly as the surgeons could manage. Infirmity was no excuse. If you weren't robust enough for home, there were a thousand ways to turf you into the hands of a less single-minded speciality, with the acute general medics invariably being targeted as the dumping ground of least resistance.

This surgical stereotype neglects, of course, the systemic factors that can force such a dizzying throughput of patients. One reason an acute surgical unit turns over patients so rapidly is because, if surgeons don't do this, they cannot accept the next patient in need of an operation. Instead, surgically unwell patients who cannot get into the unit either wait inappropriately in A&E or – possibly worse – are sent to medical wards where they can receive inadequate surgical nursing and usually a longer wait before review by a surgical consultant. Acute surgical beds are acute – as short stay as possible – precisely because they are required for patients who desperately need an operation from only those clinicians, the surgeons, who can give them one.

Nevertheless in this context, one surgeon's morning ward round had been exceptional. The night before, I'd admitted an elderly man to the SEU. Brought by ambulance to the hospital in excruciating abdominal pain, Mr Skipton had been rushed straight to the CT scanner. Haggard, gaunt and frightened, he'd asked me not to leave him even as the porters were wheeling him away down the corridor.

The next morning, just prior to meeting the patient for the first time, my consultant surveyed the CT scan. Everyone jostled for a view of the computer monitor tucked away behind the nurses' station.

'Well,' said the surgeon, after a brief pause. 'He's fucked, isn't he?'

The scans were indeed bleak, though the surgeon's bluntness made me wince. My patient's pain was being caused by a huge tumour obstructing his bowel and aggressively invading the rest of his abdomen. His liver was riddled with metastatic cancer. At ninety-three, active treatment of his malignancy was not going to be an option.

Mr Skipton was now being fed and watered through a drip in his arm and a tube down his nose. He stared up in trepidation as my boss, impatient to get to theatre as quickly as possible, alighted at the bedside. I hastily drew the flimsy curtains. Without so much as an introduction, he broke the news to the patient of his terminal illness by turning away to the bedside entourage and muttering, perfectly audibly, 'Get a palliative care nurse to come and see him.' No one had even told 'him' he had cancer.

As panic began to rise in Mr Skipton's face, I remember catching the ward sister's eye to see her cringing alongside me. But trying to undo the damage would take so long and the ward round was already sweeping on. I had a moment in which to act decisively. I could have chosen to earn my consultant's wrath by remaining at my patient's bedside. Instead, to my shame, I scuttled dutifully after my boss, leaving someone else to pick up the pieces.

All that stood between Stafford Hospital and this sorry encounter was a missing family member – a wife, perhaps – who, years later, through bitter tears, might go on to describe the lack of compassion to an impassive QC, her words discreetly transcribed by a stenographer tucked away in the corner, immortalising yet another piece of damning testimony. I could blame my inaction on my lowly status at the bottom of the food chain – the most junior, and thus least powerful member of the team of doctors – but the fact remained that I'd known it was wrong and done nothing about it. All of us were complicit, including me. So were we really any different from, any better than, the staff who had allowed, even if they not actively participated in, the horrors of Mid Staffs? Like frogs who accept being boiled alive without a croak of complaint, provided they are heated sufficiently gradually, were the newest recruits to the wards of NHS hospitals being stealthily inured to unacceptable levels of brutality?

The trouble with trying to answer these questions was, I didn't have a clear grip on 'normal' any more. The moment I'd first pressed a scalpel into a human corpse, normality had ceased to mean the same for me as for my non-medic friends. And, once you start breaking taboos, perhaps you need external guidance about when to stop. You can no longer rely upon the churning in your stomach or the tingle down your spine because you've developed an abnormal steeliness that enables you to act in defiance of your basic instincts or – worse – cease to feel them at all.

My SEU was not Mid Staffs. Of that I was certain. The majority of the nurses and doctors were kind and professional. Patients were not routinely being starved or soiled. But, in one fundamental respect, my place of work felt uneasily similar. There were, from my frontline perspective, insufficient doctors and nurses. Francis had identified the root cause of the horrors of Mid Staffs as being the severely depleted numbers of frontline staff. The Trust board, determined to win from the government the coveted 'foundation Trust' status, had sought to demonstrate their fiscal prudence by saving £10 million. This would be largely achieved through draconian staffing cuts, in spite of warnings from both doctors and nurses:

I have no doubt that the economies imposed by the Trust Board, year after year, had a profound effect on the organisation's ability to deliver a safe and effective service. With hindsight it is possible to discern an ever more desperate situation,' stated Francis. 'A chronic shortage of staff, particularly nursing staff, was largely responsible for the substandard care.'[1]

In some ways, the testimony from overstretched individual members of staff working at Mid Staffs mirrored the anguish of patients and relatives. One nurse from the hospital's emergency assessment unit told Francis:

I remember at the time when our staffing levels were cut and we were just literally running around. Our ward was known as Beirut from several other wards. I heard it nicknamed that. ITU used to call us Beirut . . . I remember saying: this will have repercussions, this can't go on like this. Because relatives were regularly coming up to us and saying: my Mum has been buzzing for this long, there has been a buzzer going there for that long.[9]

Another nurse recalled her distress and guilt at being too overstretched to provide humane care for her patients:

In some ways I feel ashamed because I have worked there and I can tell you that I have done my best, and sometimes you go home and you are really upset because you can't say that you have done anything to help. You feel like you have not

– although you have answered buzzers, you have provided the medical care but it never seemed to be enough. There was not enough staff to deal with the type of patient that you needed to deal with, to provide everything that a patient would need. You were doing – you were just skimming the surface and that is not how I was trained.[9]

The junior doctor from the Mid Staffs Emergency Department who had speculated about incremental brutality building up over time was adamant that the fundamental problem in the hospital was not the quality of its staff, but their shortage and the overstretched system within which they were being obliged to work, forcing them to keep their heads down and muddle through the best they could:

There just were not enough staff . . . Very few people come to work to do a bad job and I have never met a nurse who comes to work to do a bad job. The nurses were so under-resourced they were working extra hours, they were desperately moving from place to place to try to give adequate care to patients. If you are in that environment for long enough, what happens is you become immune to the sound of pain. You either become immune to the sound of pain or you walk away. You cannot feel people's pain, you cannot continue to want to do the best you possibly can when the system says no to you, you can't do the best you can. And the system in the hospital said no to the nursing staff doing the best they could and to the doctors.[9]

This struck a disconcerting chord. Only a few months into my life as a doctor, immunity to the sound of pain was something with which I was already familiar. In some ways, it was a prerequisite for doing my job. Every time I assessed a patient's level of consciousness, for example, and they failed to open their eyes in response to my voice, I would grind my knuckles into their breastbone with such force that all but the most deeply unconscious of patients would flinch, groan or cry out loudly with pain. Those cries caused me not a moment's guilt. In provoking pain, I felt the opposite sensation – a wave of relief – since I now knew that the patient's brain injury was not as severe as I had feared. Without first causing the pain to which I graded their response, I had no way of objectively quantifying their conscious level.

More prosaically, I'd moved on from my early days of struggling ineptly to site cannulas in my patients' veins, their grimaces at my clumsy efforts making me hot and sweaty with guilt. I'd learned that treating the task as a purely technical challenge, rather than a human encounter, gave the patient the best chance of a pain-free cannula. Paradoxically, being cruel was the best way to be kind. I would talk gently and soothingly as I decisively stabbed them, but, inside, I was ruthlessly focused, feeling nothing at all. It worked. I became cold but proficient – a proficiency that spared my patients the bumbling misery of an incompetent, if kindly, practitioner. Notably, only children in our hospital had the automatic right to a dollop of anaesthetic cream that would numb the site of their cannula. And even then, this was probably more for the sake of expediency, not kindness, with distraught tots being some of the most challenging and time-consuming patients to manage. Everyone else was expected to bear the few seconds of pain, even though, for an unlucky minority with 'difficult' veins, those seconds could drag out into half an hour or more of increasingly painful attempts at cannulation. It had never occurred to me to question why, if we knew a patient had 'bad' veins, we didn't pre-empt our efforts with the kindness of a squirt of local anaesthetic.

In fact, no one at medical school had ever discussed with us the idea that inflicting a minimal degree of pain might be a necessary component of providing exemplary medical care. Nor challenged us to question when its infliction was justifiable, and when it was simply abuse. I thought back to one of my surgical inpatients who had recently become dangerously septic, his body overwhelmed with bacterial infection. The source of the bugs was unclear, so I was asked to perform a rectal examination, exploring the rectum with my gloved finger to see if his prostate gland was inflamed. Based on my examination technique, it was not. But when my consultant repeated my pitifully gentle examination, causing the patient to leap off the bed with a howl of pain, the prostate was clearly exquisitely tender. My feeble, minimalist technique – the product of not wanting to cause my patient discomfort – had wholly failed to elicit the diagnosis. In attempting to be kind, I had merely let my patient down.

While effective medicine undoubtedly entails a degree of detachment, I had a sneaking fear that, on my SEU, our patients' distress might be turning into white noise, a persistent but necessarily surmountable distraction. The fact was, there were simply insufficient doctors to manage the ward. As house officers, we barely had time to think straight. Four of us should have been looking after the hundred or so surgical inpatients, but sickness, night shifts and annual leave meant that rarely were there more than three of us, and frequently we were down to two.

As for our immediate seniors, the surgical trainees, they too were desperately short-staffed, struggling to balance on call admissions, which they were usually left to deal with on their own, along with supporting their juniors and getting into theatre for their actual training. Above them, the surgical registrars and consultants on call were often unable to get up to the wards not because they were loathe to leave clinic or theatre, but because they physically could not. The consultant in charge might appear frustrated and rushed since he or she was the sole individual in charge of over one hundred acutely unwell patients, trying to see all of them in the time it took to anaesthetise their first patient in theatre. If they were late for theatre, they would cause a whole team of often over ten staff, as well as the anaesthetised patient, to be kept waiting. In short, at every level of seniority, the system – the sheer lack of capacity for surgical beds and theatre time – was pushing all of us away from kindness and further towards callousness. It felt like a Mid Staffs in the making.

For we house officers, the sheer volume and complexity of patients daily outstripped our ability to keep then safe unless we toiled without a break from the moment we arrived at work until several hours after we were meant to have gone home. Often, this meant starting work at 7 a.m. and not stopping until 10 or 11 p.m. Not infrequently, I was filled with dread at the thought of the effort required to get through another day.

'Hey ho,' my friend would say as we changed into our scrubs each morning. 'Fancy being assaulted for the next sixteen hours?'

We laughed mirthlessly at the comment, which, though crude and inappropriate, somehow captured the sense of the physical violation inherent in a job that denies you time to eat, drink or even visit a toilet. I held the current unit record for interrupted wee breaks: no fewer than five bleeps from the nurses during one thwarted attempt at urination. Needless to say, no one was the slightest bit interested in our grumbling. In their day as junior doctors, went the consultants' mantra, it was so much worse – we didn't know how lucky we were not to be working the 120-hour weeks of old.

Perhaps. But the old days had at least had proper teams of doctors, a traditional surgical 'firm', led by a consultant who kept the same set of juniors for six months or more. We were mere shift workers, numbers on a spreadsheet who slotted in and out of days and nights on the roster almost as interchangeably as the patients. No one knew us, let alone formed a meaningful relationship with us. Left, by and large, to our own devices, we would race through our jobs at breakneck speed to try to stop them overwhelming us. We could just about survive fifteen hours of nonstop work, but, when the end of a 'normal' working day started nudging midnight, our judgement became blurred and muddy. Sometimes, towards the end of a shift, I felt so drunk with fatigue I could barely pronounce my name, let alone feel confident with patients' lives in my hands. It felt terribly unstable and fraught with risk, as though at any moment catastrophe might strike. But our warnings to our consultants fell on deaf ears. At no point would anyone above us in the hierarchy admit that the unit was understaffed. Instead, an unspoken yet implied criticism hung in the air: that we were to blame for our excessive hours, failing to conduct ourselves with the expected efficiency.

CALLOUSNESS

I wanted to care, I really did. Indeed, sometimes the only thing that gave my day meaning was the time I spent quietly talking to a patient, a moment of focused calm in the maelstrom. But – particularly when forced by another doctor's absence to do the job of two doctors – that time devoted to my relationship with my patients came at a heavy personal price. Every weekday I'd return to the house many hours after my toddler was asleep in his cot. One Saturday morning, after another 'forty'-hour week that had turned into seventy, I remember sitting numbly on the floor with him as he crooned with delight in my arms, too tired even to respond. Those extra thirty hours had, as usual, gone unpaid and unnoticed. Week by week, the cumulative effects of exhaustion made maintaining one's compassion that bit harder. If I were strictly honest with myself, on reading the testimony from the staff at Mid Staffs, I found elements with which I identified.

In one sense, none of this mattered. Plenty of people work long and hard, for a great deal less money than doctors. And plenty of jobs have no autonomy or meaning, whereas – when things go right – being a doctor brings the ultimate reward of feeling as though you have touched someone's life, helped make a difference when it really counted. It wasn't that I sought anyone's sympathy or pity. But I feared that, if my hours and workload continued as they were, I might fail to cling onto the one thing that had driven me into medicine in the first place: my compassion. That or I might just crack up.

CHAPTER 7

HAEMORRHAGE

I couldn't decide whether I possessed the energy to exterminate my companion. It had been a long night. Normally, stamping on one of the cockroaches that invaded the hospital corridors under the cover of darkness was a particular perk of my night shifts. Infestation control was everyone's job, after all. But it was approaching 8 a.m., my shift was almost over, and I felt like a dead woman walking, too bombed out to derive any pleasure from dispatching pests to cockroach heaven.

Studies show that the fatigue levels experienced by doctors at the end of busy night shifts can impair their mental acuity more effectively than exceeding the alcohol limit for driving. So, if you become unwell in hospital at the wrong moment, you might find your life rests in the hands of someone who is essentially drunk. Right now, I didn't just feel inebriated. I felt as if I were face down, fully clothed, drooling into the bedroom carpet, having partied all night and danced until my brain hurt, too tired even to drag myself three feet up onto the mattress. I was still putting one foot in front of the other, walking doggedly to the next ward that had bleeped me, but the feet just didn't seem connected to the rest of me.

Not that the shift had been devoid of entertainment. In the early hours, as I was scribbling in a patient's notes in the Emergency Department, Catherine, my favourite nurse, a brilliantly skilled and filthy-tongued young Belfast woman with the strongest Ulster accent I'd ever encountered, was trying to make herself understood. Behind the cheap cotton curtain, her profoundly deaf patient, a man in his nineties, was getting exasperated.

'What?' he shouted tetchily. 'What are you saying? Speak up, young lady. I can't hear you.'

She tried again, raising her voice. 'Would you like me to fetch you some medication for your pain, Mr Rogers? For your pain.'

'What? What's that you say?' shrieked a now furious Mr Rogers. 'Speak up, woman!'

'Pain, Mr Rogers! Pain!' shouted Catherine, who always gave as good as she got. 'Can I bring you something for your pain?'

'What?' exploded Mr Rogers. 'Porn? You mean to tell me you have porn now on the NHS? On the bloody NHS? What kind of nurse are you?'

'No, Mr Rogers! Not porn. Pain. Pain! Would you like some painkillers?'

I'd left them to it, still going hammer and tongs, relieved that Mr Rogers was unable to hear my unprofessional giggling as I disappeared back onto the wards.

Now, so close to the end of a particularly grim night on the Surgical Emergency Unit – too many jobs, too many sick patients, a workload for two being perilously managed by one – I made the fatal mistake of starting to dream ahead to the end of the shift. Coffee, bacon sandwiches, a long hot shower. The thought of it felt a little hallucinogenic. I could almost sense the bliss of sleep creeping over my limbs. An amateur error. Such indulgence is always punished by some kind of ghastly emergency. On this occasion, it was a fast bleep. Rarely used by the nursing staff, this means they are so worried by a patient that they ask switchboard to summon you urgently by name, a whisker below putting out a full-blown crash call. Unlike the crash call, when a full resuscitation team arrives at the bedside, a fast bleep is received by only one doctor – he or she alone, at least initially, is responsible for handling the emergency.

A few months into my life as a doctor, this was my first ever fast bleep. After the crackle and static, a disembodied voice hissed out of my pager: 'Dr Clarke to the Surgical Emergency Unit immediately. This is a fast bleep for Dr Clarke. Proceed to the Surgical Emergency Unit.'

The adrenaline surge electrified me. In the space of a second, I went from soporific stupor to wide-eyed hypervigilance. I found myself sprinting to whatever emergency awaited, cockroaches forgotten, heart pounding.

On the unit, the nurses had already swung into action.

'Bay 5,' someone called as I burst through the swing doors. 'It's a big upper GI bleed.'

My pulse quickened. Major bleeding – haemorrhage – is one of the swiftest and messiest routes to oblivion. A particularly distressing kind of bleeding for both patients and staff is that which arises from the upper gastrointestinal tract: the mouth, the stomach and the tube that connects them, the oesophagus. If an upper GI bleed is too rapid, too profuse, the patient ends up vomiting up their own blood uncontrollably. Old hands in the doctors' mess had told me you never forget your first time, and this bleed, my first, was a big one.

Jennifer Brownlee was a minute, rake-thin, cantankerous septuagenarian who had been keeping the entire surgical ward on its toes with her abrasive manner and continual demands – for a fresh copy of the *Telegraph*, a private side room, a better doctor, a more competent nurse. As for many patients with a history of chronic alcohol abuse, years of drinking had scarred her liver into a shrivelled, fibrous husk through which blood struggled to flow. This put her at risk from bleeding elsewhere – in particular the bulging, engorged veins of her oesophagus. Shortly before 8 a.m. that day, one of those overstretched veins had finally burst.

I flung back the bedside curtain to find three or four staff surrounding Mrs Brownlee, who was lying, looking shocked and ashen, drenched in her own fresh blood. The stuff was everywhere. Her face, her nightgown, the curtains, the bedsheets. Even the *Telegraph* was spattered. No one ever tells you how cloying the smell of large quantities of blood can be. It was like being inside a butcher's shop.

'Mrs Brownlee,' I said with as much authority as I could muster, 'don't worry, we will fix this.'

In reality, with rapid bleeds, unless you can pour blood in as quickly as it pours away, in a minute or two your patient will exsanguinate. But that wasn't what Mrs Brownlee needed to hear at this point. Already, her blood pressure had fallen so precipitously she was beginning to lose consciousness. We had very little time. The nurses had grabbed the kit for placing the biggest cannulas possible in her veins and my job was to site them. As I tied my tourniquet as tightly as I could physically manage, I asked someone to run for O negative blood and bags of fluid. If her blood pressure continued to plummet, Mrs Brownlee would have a cardiac arrest. There was no time for fumbling. My registrar arrived just as I'd managed, to my grim satisfaction, to access the veins, and we were forcibly squeezing bags of blood into our now unconscious patient. An old pro who'd seen everything a thousand times before, he calmly took her to theatre, where his expert hands would attempt to save her life.

As Mrs Brownlee was wheeled away, she left a bed-shaped gap on the floor, bordered by the bloody chaos of our footprints. Barely ten minutes after I'd arrived at the bedside, my patient was gone, scooped up by far more skilled hands than mine. My shift, abruptly, had ended. We thanked each other for our roles in the emergency. I noticed I had blood in my hair. Wearily I walked to the changing rooms, peeled myself out of my blood-soaked scrubs and stood for many minutes under the shower, as though water could wash the night away.

Having basked briefly in the satisfaction of feeling as though I'd helped, however minimally, to save a patient's life, a few days later I was back on day shifts and Mrs Brownlee was back from the dead, thanks to my registrar's expertise in theatre. But resurrections aren't always celebrations. The consultant ward round arrived at Mrs Brownlee's bedside. This particular consultant was a silver-tongued charmer who left half the women on the ward – patients, nurses and doctors alike – starry-eyed and swooning. Mrs Brownlee was one of the seduced.

'You're doing marvellously, my dear,' he crooned. 'We're so very pleased with you.'

'Doctor,' she beamed back at him, uncharacteristically docile ever since her brush with death, 'you are all marvellous too. All of you – but especially you.'

Then she paused, frowning darkly. Her eyes had fixated upon mine. 'Wait. Not that one. That one there isn't marvellous. She's a little bitch. She's a bloody Nazi. Get out of here, you filthy little Nazi! Get out of my sight, you little witch!'

'Well,' said my consultant, eyebrow raised at me, 'I expect that's the last time you save someone's life, isn't it? I'm looking forward to including Mrs Brownlee's comments in your multisource feedback, Rachel.'

I grinned as we headed off to see the next patient. The real Mrs Brownlee was back – in all her vituperative glory. Tiny, ferocious and irrepressible, I hadn't realised I had missed her.

$$\sim\!\!\!\wedge\!\!\!\sim$$

Medicine in the UK faces its own major haemorrhage. Doctors are leaving the NHS in droves, an exodus our patients can ill afford. So too are the nurses, midwives, paramedics, physiotherapists and a huge range of other allied health professionals. Currently, England, Wales and Northern Ireland are short of over 23,000 nurses, 6,000 doctors and 3,500 midwives.[11] The lifeblood of the health service, the staff without whose goodwill the NHS could not function, is rapidly draining away.

If a journalist points this out to the Department of Health

press office, its kneejerk response is to whip out some statistics purporting to show how unprecedentedly well staffed the NHS is under the current government. Jeremy Hunt likes to talk, for example, about the 'ten thousand additional doctors' the Conservative Party has brought to the NHS since attaining power in 2010. As always, though, the devil is in the detail. Those ten thousand doctors shrink to only half that when part-time doctors are factored into the mix and, once the UK's rising population is taken into account, there is no increase in doctors per head of population at all.[12] The statistic, like so many others, is a distortion, for political ends, of the yawning mismatch between numbers of staff and patients that anyone who actually works in the NHS experiences day in, day out.

Contrary to the government's spin, Britain has fewer doctors per capita than almost any other country in Europe, including Bulgaria, Estonia and Latvia. According to OECD figures, we have a paltry 2.8 doctors per 1,000 people, compared with 6.1 in Greece, 4.8 in Austria and 4.0 in Italy.[1] Worse, while first-year doctor jobs are fully subscribed, the Department of Health's own statistics show that, overall, one in ten junior doctor training posts lies vacant, exposing patients to potentially dangerous rota gaps. The exodus of young doctors from the NHS has worsened year on year since the 2010 general election. In 2011, nearly three-quarters of doctors continued in NHS training posts after completing their first two years of practice. In 2012, only 67 per cent did; in 2013, 64 per cent; in 2014, 58 per cent; and in 2015, the most recent data, a mere 52 per cent of doctors continued in NHS training posts after completing their first two years of training, the rest having gone elsewhere, often Australia or

New Zealand.[13] In some specialities, such as paediatrics, the shortage of trainees is now so critical that one in five training posts is unfilled nationally.

Some media commentators have argued that young doctors who choose to turn their backs on the NHS ought to be punished for their fecklessness by having to pay back the cost to the taxpayer of their years of training. The impression created is one of irresponsible dilettantes being lured by the prospect of a cushy surf bum's life on the Gold Coast, as opposed to being driven out of the job they love by conditions of work that have become intolerable. Yet across the NHS – spanning frontline staff with different jobs, genders, ages and locations – the chorus of distress is disturbingly uniform. Crucially, for anyone who cares about patient safety, it also chimes with the testimony from staff at Mid Staffs.

Recently, an NHS midwife's anonymous letter to her local newspaper, the *Liverpool Echo*, went viral on social media. Like many other NHS staff, I shared it widely online because it seemed to encapsulate some fundamental truths about the working conditions increasingly endured by midwives, nurses and doctors alike, ones that the government would dearly love to airbrush away.

'I am a midwife and I wish I was dead,' she began, continuing:

To the outside world I have a lot to be thankful for: house, car, food in the fridge, family who love me, steady job. The truth is that the last on that list is all consuming. It is a black hole destroying my world.

Currently, my caseload is up to 40 women and rising so that's 80 lives in total that I am personally responsible for right at this very moment. I don't get much sleep at night. I am unsupported. I have been the difference between life and death more times than I care to remember, seemingly unflappable in the eyes of the parents of the little lives I have rescued from the brink of extinction. They never knew of the tears I cried as I rocked back and forth on the floor of the staff toilet.

I dust myself off as everyone does and it's on to the next couple, the next birth, and what will that bring? I am scared to attend my next birth as I'm still shaken by the last but we are short staffed at the moment so I just keep my head down and get on with the ever-growing list of things for me to do. An impossibly long list of things to do and I know I will never reach the end, it's almost futile to try . . . The hours are endless. Most days I don't stop for lunch and I frequently get to the end of the day without having been to the toilet. Midwives often joke about having cast iron bladders. I'm not the only one. This is so commonplace I fear it's becoming an accepted norm.

I don't feel that I am able to do my job safely, let alone provide a good standard of care. I trudge my way through this wretched existence . . . I have been treading water for some time, I am out of my depth, the tide is drawing me further out and now I am drowning.[14]

—∿—

Similarly, in Mid Staffs, the impact of staffing cuts was so distressing to nurses that a group of them wrote an anonymous letter to their directorate manager in order to highlight – futilely, as it turned out – their inability to keep their patients safe given their crippling workloads:

> As a ward, despite our exhaustive attempts, we are struggling and on occasions failing to deliver the high standards of care that both ourselves and the Trust aspire to and we request that this be addressed with great urgency . . . At a recent meeting it was highlighted that our sickness rate was high and the submission of incident forms surpass others. We were asked why. We feel that it is a true reflection of the environment, the unrealistic demands and lack of resources. We all exhausted, mentally and physically. We are fed up with tackling unmanageable workloads, going without breaks, not getting off on time, doing extras with no respite. The environment is neither safe for patients or staff. As registered nurses we are professionally obliged to raise our concerns. We feel compromised, bullied and disempowered. The ward no longer belongs to us. And [on] occasion we almost feel derided.[9]

These sentiments strike a powerful chord with me today. Statistical spats may be dry and tedious, but the reality of NHS understaffing is as raw and emotionally charged as anything I've experienced in either of my two careers. Of course a great many jobs are desperately hectic, but there is something particularly stressful about struggling daily with punitive workloads while knowing that just one mistake, a momentary lapse of judgement, could cost a patient their life.

In one of my recent jobs, in 2016, I would arrive every

morning on my ward to greet the most senior nurse, the ward sister, as she grappled with how she would manage with all the nurses missing from that day's rota. She would weigh up whether she would be forced to close beds to patients or whether, with superhuman effort, her depleted band of nurses could manage to keep the whole ward open. In other words, in this zero-sum game, would it be patients or nurses who would suffer more today? Once, to my shock, this tough, uncomplaining, seemingly imperturbable colossus – the absolute heart and soul of our ward – broke down and started to cry. There is only so much fudging and firefighting even the most resilient of professionals can take.

'You know what's really done it?' she said to me. 'It's the bloody Zumba. I mean, for Christ's sake! Zumba!'

Periodically in the NHS, staff surveys reveal such abject depths of low morale among staff that Trusts are prodded to come up with 'initiatives' to lift our spirits. In 2015, Simon Stevens, the CEO of NHS England, announced various ways in which NHS organisations would be supported to help their staff 'stay well', including stress-busting classes in yoga and Zumba. Needless to say, my own Trust's newly instigated lunchtime Zumba classes were predicated on the notion that we could stroll along for a relaxing dance during our notional 'lunch hour'. Book groups and lunchtime walks were also on offer for all those doctors and nurses with an hour to spare in their day, equating to no one I knew in the hospital.

'I mean, seriously, what sodding lunch hour?' muttered the ward sister. I smiled in rueful agreement. Only managers and CEOs monumentally out of touch with what life is like on the ground could imagine that such activities, though desirable, were feasible. That they were offered nonetheless felt like an insult. We needed more staff, not a token gesture towards our 'wellbeing'. Sod yoga, sod book groups and sod sodding Zumba.

Occasionally, I too am prone to tears. When working recently in a job designed for three doctors, one of the three of us went on an unforeseen six-month absence. Needless to say, the last thing my cash-strapped Trust – itself beholden to wildly unrealistic government 'efficiency savings' – wished to do was pay for a replacement locum doctor, so the two of us who remained were largely left to shoulder three doctors' jobs, regardless of workload. It was tiring, miserable and sometimes risky.

Under these overstretched circumstances, our attention to detail was not, nor could be, up to the standard we expected of ourselves. Every day, my colleague and I were uncomfortably conscious of the fact that our patients were being short-changed. And in a system driven by top-down cuts – the government expects the NHS to make £22 billion of 'efficiency savings' by 2020 – this is not unusual, it is the norm. Ministers of state declare their heartfelt commitment to patient safety, while being fully aware that our capacity to provide safe and compassionate care is painfully curtailed by lack of resources. Unable to influence the system that constrains us, we are nonetheless responsible for making that system work for our patients. The buck stops with us and, if anything goes wrong, you can guarantee it will be the individual doctor or nurse, not a politician, who is hung out to dry.

Jennifer Middleton's voice suddenly hardened.

'The way they treated him was disgusting. You wouldn't treat an animal like that, let alone a human being.'

Briefly, her face twisted with hostility and the effort of forbidding her tears to spill. Nobody made a sound in the living room, which suddenly felt too small to contain her grief. Occasionally, even under glaring lights and with a camera rolling, a television interview ceases to feel like a production as the crew are held spellbound by the story. I had known that Jennifer's testimony was likely to be harrowing. Prior to filming, I had made a deliberate calculation not to talk through her story with her in advance, recognising how powerful its rawness might be on camera. Her late husband observed us from the photos displayed on every table, windowsill and the mantelpiece. With all our oversized equipment squeezed inside, the tiny living room felt like a claustrophobic shrine. I asked Jennifer if she would like to stop, but an impatient flick of her wrist shut me up as she continued, in the grip of her story.

It was the late 1990s, perhaps a year or two into the first New Labour government, and I had been commissioned by Channel 4 to make a film about the state of the NHS. This was the era of the postcode lottery. The health service had been underfunded for years and an array of NHS treatments were being dispensed or denied according to where a patient lived. Stories of rationing by postcode abounded. I interviewed one woman with metastatic breast cancer who was fighting her local health authority to fund the drug that, had she lived on the opposite side of her street, she would have been eligible to receive for free. In North Wales, I met a man who had been waiting over eighteen months for lifesaving coronary artery surgery. He had already suffered two heart attacks and his arteries were so clogged with cholesterol that even walking a few steps caused him crippling chest pain. Three times he had arrived at his local hospital for surgery, only to be turned away when lack of beds caused his operation to be cancelled. Another heart attack, his cardiologist had told him, would kill him, yet the hospital's Department of Surgery was in understaffed meltdown, cancelling operations daily. Only when this tough former steelworker began to cry did I appreciate how much fear was hidden behind his gruff exterior.

'I've paid taxes all my life,' he told me, 'and now I'm probably going to die because there's no money in the NHS for my operation. That's not right. That can't be right.'

The most shocking story of all concerned Jennifer Middleton's husband, David. Earlier in the year, he had been diagnosed with bowel cancer. After surgery to remove his tumour, he faced months of chemotherapy, which would be strictly timetabled in four-weekly intervals until a scan would determine whether he remained cancer free.

'He was quite positive at the start of the chemo,' Jennifer told me. 'We both were. Our attitude was that the cancer was gone and the chemo was going to keep it that way.'

But, in David's hospital, rationing was biting in a different way. The oncology day unit he was due to attend for his chemotherapy was in the grip of a funding and staffing crisis. Almost every day, there were insufficient nurses and doctors to put up the drips and administer the drugs, meaning patients would arrive for treatment only to be sent back home again. It was every bit as brutal as it sounds.

'The first time it happened,' said Jennifer on camera, 'we thought it must be a one-off. David was disappointed because he knew the chemo was what was going to kill the cancer, but, when the nurse explained they just didn't have enough staff that day, we actually felt a bit sorry for them. But then it happened the next time, and the one after that. We realised it was just routine. Literally every time we arrived for David's chemo, I would sit there panicking every time a nurse came round, thinking, Please don't stop in front of us; don't let it be him today; please don't let it be him. Everyone was the same, just thinking, Please let me get my chemo; don't let me be one of the ones who get sent home. It happened all the time. It was disgusting.'

A consultant oncologist who worked at the hospital, deeply distressed at what his patients were being forced to endure, agreed to speak to me off the record. The hospital had cut staff numbers, he explained, and, no matter what they did, the remaining doctors and nurses could not safely treat everybody.

'You have to understand,' he told me, 'this isn't just horrendous for the patients on the day, it is potentially affecting their chances of survival. If chemotherapy is delayed and not given according to schedule, there's no guarantee it will be as effective. It's entirely possible that patients are dying because of these delays.'

'Why isn't the number of patients being reduced to match the number of staff?' I asked.

'They just expect us to manage,' he answered. 'They don't want to know about patients being sent away. They're not the slightest bit interested in us trying to tell them.'

Several months into his chemotherapy, after his cancer recurred and spread, causing increasingly distressing and undignified symptoms, David died.

'I will never know if it could have been different,' his wife told me. 'Maybe he could have lived. They treated him like dirt and I will never forgive them.'

At the time, I was so intent on exposing the story – the hospital, I believed, must be publicly held to account – it never occurred to me to imagine these events from the nurses' perspective. Nor, in retrospect, did I delve sufficiently deeply into whether external budget constraints were driving the understaffing in a manner over which the hospital had little control. Now, as a clinician myself, I find it hard not to flinch at the thought of having to work in such a traumatic environment. Imagine deliberately choosing to specialise in oncology. You have committed yourself to caring for people with the disease that is steeped in more taboo and fear than any other. But, each morning, you arrive at work to see the drawn faces of your patients packed into the waiting room, knowing – as they do – that some of them will be turned away. Maybe, like the patients, you make your own silent plea. Please don't let ward sister pick me to have to tell them. Not today, not again. But, since you are pretty good at the communication side of things, you are sent out yet again to do the dirty. Now you feel the weight of every pair of eyes as they follow you around the room. The patients know exactly what it means if you alight in front of them. As you approach the first one to break the bad news, an elderly gentleman stripped to the bone by his cancer, his wife's eyes start to fill with tears before you have uttered a word. They have been here so many times before.

'I'm so sorry,' you begin, as her sobs grow louder. 'We don't have enough staff today and I'm afraid we need to ask you to come back tomorrow when hopefully we'll have more nurses.'

As they gather their coats to depart with the cancer untreated, as so many times before, you scour the room for the next name on your list, while privately burning with shame.

When something unacceptable happens to a patient in the NHS it is never, in my view, excusable. But it does not necessarily follow that the individuals whose acts or omissions caused cruelty or harm are to blame for their behaviour. Sometimes, in spite of their best efforts, doctors and nurses are as trapped within a failing system as the patients whose care is being compromised. And there is a unique form of anguish that stems from causing – or being unable to prevent – harm to your patient when all you ever wanted to do was heal. Jennifer Middleton's anger towards the doctors and nurses who treated her husband 'like dirt' is entirely understandable. Yet, in a sense, those frontline staff were being treated with equal contempt by their own employer: forced to go out and face the failed patients, the reluctant human face of corporate disdain. Even the culpability of the hospital management is questionable. If a hospital's budget, imposed from on high by an NHS funding settlement set according to political priorities, cannot safely meet the needs of its patients, then everyone from the CEO downwards may be embroiled, whether they like it or not, in the delivery of substandard care.

In today's culture of increasing complicity and compromise – where the standard of care is too often curtailed by inadequate numbers of staff – it is small wonder our doctors and nurses are quitting the NHS. To them – demoralised, disempowered and permanently exhausted – the options are hardly attractive. Be disillusioned, be resentful, be cruel, be indifferent, be depressed, be unsafe, be a shadow of the doctor or nurse you once dreamed of, let down yourself, let down your patients, let go of treasured principles, be overwhelmed with stress, withdraw until you cease to give a damn, concede defeat, get out while you can. Like rats on the *Titanic*, staff are fleeing the NHS out of self-preservation. You mourn the loss of every good colleague – hating to think of all that expertise wasted – yet a part of you silently envies them.

Mid Staffs, in short, may have been extreme, but the dynamics that led to it are everywhere in the NHS today. At any moment, in our hospitals, frontline staff are acutely aware that our wards may be only a whisker away from disaster. As a journalist-turned-doctor, I find that the most soul-destroying aspect of this knowledge is that the politicians who lead the NHS are every bit as cognisant of the knife edge upon which the NHS teeters, yet choose, for political expediency, to deny this. The former BBC *Newsnight* arch-inquisitor Jeremy Paxman is famously misquoted as adopting as his opening premise in interviews, 'Why is this lying bastard lying to me?' Increasingly, for NHS staff, there is only one word of difference between Paxman's question and the one we ask of the political custodians of the NHS: 'Why is this lying bastard lying *about* me?' Clearly, such suspicion and hostility cannot be constructive. But, arguably, our cynicism is inevitable, born out of repeated exposure to the silver-tongued assurances fed to the public that the NHS is thriving, really thriving, when we all know it is anything but.

Typically, the dissonance between what we experience as NHS staff and the political denial of our own lived experiences surfaces most strikingly when the latest NHS performance statistics appear to reflect badly on the government's stewardship of the health service. In early 2016, for example, in response to the worst ever monthly figures from NHS England since records began, the president of the Society for Acute Medicine, Dr Mark Holland, felt compelled to speak out. All over the country, tens of thousands of patients were waiting more than four hours to be seen in A&E, more than six weeks for supposedly urgent scans, and more than four hours on a trolley before being given a hospital bed. Given Jeremy Hunt's apparent commitment to eliminating eleven thousand avoidable deaths by tackling the infamous 'weekend effect', Holland made the point that the daily overstretch within our hospitals was now so severe as to be itself potentially life-threatening:

> A government which has the laudable aim of reducing hospital deaths by 11,000 [he told the *Guardian*] must recognise overcrowded hospitals that are full of sick patients in overstretched medical units will contribute to avoidable deaths. The ability to deliver acute medical care is reaching crisis point and any other crisis affecting our society would be acknowledged and addressed. The volume of patients and disease severity is so much that we are now functioning at the edge of what is possible.'[15]

But, in a manner reminiscent of the Mid Staffs board of governors, the Department of Health's response to Holland's fears about possible patient deaths was to tartly dismiss them, while accusing him of exaggerating the problems within the NHS:

'This is patent nonsense,' a departmental press spokesman stated, 'and does a disservice to our hospitals and staff coping well under huge pressure.'[10]

Clearly, the intended audience of these glib denials is not the NHS staff who know better, but the voting public who must, at all costs, be mollified into thinking the health service is safe in government hands. Alas, their unintended consequence is to drive a subsidiary audience – the doctors and nurses fighting tooth and nail to stop the NHS going under – wild with frustration and impotence.

The official government response to Mid Staffs, published in 2014 and running to two volumes in length, emphatically vowed that finance would 'never again be allowed to come before quality of care'.[16] The irony was not lost on NHS staff that, later the same year, NHS England's 'Five Year Forward View' was also published, estimating that, if NHS funding and demand continued at current levels, the health service would be £30 billion in debt by 2020.[17] The government, in refusing to provide more than £8 billion of this shortfall, condemned the NHS to five years of the most draconian cost-cutting in its history. From my frontline perspective, it is glaringly obvious that, far from safety being placed above finance, the two are now locked in an unholy alliance in which risk increases as budgets are cut. The government has rigged the system. Staff and Trusts must excel in patient care while being denied the resources to enable them to do so.

Post-Mid Staffs, the official government mantra is candour. According to Jeremy Hunt, embracing the lead of Sir Robert Francis, the brave voices of whistleblowing staff must never again be ignored. Yet, when staff speak out about the wisdom of imposing unachievable 'efficiency savings' while expecting standards and safety to be maintained, they are batted away with casual disdain. Mr Hunt, the doctor in me wants to scream, if £10 million worth of cuts can wreak havoc like Mid Staffs, how can you not be quaking in your ministerial shoes at the misery that 2 million times that amount is going to unleash upon the nation's patients? How can your government possibly claim to care about patient safety?

In the end, trying to function as a conscientious doctor or nurse within a system governed by politicians who respond with selective deafness to your patient-safety concerns is arguably the most demoralising thing of all. Continuing to care – indeed, continuing full stop – is a tall order.

'I'm done,' my friend Hannah announced one day. 'I can't do this any more.' We'd spent three years of medical school and two years as doctors together. During that time she had evolved from brilliant student into brilliant doctor, the kind you would pray your loved ones might be treated by in hospital. Latterly, marooned in a faraway district general hospital plagued by excessive numbers of doctor rota gaps, she was being forced by her Trust to work routinely the jobs of two doctors. No shrinking violet, she didn't hold back.

'I've told them a thousand times people are going to die,' she told me. 'I can't keep people safe if I'm carrying two doctors' bleeps and have double the number of patients to look after. But they don't give a shit. Sometimes it's like a war zone. They just don't want to know.'

The prospect of Hannah quitting the profession she had once so loved filled me with sadness. I tried to persuade her to stay.

'Rach,' she said, 'you don't understand. If I carry on like this, I won't end up surviving it. I can't keep pouring my life and soul into the NHS if I'm fighting against the system to do a decent job for the patients. Not when the managers don't give a shit, the politicians are hypocrites and I get told I'm scum by the *Daily Mail* on a weekly basis. Why would I do that? It's falling apart. Everything I do is in spite of, not because of, my employers, and I hate it.'

One day, Hannah should have been a professor or groundbreaker of UK medicine. The NHS cannot afford to lose a single doctor or nurse, least of all its brightest and best. Yet, instead of addressing the gaps that blight doctors' and nurses' rotas, the government attempts to downplay and deny them. In contrast, Sir Robert Francis has been characteristically blunt about what should constitute a safe response to understaffing:

'If you haven't got the right number of people to fly an aircraft properly, you don't fly the aircraft. You should not be operating if you haven't got enough surgeons on duty who are fit to operate [and] you should not be running a ward if you haven't got enough staff on duty to feed people.'

It is simply a fact that we don't. We don't have enough of anyone. In an NHS with too few doctors and nurses being stretched too thinly across too many patients, we increasingly fear a repeat of Mid Staffs, but the politicians choose not to hear this.

CHAPTER 8

MILITANCY

In my world of princesses, heroines and unicorns, Margaret Thatcher was an unlikely addition. But, to my six-year-old self, there was something about her ascent to power that seemed to be tinged with magic. I'd had no idea certain jobs were for men. The thought hadn't crossed my mind. Then, the morning after the 1979 general election, my primary school teacher held a newspaper aloft to the class in triumph.

'Look!' she cried ecstatically. 'The Prime Minister is the most powerful person in the country and this lady, Margaret Thatcher, is the first woman in the history of Britain ever to have become Prime Minister. Listen, children. Every other Prime Minister until now has been a man. All of you, especially the girls in the class, should feel so incredibly proud. A woman can do anything a man can.'

My eyes gleamed with excitement. Fired up by my teacher's passion – and with my vision of Thatcher temporarily established as a kind of crusading female superhero, Wonder Woman in pearls and an electric-blue twinset – I must have fixed that day in my memory, because a couple of years later, now aged eight or nine, I decided to take a political stand of my own.

Maybe if Henry Bone had not been so obnoxious – he liked to chase the girls round the playground and try to pull their knickers down – I wouldn't have taken him on. But he was a thug and I hated bullies. Short, squat and prone to bashing the weedy boys, he was shaped like a dumpy torpedo. Perhaps it was this that gave him his edge in the water, because Henry Bone was some kind of swimming prodigy, supposedly destined for the Olympics, though I didn't buy a word of his bragging. One of the very best things about my primary school was its decrepit old outdoor swimming pool, tucked away at the bottom of the playing field. Though the water was greenish and icy cold, usually blighted by weed and dead insects, our precious weekly 'swimming lesson' – an anarchic, overcrowded frenzy of splashing and squealing – was the weekly highlight of our summer terms. The chance to plunge into the stagnant water could never come round soon enough. The headmistress's husband, a thin, stooped, browbeaten man known only as 'Sir', would stand on duty at the poolside, eyes glumly averted, while we unleashed merry bedlam in the water.

In contrast to our strictly rationed pool time, Henry Bone had been granted special privileges. Being a swimmer of such prodigious talent, every lunch hour, five times a week, he was given the grace of the pool. Up and down he cruised, lord of the duckweed, gloating insufferably afterwards. Perhaps I really just wanted to cut him down to size – punish him for all the times he beat up the little kids – but the injustice of it festered within me. I couldn't see why he should enjoy daily private pool time just because he happened to be good at swimming. If anything, the kids who couldn't swim should be in there, learning how to improve.

Somehow I rallied the rest of the children in my class to the cause, and for one entire lunch hour, instead of playing tag and scaling the climbing frames, we all sat cross-legged on the grass in front of the swimming pool, silently observing Henry Bone swim his lengths. It was swelteringly hot, itchy and boring. Our polyester shirts stuck to our backs with sweat, but I wouldn't let anyone leave. The teachers, observing this unusual spectacle from the terrace where they ate their packed lunches, dispatched Sir to find out what we were up to. I stood up and spoke.

'We don't think it's fair that Henry Bone is the only person in the school who's allowed to swim at lunch just because he's better at swimming than us. We think everyone should be allowed to swim even if they aren't very good at it.'

Sir reported back to the rest of the teachers. When the school bell rang at the end of lunch break, they all remained seated, curious to see what we would do next. None of us moved, though mutterings of unease spread through the ranks. Collectively breaking the school rules was unnerving.

'Stay,' I urged. 'I'll take the blame. We won't get into trouble.'

This time, the headmistress herself strode over to our protest. Notoriously fierce, she had a prominent wart on her chin that sprouted black hairs, which she would stroke unconsciously when not tearing strips off a miscreant. We all lived in fear of her temper. Sometimes I'd spend whole lessons spellbound by the wart and what it might represent, unable to tear my eyes from it. It seemed entirely possible that our headmistress was in fact a witch. Now, as she towered over us, glowering, I started to feel sick inside.

'The teachers and I have discussed your protest,' she announced with the utmost gravity. She paused. The wart was distracting me. 'And we have decided that you are quite correct. If one child is allowed to swim at lunchtimes, then all children should be allowed to swim at lunchtimes. From now on, we will start a timetable and each class will take it in turns to swim.'

The class erupted into shrieks of delight, the concept of a gracious victory meaning nothing to a bunch of nine-year-olds who weren't even sure what a protest was. Justice felt sweet, even if we couldn't spell it. It was a triumph for mediocre, underaged swimmers everywhere and our cheering seemed to last for ever. Though Henry Bone never stopped tormenting me afterwards, it was deliciously, magnificently worth it.

—∿—

I'd forgotten all about the children's stand against Henry Bone until, as the junior doctor dispute got under way, the press started branding junior doctors as 'militants'. The label was clearly a tactical smear aimed at delegitimising campaigning doctors, but – who knew? – perhaps I'd had a dormant militant tendency all along, having acquired a taste for it in childhood.

A slew of similar insults followed. Doctors who backed going on strike against the government's new contract were labelled 'radicals' and 'extremists', as though the behaviour of the country's doctors in some way echoed that of terrorists. Jeremy Hunt apparently approved of these insinuations, retweeting some of them on his personal Twitter account. Not once, in all those years of medical school, could I have imagined that one day my status as a doctor in training would become, for certain journalists, a term of abuse, nor how painful it would be to confront that.

Since the Health Secretary had launched his seven-day crusade, relations between doctors and the government had imploded. Hunt had renewed his vow to impose the contract if negotiations failed and the BMA Junior Doctors Committee, in response, had announced a ballot of its members over strike action. Huge numbers of ordinary grassroots doctors – those, such as myself, with no formal role or involvement in the BMA – had been galvanised by Hunt's speech into action. Prior to this, like most of my colleagues, I was only dimly aware that doctors' contracts were up for negotiation. I belonged to the BMA only to enjoy my copy of the *British Medical Journal* every weekend.

Typically, doctors are not exactly renowned for our insurgency. We're people-pleasers, not revolutionaries. We've spent our lifetimes obligingly jumping through hoops. When the rebels among our schoolmates went behind the bike sheds, we went to the library to swot up on our A levels. Then, after choosing five or six years' worth of further exams at medical school, we accepted with passive subservience working conditions that in any other profession would be met with incredulity. I have friends who have asked their hospital a full year in advance for annual leave for their wedding and honeymoon, only to discover nearer the time that they have been rostered on call for that particular fortnight. I have begged in vain for a rota in advance of starting a new job in order to plan my childcare, to be told on my first day in post that I am in fact starting on night shifts and will be expected to be on call that evening. I've worked in a hospital whose doctors' mess was infested with rats in the ceiling and cockroaches in the skirting boards, despite years of efforts by the juniors to press the hospital management to address this.

We used to take this kind of treatment with remarkable docility. But Hunt achieved something unprecedented. He politicised junior doctors, turning us *en masse* from compliant NHS rota fodder into accidental militants. Some of us gave television interviews that went viral, viewed online hundreds of thousands, or even millions, of times after they had been broadcast. Others started to plan mass demonstrations in London, Leeds and Belfast. Five junior doctors would go on to fight Hunt in court, their judicial review becoming the most successful example of crowdfunding in UK legal history, receiving over £50,000 of public donations in less than twenty-four hours. Most successfully, we harnessed social media to counter the government's narrative that this was simply a pay dispute. When a small group of non-BMA juniors set up a Facebook forum, word quickly spread and everyone started joining. At its peak, the so-called 'Junior Doctors Contract Forum' had over 60,000 members and, though infiltrated by the press and the Department of Health, the majority of these were doctors. We used it to share freely our opinions, ideas and reactions to the unfolding saga. For the first time, the country's 54,000 junior doctors had acquired a common identity, a sense of solidarity and a strong desire for collective action.

On a bitterly cold Saturday in mid-October, 20,000 doctors and their supporters marched on Downing Street in the London protest against the contract. I'd only ever been on one protest march before – when a million people demonstrated against the Gulf War in 2003 – but that was in order to film it for a documentary I was making about Al-Qaeda. So, technically, this was my first protest. The Metropolitan police were out in force as doctors in scrubs, pensioners and children all flocked to Westminster. There were family zones, an NHS choir, banners and placards, one of which was immortalised in the next day's press, saying, 'I may not be a gynaecologist but I know a Hunt when I see one.'

I'd never seen police officers beaming so supportively. One of them made a point of coming up to me to say, 'Don't give up. You keep on fighting. We don't want to see them doing to you what they've already done to us.'

It made me feel humbled. As protests go, this was a frightfully polite one. Having arrived outside Number 10, chanted a little and brandished placards, the crowd peacefully dispersed, leaving a few stragglers, myself included, who felt duty-bound to retrace their steps, carefully removing any traces of litter. Clearly, even when driven to extremism, doctors' innate obedience lives on.

At home, Dave and children took a dim view of my 'militancy'. I'd started setting my alarm half an hour early every morning to give me time respond on Twitter to the latest government spin before getting the children to breakfast club and myself to the hospital. I wrote blogs and newspaper columns in the early hours, and regularly caught the train to London to give live television news interviews. Occasionally, a film crew invaded our kitchen and, to my children's delight, I would bribe them into silence with the family iPad. Once, my husband asked my five-year-old daughter whether she would like, as a treat, to stay up late at bedtime to watch

Mummy give an interview on the news. She gave the matter some thought before delivering an uncompromising verdict.

'Well,' she said at last. 'Will the news have My Little Pony in it?'

'No, it probably won't, I'm afraid,' replied my husband.

'Oh. No, then. I'd like it if there was My Little Pony, but Mummy's boring.'

She was right. I was. People in the grip of an obsession always are. The more aggressively the government spun the conflict as merely a pay dispute, the less able I felt to sit passively by. Hunt believed the wrath of junior doctors had been provoked not by anything he had said but by the BMA, which had maliciously duped its members into misplaced fury by claiming that he planned to slash our salaries, when in fact he had no such intention. He therefore set out to divide and rule the union from its members, reserving his attacks for the 'politically poisoned' BMA, while seeking to appease and flatter ordinary junior doctors:

'Working on the NHS's front line is one of the toughest jobs in Britain today,' he wrote in the *Telegraph*, just prior to our strike ballot. 'Our junior doctors are at the forefront of dealing with those pressures. They work the longest, most unsociable hours and staff our hospitals over the weekend – in short, they are the backbone of the health service.'[18]

These soft words cut no ice, being undermined by the occasions when the Health Secretary said something in public that we knew to be inaccurate. Early on in the dispute, for example, he claimed on the news during the BBC's *Breakfast* programme that a minority of doctors working over fifty-six hours a week were 'paid what's called colloquially in the NHS "danger money".'[19] The insinuation – that some among us were willing to jeopardise our patients for the sake of lucrative overtime – conjured an image of junior doctors as reckless opportunists. The trouble was, it was cobblers. Not once had any doctor, even those in retirement, ever heard of the fictitious phrase 'danger money', let alone been paid any. Hunt's claim, broadcast live to the nation at breakfast, was entirely disingenuous – or what is colloquially known as a barefaced lie. He'd literally made it up. And, the more he spun to the public using fabricated soundbites, the more successfully he alienated the country's doctors.

More subtle versions of divide and rule were deployed by various newspaper columnists, who looked to separate grassroots doctors into two opposing camps, inviting 'moderates' to perceive themselves as different from and better than their more 'militant' peers. In his column entitled, 'Moderate doctors must defeat the militants', the *Times*'s chief leader writer and former director of the Conservative Research Department, Danny Finkelstein, claimed that 'threatening patients' wellbeing for the sake of overtime pay is typical of the BMA's cynical rabble-rousing behaviour.'[20]

He argued that no doctor with honour should be willing to contemplate striking, ending with the impassioned plea:

> Where are you, brave moderate doctors, to tell the leadership that this has gone far enough? When all your associates are in such a lather, of course it is hard to stand up against it. But it's your duty. To harm patients over your pay is outrageous.[20]

Ironically, even as his cheerleaders in the media urged us not to be motivated by pay, Hunt himself attempted to buy us off with financial sweeteners. On the morning the strike ballot opened, every front page was dominated by headlines about an extraordinary concession on his part, a whopping 11 per cent pay rise for junior doctors.[21] It was a masterclass in political spin. Not only did it make him appear magnanimous but, if we voted nonetheless to strike, we really would be showing ourselves up to be the money-grabbing individuals he had implied all along.

But, if his new-found largesse sounded too good to be true, that's because it was. The 11 per cent increase was in basic pay only, offset by huge cuts elsewhere in pay for antisocial hours, and, since most of us worked a great proportion of those, the overall effect was likely to be a pay cut for many. Perhaps Hunt had hoped to avoid strikes by duping us with an apparent pay rise, but what he actually achieved with his engineered headlines was to reignite doctors' fury. Trust, honesty, candour. Those values at medicine's core were not, apparently, shared by the Health Secretary. Unsurprisingly, 98 per cent of us voted in favour of striking.

Perhaps most frustratingly, in working so hard to present the conflict as a pay dispute, an objective he achieved with aplomb, Hunt had failed to grasp what really motivated many of us. It was fear, fundamentally, that stoked much of the anger. Not, primarily, fear of losing out financially – though the idea of being paid less for our work was clearly inflammatory – but of being forced to work longer and harder than we already did, of being stretched even more thinly. I knew my limits. They were already being tested. More than anything, I feared being driven out of the job I so loved by intolerable increases in my workload.

Hunt insisted no doctor would work longer than currently.

Indeed, the new contract would reduce overall hours from ninety-one to seventy-two per week, he claimed, so we ought to be embracing it. But his assurances were undermined by his insistence that the new contract had to deliver seven-day services 'cost-neutrally'. The public were being promised something for nothing, seven days for the price of five. Weekends would be transformed, allegedly, without any additional doctors or resources. Yet the original Conservative Party manifesto commitment in 2015 had recognised that staffing was critical: 'We want England to be the first nation in the world to provide a truly 7 day NHS ... with hospitals properly staffed, so that the quality of care is the same every day of the week.'[22]

The crux, for junior doctors, was the phrase 'properly staffed'. We knew we were barely delivering a safe five-day service and yet, in Jeremy Hunt's parallel universe, we now had to provide a seven-day one. The maths was simple. In the absence of additional doctors, the only ways to deliver new weekend services would be for our overall hours to increase, or for us to be removed from our patients from Monday to Friday in order to beef up the weekend workforce. Either way, Mid Staffs-style overstretch seemed inevitable, unless, that was, the 'seven-day NHS' was less a genuine commitment than an empty soundbite, a piece of slick electioneering with no underlying substance. Respected health commentators such as Nigel Edwards, the chief executive of the health think tank the Nuffield Trust, appeared to suspect the latter:

Even if there were significant extra funding available for the NHS, getting the critical mass of specialist staff needed to make seven-day working a reality would be likely to mean closures or mergers of local services, such as emergency surgery or maternity units.[23]

Later, when the junior doctors' dispute was all but over, parliament's spending watchdog, the Public Accounts Committee, issued a report excoriating the government and Department of Health for having no idea how many additional staff would be required for a seven-day NHS, let alone budgeted for them. It stated, 'The department has not adequately assessed the impact on the clinical workforce of implementing seven-day services and so does not know if there will be enough clinical staff with the right skills.'[24]

The committee's chair, MP Meg Hillier, encapsulated what many junior doctors had felt and argued throughout the preceding year, their concerns dismissed as self-interest: 'It beggars belief that such a major policy should be advanced with so flimsy a notion of how it will be funded.'[24]

Militancy came at a price. The attacks in the press grew nastier. In one memorable diatribe, the *Telegraph*'s executive political editor, James Kirkup, variously described junior doctors who supported strike action as 'stupid', 'selfish', 'self-indulgent', 'self-righteous', 'inept', 'dishonest' and 'infantile and self-deluding idiots'. We were childish, petulant and politically naïve: 'How else to describe the howling anguish of people who don't get their way?'[25]

Kirkup objected to doctors dabbling in politics, dismissing our linkage of contractual negotiations with the broader issue of how seven-day services would be staffed and funded as nothing more than a petulant strop:

Many, engaged in politics for the first time, cannot understand why the Government will not do exactly as they want; for them it's unthinkable that others would not accept the doctors' word on how to fund and structure the NHS as final.[25]

Sometimes, it felt as though the political columnists were revelling in the chance to take down the know-it-all doctors a notch or two. 'When doctors go on strike we enter lands not of medicine, nor hospital management, nor even industrial relations,' wrote Hugo Rifkind in *The Times*, and continued:

This, rather, is a place of politics. It is a battlefield of pressures and ideas; of public mood and political reality. And here, my medical friends, you are no longer the experts. You're not even informed hobbyists. You're day-trippers, and you're out of your depth, and you're in for a shock.[26]

At one stage, Danny Finkelstein went as far as claiming that the dispute for us had never been about the contract at all. Instead, it was:

simply a loud, angry protest about a very difficult job, which is emotionally taxing and physically wearing and sometimes just seems a bit too much. It's impossible not to feel a little sympathy and impossible also not to feel a little bewildered about what to do about it.[27]

While I appreciated the sympathy, the mildly patronising tone was less welcome. As a forty-three-year-old mother of two who had spent a decade working in current-affairs journalism, my patience had worn thin pretty quickly with journalists' gleeful disdain for the 'tragic naïveté' of junior doctors. On the other hand, I could see why the commentators were exasperated. I knew what I was personally willing to strike for: the dangers, as I saw them, of stretching the same number of doctors more thinly across seven days, not five. I was absolutely in favour of better weekend services, but only if they were coherently modelled, planned, funded and staffed. The BMA, on the other hand, had conceded behind closed doors the principle that our contract must deliver seven-day services 'cost-neutrally'. Indeed, albeit under duress, it had signed up to cost-neutrality as one of the preconditions of contract negotiations. This made it look as though it had tacitly accepted that it was possible to deliver a seven-day NHS in the absence of seven-day funding.

Inevitably, given this fundamental concession, the BMA appeared fixated on Saturday pay, while grassroots doctors like myself and many others continued to give interviews in which our key concern was the perils of expanding services across seven days without an appropriate expansion of staff. No wonder overall our messaging sounded muddled, or that the Department of Health press office often ran rings round us.

Long before we even went on strike, it was clear that many commentators regarded junior doctors' arguments about safety as nothing more than our own clumsy efforts at spin, a cynical strategy to transform a grubby pay dispute into something more noble and admirable. After all, they intimated, we were contemplating using what was, fundamentally, the weapon of our patients' misery – denied their operations and appointments on strike days – to contest the contract. But I didn't want more money. The salary I'd chosen to give up when I'd left television ten years previously was three times the one I earned now. What I desperately wanted was for the understaffing that already plagued my working life not to be exacerbated. If it were, I feared not only for my patients but also for my future in medicine.

CHAPTER 9

OESTROGEN

It is always around 4 a.m. that my brain begins to malfunction. I can walk, talk, perform medical procedures, but my ability to synthesise and weigh information briefly grinds to a halt. Once or twice, while writing an entry in a patient's notes at this time, my pen has started to veer off the page as my eyes have drifted shut mid-sentence. Clearly, from a patient-safety perspective, this is far from ideal. Diet Coke, a chocolate bar, cold water on my face, a quick slap to the cheeks all help. But everyone has a point in their night shifts at which they are at their most tired and vulnerable.

A few weeks into my first year as a doctor, I was called one night to cannulate a patient at my 4 a.m. nadir. Almost sleepwalking towards his bedside, I hoped for easy veins. He was, I suppose, in his early fifties. Well enough to twinkle with delight at the arrival of the female house officer. I should have noticed that his smile was more of a leer, and that licking one's lips was an unconventional way to greet the arrival of the doctor at your bedside. But I was exhausted and the warning signs escaped me. Crouching down in concentration, with the curtains closed around me, and the ward in darkness, I was oblivious to everything but the veins I scrutinised beneath the feeble NHS sidelight. As I was on the brink of piercing the skin of his arm with my needle, a hand suddenly gripped mine. Startled, I stared up at a sneer.

'Ooh. I bet you like being down there, don't you? Down on your knees in front of me?'

Slowly, deliberately, again he licked his lips. I realised his other hand was rubbing his genitals. Without making a sound, I stood and walked away from the bedside. Had it not been 4 a.m., had I been my normal self, I like to believe I would have torn strips off him, not least to make him think twice before sexually harassing the next lone female doctor. But I'm not certain. Humiliation is a powerful thing and my overwhelming impulse was get away from him. I told no one, cried briefly in a corridor, felt grubby and defiled, and moved on.

Though this is exceptionally unusual behaviour from a ward-based inpatient, in the cut and thrust of the Emergency Department, we are steeled for every shade of abuse, particularly after the pubs close. I've seen doctors spat at for the colour of their skin, nurses physically assaulted, porters restraining someone who threatened to kill them, the list goes on and on. A few weeks before starting my first six-month stint in emergency medicine, I ran into a friend one morning, just as she finished an A&E night shift.

'Are you OK?' I asked, concerned. She looked on the brink of tears.

'I just wish,' she said bitterly, 'that I could get through one shift in this place without a member of the public calling me a cunt.'

I found the more abusive visitors to the Emergency Department less of a problem than I'd expected. At night, invariably, there would be some kind of racism, misogyny, ignorance or filth to deal with – sometimes all of it at once – but usually from patients who were drunk, high or in the grip of a mental or physical illness that rendered them distressed, aggressive or disinhibited. It was an unpleasant part of the job, but I never took it personally. Once, though, while I was in my third trimester of pregnancy, the most senior nurse in the department that night refused to let me see the next patient.

'Seriously, Rach, go and see the next on the list,' he told me. 'Believe me, you don't want to see this guy.'

It turned out that the man in question had just traumatised a young and inexperienced student nurse who had pulled the curtains shut around his bed in order to check his observations. While sequestered out of sight with her, he had inveigled her into examining his penis, which, he assured her, was in need of medical attention. Around the root of his grotesquely swollen, purple member was wrapped not once but three times a 'Britain First' rubber wrist bracelet – an idiosyncratic expression of patriotism, to say the least. The nursing staff were livid. The perception that someone had preyed on one of their own brought out a fierce, almost familial loyalty. And, in truth, the bonds you form with your A&E family – the people with whom you witness all the trauma and sorrow and ugliness that life can hurl your patients' way – are as strong as any. The camaraderie forged from this shared experience is second to none.

When it comes to sexism, every group has its outliers, and doctors, like patients, are no exception. Rarely have I encountered overt misogyny among my medical peers, though the few occasions on which I have done so are memorable. Once, just before I sat my finals, an old-school male breast surgeon, close to retirement, gave us a revision lecture on breast cancer. Amid the bleak statistics about the second-biggest cancer killer of women in Britain, he suddenly flashed up a slide of a young blonde woman sitting coquettishly in front of a mammography machine, her naked breasts displayed prominently.

'Of course,' the surgeon commented ruefully, 'most of the patients I see in my clinic are in their fifties at least.' He paused, eyes twinkling mirthlessly at his student audience. 'Nothing like as nice as this one is to look at.'

The gasp from the student audience was audible. The sole purpose of the slide appeared to have been to enable the consultant to crack this joke. He continued as though he had said nothing abnormal. Quite apart from the fact that I knew that the mother of at least one of the students in the room was currently receiving treatment for breast cancer, this apparent contempt for women from a man who performed mastectomies for a living was difficult to stomach. To their credit, the medical school leadership took seriously the deluge of complaints that followed and the surgeon in question never taught medical students again.

The old-school are still at large in the medical hierarchy and often, on account of age and seniority, residing near the top of it. Recently, Jen, one of my female junior doctor colleagues, attended a medical dinner at an Oxbridge college. She remarked in passing to her fellow guests that it was striking to observe the low proportion of women seated at the high table. Only two of the forty or so spaces were occupied by women and these, Jen noted, were not present due to academic merit but because they were married to fellows of the college. The implication that medicine might in any way be sexist infuriated Jen's neighbour, himself a consultant in orthopaedics who led a prestigious department of spinal surgery.

'The trouble with women in surgery,' he said, 'is that they haven't got the temperament for it. Surgery requires hard work and dedication that women are incapable of. The reason they don't get to the top is because they're not cut out for it.'

That such views still exist in Britain's biggest employer in the twenty-first century struck the surgeon as entirely unremarkable. He was simply stating facts, he argued, and could certainly not be described as sexist himself since he had female juniors working in his service. When challenged with the argument that perhaps attitudes like his own might be driving women away from his speciality, rather than seeking to excel in it, he dismissed this as mere political correctness.

'There is a temperamental difference between men and women,' he insisted, 'that means women do not make good surgeons.'

Later, over drinks in the senior common room, another male consultant who had overheard the conversation sought Jen out to express how greatly he admired her forthrightness.

Alas, his approval came with its own particular kind of gender stereotyping. Without a trace of irony, he told her, 'You really are a feisty hussy, aren't you?'

'Honestly,' she told me afterwards, 'it was like being in a bloody nineteen-fifties gentlemen's club. Without the gentlemen.'

The vast majority of the doctors I have encountered respect their male and female colleagues equally. Indeed, medicine has a justifiable reputation for being one of the UK's more progressive professions when it comes to gender equality. But that does not mean medicine is a level playing field. As with so many jobs in Britain, it has an established gender pay gap as well as a gendered distribution of doctors among the various medical specialities, with many of the more 'prestigious' roles such as neurosurgery and cardiology remaining predominantly male. The disproportionate number of men in these roles increases the higher ones climbs up the hierarchy. While 57 per cent of junior doctors are women, only 30 per cent of surgical trainees are female, for example, and a mere 11 per cent of consultant surgeons are women.[28]

Though it takes a special kind of doctor to argue these days that women are temperamentally inferior to men, I have frequently heard colleagues explain away the existence of a glass ceiling in medicine as the result of women choosing to prioritise having a family above their career, rather than being the product of any structural or societal inequality. If, so the argument goes, we will insist on taking time out for maternity leave or to work part-time in order to be with our children, then our relegation to lesser roles within the profession is only to be expected.

With its long and unpredictable hours, hospital medicine is undeniably difficult to combine with family life. Indeed, the first hurdle is often making a family in the first place. I have two friends, Sarah, a female orthopaedic surgeon, and Nick, her anaesthetist husband, whose little girl is the same age as mine. Their daughter's conception required such relentless commitment, such spirited defiance of impossible odds that I secretly wish they had named her 'Immaculate'. Both parents at the time were junior doctors who worked punishing on-call rotas, often spending seventy-two-hour stints at a time inside the hospital. They quickly realised that attempting to align the rare moments when they were both at home with Sarah's ovulation was a strategy doomed to failure. Statistically speaking, the only reliable route to parenthood was sex inside the hospital.

This undertaking was not for the fainthearted. Contrary to the impression given by *Grey's Anatomy*, doctors' on-call rooms in the NHS are at best shabby, at worst a squalid health hazard. Nonetheless, at precisely the right time of the month, Nick and Sarah arranged an on-call-room tryst at six o'clock that morning. He was finishing his night shift, she was due to start hers an hour or so later. With a bit of luck, there would be a sufficient lull in the night's anaesthetic emergencies to permit the act of procreation.

Sarah waited impatiently on cheap hospital sheets whose cleanliness she chose not to question. A cockroach squatted in a corner of the room. She bleeped her husband. Stuck in theatre, said the scrub nurse. She tried again half an hour later. Still stuck in theatre. By now, her own on-call shift was close to starting. Irate, frustrated, another month squandered, she was about to change into her surgical scrubs when there was a frantic tap on the door. Sweaty and dishevelled from sprinting up seven flights of stairs, Nick had finally made it.

'Quick! I'm going to be late for my shift. Come on!' she ordered.

'I – I don't know if I can,' he told her and, under the circumstances, who could blame him?

'Oh, for God's sake! There's no time for that. Just get over here and do it.'

In an act so swift and primal it was surely worthy of narration by David Attenborough, Nick and Sarah mated. Immediately afterwards, she leaped up to pull on her scrubs.

'Shouldn't you, you know, lie on your back with your legs in the air for half an hour or something?' he asked her.

'Are you kidding? There's no time for that: my list is about to start in theatre.'

With that, she was gone and the rest is history, the phrase 'doing a level seven' immortalised in one particular family from that moment for ever more.

I was the first student in my medical school to have a baby, the first house officer in my Trust to be a parent, and the first to ask permission to work part-time. To my relief – and I'd felt uneasy about how the news would be received – not once was I aware of my medical school judging or frowning upon me. Quite the opposite. In a supportive and liberal university environment, combining my studies with motherhood felt, if not quite easy, then certainly manageable. The local nursery hours meshed with mine and the sleep deprivation felt like early training for all those imminent nights on call.

Only once I started my first year of practice, now as the mother of a toddler, did I discover how rigid and indifferent the NHS could be in its treatment of doctors in training. It was not that I wanted special treatment. I hadn't slogged away for six years to be anything other than a devoted doctor, as committed and industrious as any of my peers. I just hadn't banked on hospital management disregarding quite so blithely the way in which its approach to its staff could be, on occasion, unintentionally punitive.

The excuse always given is 'service provision'. Individual employees must be subservient to providing the service our patients need and what, in the NHS, could sound more reasonable than that? The problem arises when 'service' is used to justify an unnecessary blanket approach to treating staff as mere numbers on a roster, their own lives and needs being entirely disregarded. As any decent manager should know, this is a fast track towards a disaffected workforce.

Junior doctors in particular – moving as we do from job to job every three, four or six months – live in perpetual frustration at being unable to plan our lives. Leave is frequently 'fixed' – handed out at the last minute, with no capacity for adjustment, making even booking a holiday impossible. Rosters can be allocated without any notice, so that one's nights, weekends and evenings on call are not known until the first day of a new job. On occasion, a doctor will prepare for a new post by setting themselves up with a new home and amenities in their new town of work, only to find, days before they start, that they are now being sent somewhere a hundred or more miles away to do something entirely different. No explanation, no apology is ever given. Service provision requires it, so get over it.

None of this is necessary, let alone dictated by 'service needs'. It could all be avoided with a little forward planning. But, while some managers strive to provide this, many, in my experience, do not. All the doctors I know are more than happy to devote long working hours to their patients, but the casual thwarting of any attempt to plan one's life by departments too disorganised to email out advance rotas is infuriating. And, since hospital medicine – with its long, erratic and antisocial hours – is one of the most child-unfriendly careers, this can generate particular obstacles for parents who are attempting to combine being a doctor with caring for a family.

Dave and I swiftly discovered that the net financial benefit to our family of my working was less than zero. By becoming an NHS doctor, I was losing my family around £5,000 a year since our childcare costs outstripped my income. One weekend on call could last thirty-five hours and cost close to £500 in childcare. Antisocial hours were only a part of it. To avoid being a clock-watching doctor, someone who raced out of the ward on the dot of five to reach the nursery before it closed, we paid for childcare that ran on into the evenings, since the workload invariably did the same, regardless of what were, on paper, our official hours. There was no other way to avoid becoming the kind of doctor who dumped on her colleagues or abandoned her patients if they took a turn for the worse at the end of the day. I simply could not do that. But paying for the privilege of working hours that I myself worked for free understandably exasperated Dave, who now found himself in the unenviable position of trying to provide for his family and subsidise his hardworking yet financial drain of a wife.

'Why are you doing this, Rach? You come home exhausted and stressed, always three hours after you should do. You never see your son. You're costing your family thousands of pounds. It's completely insane.'

I had no convincing answers. I loved my patients and I

loved being a doctor. But, financially and emotionally, my family were paying for my decision to eschew time with them for endless hours in the hospital. On bad days, perpetually torn between my children, my husband and my patients, medicine felt less like a vocation than a folly. Cutting back my hours after my first year as a doctor felt like the only way to balance life, though an ostensibly 60 per cent job-share often resulted in my working in excess of the forty hours a week that typically constitute a full-time job.

As the junior doctor dispute hotted up, I wondered how long it would take before gender surfaced as an issue. Sure enough, writing in the *Sunday Times*, columnist Dominic Lawson devoted his provocatively entitled piece – 'The one sex change on the NHS that nobody has been talking about' – to explaining why the real cause of the dispute was not chronic NHS underfunding, inadequate workforce planning, or inflammatory sniping from the Department of Health press office but, more surprisingly, oestrogen. According to Lawson, a hidden debate had been 'raging for years' within the profession about the malign effects of the 'feminisation of medicine'.[29] Oddly, in seven years of practice, the rage had passed me and all my colleagues by. Nonetheless, his argument centred on the alleged crisis in the NHS caused by the presence of too many female doctors.

Once upon a time, all doctors were men. Women, as we know, used to be judged incapable of medicine. That changed in 1876, when, after a tenacious fight led by Britain's first female doctor, Elizabeth Garret Anderson, the law was changed to prohibit women's exclusion from medical schools. Now, more than 140 years later, female medical students outnumber men. Yet, according to Lawson, our predisposition to avoid antisocial hours and put family before career means we are more likely to work part-time, generating unsustainable staffing shortfalls. In essence, he seemed to be arguing, junior doctors were threatening the country with strikes because the fairer sex wanted to stay at home, cuddling our babies, at weekends. Worse, since each doctor costs so much to train, we part-time female doctors were overburdening the taxpayer with our inadequate productivity.

As evidence to back up his claims, Lawson cited a Dr Chris Heath, a '40-year NHS veteran', who had written to him to say, 'Women doctors don't like weekend rotas ... This is one of the reasons why paediatric units are failing: 70 per cent of their junior staff being women and therefore frequently off on maternity leave.' It's true, I'm afraid. When you pop out twenty or more babies over the course of a career, that's a significant proportion of your time spent breastfeeding. Clearly, the main issue facing the NHS was women like me who first flooded our medical schools, then spawned babies with impunity, and finally abandoned our patients for a lazy part-timer's life.

Inspired by the phenomenally successful 'Like a Girl' video from Always, the sanitary-towel company, which was screened at the 2015 American Superbowl[30], I decided to lampoon Lawson on social media by starting a satirical hashtag, '#likealadydoc'. To my immense satisfaction, I watched #likealadydoc trend internationally as female and male doctors from all over the world expressed what they thought of such sexist claptrap. Some of my favourite #likealadydoc tweets from fellow doctors included:

I apologise on behalf of my uterus for its role in NHS under investment and fragmentation of services.[31]

'I got all confused & got 3 degrees + 2 royal college memberships. I only popped out for a new frock.[32]

'Poor husband left to do all the women's work at home while I've spent 26 hrs at the hospital this weekend covering a rota gap.[31]

This weekend, I checked every major decision about a patient with a woman. My consultant. My boss. My role model.[33]

Beneath the scorn, of course, was a serious point. Once, men deemed women too weak-minded to be capable of medicine. Now, apparently, our fatal flaw was to be insufficiently economically productive, lured by our ovaries towards part-time working. Lawson's argument neglected to consider the notion that perhaps, in twenty-first-century Britain, some fathers as well as mothers longed to share in childrearing. Many modern men – men like my husband – would dearly love to have the option of balancing their workplace commitments with spending time with their children. Flexibility in the workplace is not, in short, a *woman* problem: it is a *human* problem. But in a society bereft of affordable childcare in which part-time working is the exception, not the norm – and cultural expectations are largely that men should be full-time breadwinners – the burden of sacrificing career for children continues to fall disproportionately on women.

When Dave and I considered our options, part-time

working was unavailable in his workplace. So either he quit work, which was financially untenable for us, or I worked part-time, or both of us accepted that our children would grow up spending more time in care than with their parents. My 'choice' to cut back my hours was framed accordingly. Arguably, if social and cultural barriers did not deny men the choice to work as flexibly as women, the 'problem' with women in the medical workforce would cease to be a gendered one.

Lawson's implied solution to the problem of the 'feminisation' of medicine – though he chose to insinuate rather than state it explicitly – was to address the diminished productivity of female doctors by reversing their increasing prevalence in the NHS. Perhaps, to ensure the taxpayer received the biggest bang for their buck when subsidising doctors' training, it would indeed be better to revert to a more virile time when medicine was predominantly male. After all, limiting women's encroachment on the profession would certainly minimise the problem of part-timers. One of the most disappointing aspects of the junior doctor dispute was that the government, far from ensuring the NHS remained a trailblazer for gender equality, turned out to be just as willing as Lawson to cast female doctors as a financial barrier to a seven-day NHS.

—⋀—

After his 2015 general election victory, David Cameron briefly sought to present himself as the face not only of compassionate conservatism and family values, but also of female emancipation. He took an impressively progressive lead on gender equality by vowing unequivocally to 'end the gender pay gap in a generation'.[34] But the insincerity of that commitment was swiftly exposed when, in early 2016, the government belatedly published its equality assessment of the new junior doctor contract. The assessment, a legal requirement under European law, analysed whether any specific groups were likely to be systematically disadvantaged as a result of the new contract.

Surprisingly, given the government's apparent advocacy of gender equality, the Department of Health did not attempt to hide the discrimination against women at the heart of the new contract. In fact, the Department's own analysis admitted that women might lose out disproportionately, while dismissing that fact with the statement that, 'Any adverse effect on women is a proportionate means of achieving a legitimate end.'[35] In essence, the pay of part-time doctors, 80 per cent of whom are women, was set to rise more slowly under the new contract, even though their antisocial hours would increase, creating a need for expensive additional childcare. The new contract would therefore widen the very gender pay gap the Prime Minister had pledged to eradicate. Women's salaries, it turned out, were mere collateral damage and women, in David Cameron's eyes, were almost equal to men – just that little bit cheaper.

While admitting the new contract would, 'disproportionately disadvantage those who need to arrange childcare',[35] the government proposed an outlandish solution. They helpfully invited doctors who were carers to find, 'informal unpaid childcare arrangements in the evenings and weekend' – as if the country were littered with people clamouring to do ad hoc, unpaid nannying at three o'clock on a Sunday morning. To someone who had lost count of the number of times she had scrabbled in panic to find childcare for her erratic shifts, whose job had put considerable strain on her marriage, and who had become a net financial burden to her family by working as an NHS doctor, this statement – and its utter ignorance of what life was like on the ground for junior doctors – could not have been more demoralising to me. Even under the current contract, I had already discussed with my husband whether I would be forced to quit medicine, given the financial hit of my career to my family. If the new contract meant that women with children would become less able, financially, to continue working as doctors, then medicine, after all those years of emancipation, would indeed be set to turn more male, overturning generations of doctors' fighting for gender equality.

The publication of the equality assessment provoked a storm of condemnation. Professor Jane Dacre and Miss Clare Marx, the presidents of the Royal College of Physicians and the Royal College of Surgeons respectively, said in a joint statement,

> We are very concerned by the language in the government's own equality analysis of the contract, which warns that features of the new contract 'impact disproportionately on women'. Recent commitments from government to support women in business are greatly welcome. We view the wording of the equality analysis as incompatible with this approach.[36]

Dr Maureen Baker, the chair of the Royal College of GPs, said, 'I've always been incredibly proud of our NHS – general practice in particular – for being streets ahead of the corporate world and being true leaders in terms of gender inequality, so anything that threatens this must be taken very seriously.'[37] The Shadow Health Secretary, Heidi Alexander, encapsulated many doctors' anger when she commented that the equality assessment had led to 'women rightly questioning whether they've woken up in a different century'.[38] We were enormously proud of the strides our profession had taken towards gender equality, in spite of the problems that remained, and to watch the government riding roughshod over this felt – to a great many male and female doctors alike – sickening.

To the government's embarrassment, the condemnation provoked by its casual acceptance of gender discrimination spread beyond the UK. One of the directors of the World Health Organisation, Jim Campbell, stated on Twitter that, in his opinion, the government's new junior doctor contract contravened the United Nations Commission on the Status of Women. Its 'regressive policies', he stated, meant 'gender equity for junior doctors is at risk' and 'female doctors will face widening pay gaps with male colleagues and may be forced to quit medicine'.[39]

Even if the government didn't care a jot about gender equality, in crude economic terms it seemed exceptionally short-sighted of them to increase the risks of driving away female medics while in the midst of the worst doctor recruitment and retention crisis the NHS had ever seen. After all, women currently make up 60 per cent of the profession. One might have hoped that the imperative of safely staffing the NHS front line would have caused ministers to think twice about imposing regressive working patterns that made it harder for female doctors to continue working. But apparently not. A Department of Health source told me off the record that our outrage against the gender discrimination was regarded by ministers as manufactured – it was, they believed, nothing more than an opportunist stick we had latched onto in order to bash the new contract in the media.

If that was true, it could not have been more wrong. As a child, a student, a journalist and a doctor, not once had I doubted I was as capable as a man. It took a dispute between doctors and the government for me to discover that, regardless of whether ministers viewed men and women the same way, when the principle of gender equality conflicted with that of reducing the size of the public-sector wage bill, they were willing to throw women under a bus.

CHAPTER 10

RESILIENCE

You know something is not quite right in the NHS when the head of the General Medical Council likens modern medicine to war in Helmand Province.[40] In 2016, after an internal inquiry revealed that twenty-eight doctors had committed suicide while being investigated for professional misconduct by the GMC, the doctors' regulator announced new plans for would-be doctors to have to demonstrate their 'emotional resilience' before being allowed to practise.

The GMC chair, Professor Terence Stephenson, stated that medics needed to learn from the armed forces, being formally trained, just like servicemen and women, in coping strategies for handling the pressures of practice. He told the *Telegraph*,

> Doctors see things that many other people will never see in a lifetime. Just as when soldiers go to

Afghanistan, you don't want the first time they see somebody who has suffered terrible injuries to be when they're dealing with an emergency in the heat of the moment . . . Army personnel have told me that they would not begin resilience training just as they're about to deploy and I fully understand that. The army discovered some time ago that soldiers under pressure aren't helped if they are just told to keep a stiff upper lip. It's time medicine reached a similar conclusion – and acted on it.[40]

At the time, being intimately acquainted with a member of the military myself, I turned to my long-suffering husband and asked him, 'When you went through officer training, did they teach you how to be resilient?' Dave's snort of laughter was telling.

'Are you kidding? We got taught how not to get bollocked by the drill sergeants whose main purpose in life was to whip us into shape and toughen us up the hard way. We got taught how to drag ourselves out of bed at five a.m. and be screamed at for a speck of dust on a windowsill without breaking down and crying in front of our mates. So, no, we did not get taught resilience. But we learned it pretty quickly, or we left.'

Perhaps, in these times of austerity, the most efficient way for the NHS to deal with its haemorrhaging staff would indeed be, first, to weed out the weaklings through compulsory boot camp, ensuring only the toughest were permitted to take on employment in the NHS; but one senses the GMC had something else in mind. In fact, since my husband's officer-training days, UK Armed Forces does now run courses on resilience and has even built a Stress and Resilience Training

Centre at its defence academy in Shrivenham. But the NHS is not a battlefield, doctors are not soldiers and caring is not armed combat. Moreover, implicit in the GMC's approach to doctor burnout and suicide is the assumption that the fault lies within the individual doctor, whose psychological inadequacies have somehow rendered them incapable of coping with the stresses and strains of medicine.

What if, instead of individuals' emotional failings, it is warped conditions of work within the NHS that are driving doctors and nurses to the edge? The debilitating pressures of constantly operating in an environment that denies you the resources to do your job safely? A little like facing Helmand with peashooters, to borrow the military analogy of which NHS leaders can be so fond. Under those circumstances, an online course in tick-box 'resilience', while welcome, may be doomed to failure, ignoring as it does the fundamental factors eroding doctors' and nurses' capacity to bounce back.

'Resus' is where patients are sent when doctors worry they might die. We were waiting around this particular empty resuscitation bed like predators poised to pounce. Emergency attempts to save a life are often brutal, and resuscitation, when the team first descend, can horrify any next of kin who witnesses it. None of us spoke. The paramedics had called in the trauma to A&E with sufficient warning for a full team to be assembled, our roles pre-assigned and displayed on the cardboard signs we now wore pinned to our scrubs. Our team leader, a seasoned trauma consultant, had the kind of battle-weary composure that inspires total calm. It was, as so often, a road-traffic collision. All we had been told was that the victim was young and unconscious. She had been hit by a lorry while walking through town. A mobile phone was rumoured to have been involved. No one knew anything for certain. But we were ready to launch into coordinated action the moment she swept through the swing doors.

I was 'Doctor 2', the most junior doctor in the team. I felt awkward in the bulky lead apron I wore to shield me from radiation, should bedside scans be required. This was my first time in a trauma team and I was desperate to do a good job, staying calm and focused no matter how bloody the unfolding events proved to be.

As the paramedics rushed the patient into resus, we descended *en masse*, as one. Seamlessly, one nurse attacked clothing with scissors to expose bare flesh, while another applied electrodes and oxygen. The anaesthetist assessed the girl's level of consciousness, deciding whether or not she required urgent assistance with breathing. Several policemen hovered in the background. I shoved a cannula in the largest vein I could find, then stabbed the main artery in the wrist to provide a sample of arterial blood. In under a minute, a fifteen-year-old girl – her name was Chloe – lay naked but for her knickers, the plastic collar protecting her C-spine and a tangle of plastic tubes and wires. There was no blood, no bruising, no mangled limbs, nothing to suggest her recent impact with a twelve-tonne truck. She was, in a word, perfect. Her body was flawless – it had the kind of litheness and beauty possessed only by the very young – save for one devastating detail. From her nostrils trickled a trace of clear fluid. You might barely have noticed, had you not set out to find it. Cerebrospinal fluid – the liquid that surrounds and cushions the brain and spinal cord – was leaking out of her skull through her nose. Beneath its immaculate exterior, her head had suffered a blow of such force it had fractured the skull into pieces, allowing the telltale seepage of fluid. Who knew the state of the brain beneath? She began to groan and flail at the hands that accosted her. Probably, she was cerebrally irritated – blood was inflaming the meninges, the protective layers in which the brain is wrapped.

An urgent CT scan of her head confirmed everyone's worst fears. Chloe's skull was shattered in five separate places, her brain swollen and clouded with blood. Though her body lay unblemished, we had no way of knowing if the person she had been was preserved. I was not there when her parents burst into resus, but I heard their screams, reverberating all the way to the other side of the department. The father, one of the nurses told me afterwards, had collapsed to his knees at his daughter's bedside.

In an NHS Emergency Department, the queues of patients never end and there is no time to dwell upon any of them. You move on, do your job, refuse to indulge your own feelings, because your next patient deserves better than an emotion-addled doctor. But that night, and for several more afterwards, Chloe's image – this pale, perfect girl on the cusp of adulthood – floated into my dreams. We would be crowded round her bed again, fighting to save her, while knowing she was slipping away. I held my children extra tightly that week and chose not to follow her progress on neuro-intensive care, preferring instead to believe in those uplifting patients who once in a while defy their doctors' pessimism.

It was by no means the bloodiest or ugliest of my early medical experiences, yet for a while Chloe continued to haunt me. I imagined the banality of her chitchat with a schoolfriend, giggles and gossip about last Saturday night; then, from nowhere, never glimpsed, twelve tonnes of truck bearing down, a mobile phone bouncing off the pavement, a body lying still in the road. The mother in me recoiled. No quantity of parental love, hope, fear or grief ever protects against the casual indifference of whom A&E decides to summon to its bays.

It is this, in one sense, that the GMC was latching onto – and rightly so. As Terence Stephenson put it,

> During one day last week seeing emergencies, I cared for a child of seven with an incurable life-limiting condition who will not survive until 17, and a 17-year old who took a life-threatening paracetamol overdose because she cannot face the next day. Despite 32 years as a doctor, seeing patients suffering is still very stressful for me so how much more difficult must it be for a recently qualified doctor? ... Without developing a psychological 'carapace' or some 'emotional armour' which allows one at the end of the day to hand over care of patients to the night team, to go home and not agonise over these worrying patients, doctors can burn out.[76]

Stephenson is partially right. When you are a doctor, a bad day at the office might mean, 'She has catastrophic brain damage'; 'He won't walk again'; 'We lost the baby'; 'We did everything we could, but we couldn't save him.' A bad day is disability, death or grief of an order that cuts through the routine hospital backdrop of recurring loss and pain. A bad day makes you want to tell the world to please go to hell because only cursing, or maybe alcohol, makes you feel better. If you cannot face raw human suffering, medicine is not for you. But, equally, when your job is not killing but healing, the notion that good doctors must be clad in 'emotional armour' risks the unintended harms of numbed and battle-scarred clinicians, all too evident in the drivers of the scandal of Mid Staffs.

In my experience as a junior doctor, what makes me resilient – able to function with the mental elasticity to absorb the stresses of the job I chose, weaving them positively into my working life – is, above all, other people. My colleagues, my mentors, my team. I am nothing without the doctors and nurses with whom I work every day. Break down the human relationships that sustain and nurture a medical workforce, and you risk creating doctors who first lose their compassion, and then become too brittle to remain in work. Patients are best served by neither.

—⋀—

'What the hell is going on with our patients?' asked Sally, my fellow junior doctor, as we worked our way through a bottle of wine. 'You do realise more of them have died this month than lived?'

It was our first month on haematology, the speciality that, more than any other, is accused by other doctors of inappropriately poisoning its patients, refusing to pull out and permit dignified deaths. Sometimes, this boils down to misunderstanding. Blood cancers such as leukaemia are not like other malignancies, where cure rests on cutting out a tumour. In leukaemia, where the cancer is spread throughout the blood from the outset, it is often only the 'poison' – aggressive, even life-threatening chemotherapy – that gives the patient a shot at a long-term survival. But the stakes are high. Chemotherapy attacks not only the leukaemia cells but also the healthy bone marrow where all the other, noncancerous blood cells are made. If a patient's bone marrow begins to fail, this puts them at risk of potentially fatal bleeding or infection.

I had never seen such a collection of desperately unwell patients as in my first few weeks on a haematology ward. Most of my patients were there for bone-marrow transplants, where someone is subjected to chemotherapy so devastating their entire bone marrow is wiped out, including – or so we hope – every trace of leukaemia. Marrow from a donor, perhaps a sibling or another closely matched relative, is then transplanted into the patient, replacing what we have destroyed. If the marrow successfully 'takes', and if the patient does not die from bleeding, infection or the powerful immunosuppressants they will now have to take for the rest of their life, then maybe, just maybe, they will be cured. Poison, I had to admit, was rife here, and with the poison came the deaths.

First, a mother to three young children succumbed, in increasing pain and fear, to the ravages of what can be one of the most brutal blood cancers, multiple myeloma. Next, in swift succession, several of our patients with bone-marrow transplants died. But the most searing experience, for me, in this relentless month of deaths, was a night spent looking after an unusually young patient admitted earlier that day onto our ward. At eighteen, Azra had never really known life without leukaemia. Diagnosed while still a small girl, she had spent years in and out of hospitals receiving chemotherapy, radiotherapy and transplants. Now, she had arrived with her father, gasping for air and clutching a small, scruffy bunny, a much-loved comforter since birth. Her leukaemia may have been at bay, but her lungs were overwhelmed with infection. In someone with a normal immune system, the bug in question, cytomegalovirus, is rarely even noticed, but, in the lungs of an immunosuppressed patient, it can wreak absolute havoc.

As the night wore on, Azra's temperature soared and her breathing became more ragged. Her father's face wore the drawn expression of someone who confronts the abyss. In spite of giving powerful antiviral medications through a drip and the most concentrated oxygen we could administer, Azra's oxygen saturations continued to fall. I could see the fear in her eyes every time I came towards her, doctors at her bedside invariably meaning limbs stabbed with needles or worse. She clutched her threadbare bunny to her side, as if a talisman against the pain I might inflict. She did not know it, but my pleas to allow me to take a sample of her arterial blood – a procedure that is invariably painful, sometimes exquisitely so – had her best interests, her life, at heart. Without an accurate recording of her oxygen levels, Intensive Care would never agree to giving Azra a bed. Even when finally armed with the dire oxygen readings, I faced an ICU registrar who bristled with hostility.

'The trouble with you haematologists is, you just can't stop poisoning your patients, can you?' he glowered.

My own registrar was managing another equally unwell patient, the ICU registrar didn't want to know, and Azra, I feared, was going to die on the ward without the invasive therapy only ICU could provide. I felt alone before a father's beseeching stares and his daughter's naked fear. Finally, mercifully, the daytime haematology registrar arrived, took one look at me and asked what was wrong.

'It's Azra,' I told him. 'I think she's going to die if we can't get her to ICU. Please, please try to get her there.'

We exchanged a look. In that instant, I knew he knew what the night had been, the desperate scrabbling to hold onto a life that you fear might be slipping through your hands. Of course he knew. Like every seasoned registrar, he had been there a hundred times before.

'OK. Just go home, Rach. Get some rest. I'll sort this out.'

My gratitude, exaggerated by sleep deprivation, left me close to tears. I knew Azra was now in safe hands. Returning to the ward that evening for the next of my night shifts, I found she had been sent to ICU shortly after I had left, where she now lay attached to a ventilator machine that mechanically inflated her ravaged lungs. She never managed to breathe again by herself and died, still ventilated, several days later. You could argue that ICU had been perfectly correct in their original assessment not to admit her, whereas my judgement had been clouded by sentiment. When ICU beds are like gold dust, only those patients with a genuine chance of survival earn the right of occupation.

Back in the pub, as I discussed with Sally the trials and tribulations of haematology, even Azra's death lost its sting. No explanations were needed. We had already shared so many deaths, bad deaths, the ones where you cannot shake the feeling that your years of toil and study have failed you, failed, above all, your patient. Our camaraderie was forged in each other's worst moments – the angry, exhausted, bitter, hollow times – and the solace this afforded, more than anything else, was what kept us cheerfully going on. Nothing helps resilience quite like knowing you are in it with your comrades-in-arms. Before long, we were laughing. Black humour, certainly. Jokes you could never repeat to a non-medic. The slightly twisted take on dying that brings you back to the wards, renewed, heartened and ready for more.

Sometimes, on returning home after a long shift on call, the first thing I need to do is wash it away under a scalding shower. Then, an obligatory large glass of wine to take away the hard edges. Talking to my family is not an option. A husband neither wants nor needs to know that today you were called to a crash call where the patient was vomiting up blood so profusely his circulation crashed and he suffered a cardiac arrest; that security guards scrambled to clear the public from the route between the ward and the operating theatre; that, as the crash team ran with the bed down the corridor, you knelt atop its blood-soaked sheets, pumping the patient's chest with such force you feared you might lose your balance and topple to the floor below; that in theatre, despite the surgeons cracking the chest, wrenching the ribcage apart and manually compressing the heart, it never regained a rhythm; that later, long after the time of death had been called, when you stripped off your sodden clothes, you found even your underwear was bloody. Why would he want to hear this? Why, frankly, would anyone? They say nothing is thicker than blood. But even genealogical ties do not bind as tightly as those blood ties to my other family, the one with whom I share the daily sorrows and trauma of life inside a hospital.

—∿—

These days, when not calling for compulsory resilience, NHS leaders are invariably agonising over rock-bottom morale among NHS staff. And rightly so. Low morale is linked not only to sickness but also to lower standards of patient care. NHS

England has estimated that sickness absence costs the NHS a staggering £2.4 billion a year. If that sickness absence were reduced by only one day per person per year, the NHS would manage to save £150 million, enough to pay for six thousand additional full-time staff.[41] Put simply, there is an enormous financial incentive to cheering us up. In 2015, the chief executive of NHS England, Simon Stevens, summarised the economic argument for improving staff morale and wellbeing:

> NHS staff have some of the most critical but demanding jobs in the country. When it comes to supporting the health of our own workforce, frankly the NHS needs to put its own house in order. At a time when arguably the biggest operational challenge facing hospitals is converting overspends on temporary agency staff into attractive flexible permanent posts, creating healthy and supportive workplaces is no longer a nice [thing] to have, it's a must-do.[42]

But Stevens's implicit accusation that the NHS is to blame for its own morale issues is somewhat rich, given the political and financial constraints under which every NHS institution is forced to operate, and over which the government and Treasury exercise control. While I would dearly love my hospital to treat me with a little more kindness, a little less indifference – and undoubtedly there is much work to do here – a Zumba class or two is never going to come close to addressing the corrosive impact on our daily working lives of navigating the gruelling workloads caused by insufficient numbers of frontline staff. And, in an era when hospitals are being expected to slash their expenditure under the guise of 'efficiency savings', the pressure is on them to shrink, not expand, the size of their wage bill.

Recently, a doctor writing anonymously in the *Guardian* encapsulated perfectly the conditions that can defeat the most resilient of doctors:

> It's the start of my night shift in the district general hospital as the medical registrar. I'm on my own and I know it ... All six beds in resuscitation are full. Two patients require machines to breathe: one is alert, the other is already anaesthetised. Anyone who can't talk, as a general rule, needs to be seen immediately. However, these sick people cannot be moved from their temporary beds in A&E – there are no beds free in the hospital ... It's going to be a long night. I see the exasperated paramedics in a queue; they can't drop patients off. My juniors, just two of them for 150 patients, get to work, but it is hard. There is nowhere private to see people. They are reduced to clerking patients on trolleys and chairs – it's not dignified.[43]

The stamina required to get through a shift like this – and every doctor has worked them – fills you with anticipatory dread. The chaos, the pitifully small number of on-call doctors to tackle the onslaught of patients, the potential risks of the lack of bed space, the fact that no one in the hospital wants to hear about any of it. Perhaps most soul-destroying of all is that, too often, at the widest level – in the national conversation between politicians, journalists and commentators about the state of the NHS – it can sometimes feel as though no one is willing to confront head-on what is actually happening on the ground. This is precisely the sort of denial, a kind of wilful collective blindness, whose dangers Sir Robert Francis warned of, except that, in this case, it operates at a governmental rather than Trust board level. Morale is built on belief. But how can NHS staff maintain theirs in the institution they love and serve when its political masters appear to be turning a blind eye to its slow, inexorable demise? As the medical registrar in the *Guardian* put it,

> In a moment of clarity, at 1am after I have barely stopped to breathe and an elderly lady has died in my arms, I ask myself: 'Is this not supposed to be a developed country? Do we not care for our people? Do we really accept that this is the way it needs to be? Doesn't anyone out there care that there are no beds?'[79]

In military circles, morale – or a unit's *'esprit de corps'* – is often defined as the capacity of a group's members to maintain their belief in an institution or goal, particularly in the face of opposition or hardship. If a unit's morale is depleted, they are at risk of cracking and surrendering. A Pulitzer prize-winning American military journalist, writing during the Second World War, gave a stirring definition of high morale as being when 'a soldier thinks his army is the best in the world, his regiment the best in the army, his company the best in the regiment, his squad the best in the company, and that he himself is the best blankety-blank soldier man in the outfit'.[44]

How does that compare to the NHS? My army (my health service) is crumbling around me. Year on year, the government's underfunding undermines the collective efforts of my colleagues and me to provide the public with exemplary care. Waiting lists balloon. My inpatients suffer the perils of rota gaps – arising where doctors have either fled the NHS or been signed off sick, leaving the remaining staff to carry their workloads. My regiment (my hospital) is in deficit. My squad (my fellow junior doctors) was recently reduced by sick leave from three to two. And me? I'm too tired to believe in much these days: it takes all my efforts to be safe and competent.

Recently, I witnessed a stark example of the caustic effects of understaffing on morale. My team and I were discussing our patients prior to setting off on our morning ward round when a house officer walked into the doctors' mess looking so broken and stunned he was almost staggering. We stopped our conversation in alarm. 'I know him,' I said to my consultant. 'I'll have a chat and find out what's wrong.'

Samir had just completed a night on call, attending to the emergency needs of a hundred or so medical inpatients. We sat side by side on a stinking sofa and I pressed a hot coffee into his hands. After a while, tears began to trickle down his cheeks and I could see how much he hated being seen to cry. At age twenty-four, he was two or three months into his career as a doctor.

'I just couldn't do it,' he eventually muttered. 'There was too much to do and I tried to ask the med reg for help but she was flat out in A&E and she couldn't leave the sick patients.'

'Did you have sickies?' I asked him, this being the code for patients so unwell you fear their illness might end up being life-threatening. Silently, he nodded, the tears flowing.

'I know it wasn't her fault,' he continued. 'She wanted to help me but she had all the new admissions in A&E to sort out and they were sick too.'

I knew precisely what he had been through. The feeling of abandonment, through no fault of his senior doctor, who herself had spent a night fighting fire in an equally overrun part of the hospital. The fear – a deep-seated foreboding that someone that night was going to die on your watch.

'I don't know if I can do it any more,' he told me. 'I don't even know if I want to.'

I assured him that it was not that he was slow or incompetent or feeble or useless, that he had been defeated all night by an impossible workload, that if I had worked his shift I'd be feeling just as he did, that the law of nights meant that after this shocker he'd earn at least one gentle shift before the week was out. I could see he did not believe a word of it, but he smiled half-heartedly, appreciating my efforts, and hauled himself off to bed.

It cannot be right that, only a couple of months after six years dedicated to learning how to be a doctor, a young medic is left sobbing on a sofa. It was not Samir's proximity to suffering that broke him that night, but his responsibility for too many patients. It was not that he lacked resilience, but that the workload to which he had been subjected had been unsafe, unfair and inhumane. The remedy, on this occasion, was glaringly obvious. Not a tick-box course designed to toughen him up, just another doctor on the rota.

—√\—

After his dismal set of nights, Samir managed to rally and move on. But not every young doctor is so lucky. Some quit the profession before their first year is out, others end up lost beneath the feeling that life is no longer tolerable.

In February 2016, the day after Jeremy Hunt announced the

imposition of his contract, Rose Polge, a junior doctor only six months out of medical school, took her own life. Her job and its workload had become too much to bear. As her mother, Heather, put it, Rose, 'became overwhelmed with acute anxiety about the expectations, demands and responsibilities of her job. This broke her spirit.'[45] When news of her suicide broke in the media, junior doctors nationally were horrified. Every one of us at one time or another has either felt sheer desperation ourselves or known another young doctor who has. I thought of Samir and his shame at his tears. Of another doctor friend who called me once to tell me he was going to hang himself. The near misses, the prevalence of desperate distress. Rose could have been any of us.

It emerged that Rose had been midway through a shift at her hospital when she vanished one Friday afternoon, leaving a suicide note in the glove compartment of her car, then walking into the sea and drowning herself. The note mentioned Jeremy Hunt. During the inquest into her death, her boyfriend described how, the night before her disappearance, Rose had talked about quitting medicine and, finding sleep impossible, had walked alone on the beach where, the next day, she took her own life. Her online history showed she had visited suicide sites.

At her inquest, Rose's family called for action to address the crisis in the health service precipitated by doctors' fatigue and punishing workloads. The words Rose's mother would later write about her daughter's death struck a painful chord with us all:

> Exhaustion due to long hours, work related anxiety, despair at her future in medicine and the news of the

imposition of the new contract on junior doctors were definite contributors to this awful and final decision. The hours that some junior doctors have to work are, in my opinion, terribly cruel and inhumane. Rose was working 12–14 hours a day for up to 12 days, often without breaks and staying late to get the work done. Leaving little time to get home, sleep, eat and shower before the next day began. This type of existence is seen by many as a right of passage for young doctors and takes a terrible toll on them, their families and loved ones. Until this state of affairs changes significantly, more doctors will be mentally broken and leave the profession, the country or life itself. The importance of caring for those who work so hard to provide care for others seems so neglected. We have paid the ultimate price in the loss of our wonderful Rose.[45]

I thought back to my time on the understaffed Surgical Emergency Unit, tears dripping onto my young son as I tried to shake away the toll of a hundred-hour week and be a semblance of the mother I wanted to be; I wondered whether, without him and my husband to love me, it might have been horribly different. And I could not shake the thought from my head of the beautiful twenty-five-year-old woman who beamed radiance and life from the photos in the press, yet placed her clothes in a pile on wet sand and walked away her life in the spray.

CHAPTER 11

INSURRECTION

You know events have taken a surreal turn when a Canadian pop star with more Twitter followers than the entire UK population decides to campaign publicly for the NHS.

Just before Christmas 2015, Justin Bieber – one of the most successful musicians in the history of pop music, a 23-year-old with four times as many Twitter followers as even the tweeting US president, Donald Trump – became the most improbable player in the junior doctor dispute.

A couple of months earlier, a young doctor called Harriet Nerva had started a campaign on Facebook to try to get an NHS choir to the coveted Christmas Number One spot in the charts. Her online post won nearly 100,000 fans in a week, captivating the imagination of NHS staff and the public alike. 'I qualified 15 months ago,' Harriet explained to the press, 'and I love the NHS, I'm very proud of it. And I feel getting it to number one would bring to the public's eye the fantastic service it provides in very challenging times. Junior doctors in particular feel very let down this winter by this government. They're the backbone of the NHS and they will continue to fight for a contract that's safe and fair.'[46]

The choir in question, London's Lewisham and Greenwich NHS Trust Choir, had originally recorded their single, a reworking of Coldplay's 'Fix You' and Simon and Garfunkel's 'Bridge Over Troubled Water', for a BBC Two documentary series in 2012. Their song, 'A Bridge Over You', featured a moving video of the doctors, nurses, physiotherapists, midwives and other healthcare professionals who made up the choir both singing and also carrying out their everyday work tending patients in the hospital, from newborn babies to frail great-grandparents. The footage encapsulated the tenderness and compassion that define, for so many members of NHS staff and the public alike, the essence of our health service.

Although not overtly political or allied to the junior doctors' cause, the video ended with a powerful quotation from Aneurin Bevan, the politician who founded the NHS, stating that, 'The NHS will last as long as there are folk left with faith to fight for it.' Junior doctors, already campaigning furiously against a contract we perceived to fundamentally threaten our ability to provide safe care, were captivated by the challenge of getting the NHS to number one and threw all our energies behind the cause. 'It's a proper charts battle,' enthused Katie Rogerson, a trainee paediatrician and member of the Lewisham choir. 'It's just ridiculous that it's the NHS versus Justin Bieber, but that's all in the jolliness of it.'[47]

It was indeed completely ludicrous. Only in feel-good fantasies do small NHS choirs defeat global megastars. But, with ferociously campaigning junior doctors, overwhelming public support and an enormous amount of media attention in the run-up to Christmas, 'A Bridge Over You' trailed Bieber's single by only a few thousand sales. Still, it looked as if he would just win out. Until, that is, someone managed to communicate to the superstar how much this unlikeliest of battles mattered to the British public. When Bieber discovered whom he was up against, he graciously tweeted a series of messages to his fanbase urging them not to back his own single, but instead to buy the NHS choir's: 'I'm hearing this UK Christmas race is close,' he wrote, 'but the NHS choir single is for charity. So for one week it's OK not to be number one. Let's do the right thing and help them win. It's Christmas. This is what it's all about. Merry Christmas.'[48]

On Christmas Day, I quietly crept away from the mountainous lunch Dave and I had cooked for our family to put on *Top of the Pops* for the live Christmas Number One announcement. Like every junior doctor I knew, I was desperate for the choir to win. Somehow it felt totemic. If doctors like Harriet and Katie, among so many others, could propel the NHS to chart-topping success, then it felt as if we were capable of anything, including enabling the government to see the folly of promising the public a new seven-day NHS without funding it. Tucked away by myself on the sofa, I held my breath. You could put it down to seasonal fizz but, when 'A Bridge Over You' was announced as Christmas Number One, I could not stop crying. The video expertly tugged at the heartstrings – the cannula in an infant's hand, a tiny wrist encased in plaster of Paris, an emaciated, elderly gentleman hesitantly walking with the help of a frame and encouraging smiles from his physiotherapist. But it also encapsulated why I had become a doctor. This was what I both ached for and had already lost. Conditions of work that allowed me to care. And I was damned if I would let the government denigrate them any further without a fight.

Just after dawn on 12 January 2016, I slowly walked towards a hospital picket line with too many questions dragging me down. Was I doing the right thing? Or, as some of the newspapers believed, were we really stroppy, selfish, naïve little upstarts, willing to sacrifice our patients to get our own way? As the first strike by junior doctors in over forty years began in subzero temperatures, I thought of my patients, whom I had chosen – though it felt less a choice than an act of desperation – to abandon in order to stand outside the hospital. Shame mingled with relief and pride that we were finally standing up for what we believed in. It was bitterly cold. I imagined a more experienced industrial activist would have known to bolster flimsy hospital scrubs with a pair of decent thermal long johns.

We were an awkward bunch. Initially, we were positioned by the entrance to the hospital, but a senior manager promptly kicked us off the premises, forcing us to trail uncertainly with our homemade placards to the edge of the hospital site, a windswept mini-roundabout. I took mild satisfaction from the fact that our curt ejection was filmed from the roundabout by a fortuitously positioned BBC film crew. A picket line was unnerving territory and none of us really knew what to expect. We were, I suppose, thirty or forty doctors, but the group swelled in size as various local trade-union representatives arrived, armed with professional banners and essential striking kit such as a megaphone for effective chanting.

'You have to chant,' said one of them. 'You must know some chants.'

'Chants?' We hastily discussed this among ourselves, amateurs who were new to this game. 'What chants do we know? Come on, guys. What rhymes with NHS?'

It felt like militancy for dummies. Faintly embarrassed, we started shouting loudly about the future of the health service. On the plus side, chanting kept us warm. The traffic streaming by tooted its support, sometimes so enthusiastically the horns were deafening. The irony was not lost on me that the passing public seemed to know what to do in a strike far more intuitively than we did. Every time an ambulance drove in or out of the hospital, the paramedics blasted their sirens in solidarity, to cheers of delight from the crowd.

Even more heartening were the members of the public who travelled to our picket line to support us in person. We knew in theory that the public backed us – in polls, there was 66 per cent support for our strike – but, when this translated into a beaming grandmother pressing steaming hot coffees into our hands, or a preschool tot proudly presenting homemade biscuits to us all, the human touch meant everything. I couldn't feel my feet, my legs would not stop shivering, but the public radiated warmth.

My profound discomfort at striking – the tug of the patients I had left in other doctors' hands – was somewhat assuaged when, to my great surprise, one of those patients appeared on the picket line beside me. Sammy Rogerson, a frail young man trapped in a wheelchair after infection had ravaged his legs, was determined to defy the freezing temperatures to stand beside his doctors. Despite the best efforts of his nurses, fearful of his ability to withstand the arctic winds, he had refused to stay on the ward, so they had protectively mummified him in NHS blankets, some of which now trailed like banners behind his wheelchair. The television crews clustered around him, eager for commentary from an NHS inpatient so defiantly committed to his doctors' cause.

'Sammy,' I said. 'I can't believe you came. Can I take you back to the ward? You must be absolutely freezing.'

'No. No way,' he replied. 'I've been in this hospital for six months and I know how hard you all work. I want to be here with you.'

Throughout the day, the government spin machine was in overdrive. Jeremy Hunt, speaking on BBC Radio 4, described terrifying increases in hospital mortality at weekends – deaths from strokes rising by 20 per cent, from emergency surgery by 11 per cent, and deaths of newborn babies by 7 per cent. All these data were contentious and had been challenged by some of the country's leading academics, but on air they sounded indefensible, as Hunt had known they would. To perpetuate these thousands of avoidable deaths by clinging to our weekend 'overtime' was, he insisted, wholly unreasonable:

> We recognise that if doctors are too tired they are not going to be able to give safe care to patients. Right now what happens is when a junior doctor is asked to work at weekends, which they do a lot, they go into an A&E department where there will be half as

many consultants working on a Sunday compared to a weekday despite it being one of the busiest days. It is a pretty exhausting day. You wouldn't, as a pilot, like to turn up at Heathrow airport and be told: 'I'm really sorry but because it is a Sunday you don't get a co-pilot but off you go to New York.'[49]

Aside from the fact that the number of consultants on call at weekends had nothing to do with junior doctors' contracts, Hunt was again ignoring the real barrier to improving weekend services: the finite number of doctors, not to mention all the other staff – nurses, porters, radiographers, administrators – required for extra weekend activity. Not once had he addressed how – in the absence of any additional doctors – safer weekends could be engineered without removing us from our patients from Monday to Friday. Nor had he produced any actual evidence to corroborate his claim that additional junior doctors at weekends would increase patient safety. Perhaps most frustratingly of all, the alarmist analogy he drew between jumbo jets missing pilots and hospitals missing doctors was precisely what was already happening in hospitals up and down the country, a fact he chose to ignore. Rota gaps were commonplace – each one analogous to a plane without a co-pilot – yet Hunt still wanted to stretch junior doctors more thinly. It was fantasy politics.

$$-\!\!\!\bigwedge\!\!\!\!\bigvee\!\!\!\!-$$

As the first strike drew to a close, patients remained caught in the political crossfire. Though stop-start talks between the government and the BMA continued fitfully, they failed to avert a further seven days of strikes, each of them causing thousands more cancelled operations. Throughout it all, Hunt insisted his 'door [was] always open' to junior doctors, yet took exquisite care not to meet or debate a single one of us in public. Shortly after announcing to the House of Commons that, in the absence of agreement with the BMA, he would impose his contract upon juniors, Hunt happened to arrive at London's Millbank Studios just as Dagan Lonsdale, a speciality registrar in intensive-care medicine, finished an interview there with Sky TV. The breakdown in communication between the Health Secretary and junior doctors was starkly illustrated as the Sky News crew filmed what happened next.

Dagan, having spotted Hunt entering the building, walked alongside him, attempting to raise in measured terms, 'the concerns we have about patient safety'. Unperturbed by Hunt's brief attempt to explain that he was, 'just on his way to do an interview', Dagan accused him of, 'taking a massive gamble with people in the NHS,' stating that he had, 'absolutely no evidence whatsoever that these [contractual] changes will have a positive effect'. Hunt then simply ignored Dagan, who continued to follow him down a corridor and up a staircase, asking, 'Why won't you sit down to talk to junior doctors – what if you've got this one wrong?'[50]

The visual potency of the Health Secretary actively fleeing a member of NHS staff ensured Sky's footage went viral immediately after being broadcast, watched online by hundreds of thousands of viewers. Afterwards, in an interview with the *Evening Standard*, Dagan commented,

I was a bit worried I was going to look like a bit of a fool walking after the Health Secretary, but I think it is telling he is just walking away from the questions. I spoke to my mother-in-law last night. She said it looked a lot like one of those episodes of *Rogue Traders* where the guy is just running away.[51]

Like Dagan, I too had strenuously endeavoured to engage Hunt publicly. Crucial to his efforts to position himself as the BMA's nemesis, yet 'ordinary' junior doctors' friend, was his repeated assurance that his door was open to doctors like me. The closest I had come to meeting the Health Secretary was when he appeared on the BBC's Sunday morning political interview programme, *The Andrew Marr Show*. I had provided the producers with an anonymous written comment and, knowing Andrew Marr might read this out to Hunt, settled down to watch the interview. I had my Sunday morning coffee in my hand and my wriggly five-year-old on my lap when, to my astonishment, I heard not only my words but my name read out live on air to Hunt. Several things happened in swift succession. I spat hot coffee onto the back of my daughter's head, she shrieked and writhed in indignation, I upended my coffee into my lap, and Jeremy Hunt blinked and gulped like an Amazonian python ingesting a small deer as Marr mercilessly read out yet more doctors' comments.

'Rachel Clarke,' Marr stated, 'is a doctor who says, "Mr Hunt has made me feel demoralised, insulted and cheap. He implies we are the problem. Well, I give my life to the NHS. It's so grim on the front line now, I sometimes work fourteen or fifteen hours straight without a second even to eat. I have never felt so despairing or so close to quitting medicine."'[52]

Another doctor Marr cited said, 'The profession is at absolute breaking point. I see doctors in tears because they are so despairing about what the future holds. Jeremy Hunt has done this. He is driving away a whole generation of doctors.'

'Those are the voices of doctors right now,' Marr concluded. 'That's what they feel.'

Hunt, visibly uncomfortable, responded by blaming the BMA for our anger, specifically singling out the union's irresponsibility in spreading misinformation about the contract. Later that day, invited by the BBC to respond in a live interview, I roundly dismissed this attempt to portray doctors like me as the hapless victims of BMA propaganda.[53] I was perfectly capable of appraising the evidence for myself, I argued, and the central issue was one of trust. As doctors, we are nothing if our patients do not trust us. Yet the months of spin and statistical manipulation had left us feeling unable to trust the Health Secretary, and the more aggressively he played the media game, the more corrosive the Trust deficit would become.

By now, the country's 54,000 junior doctors were following and commenting upon every twist and turn of the dispute on our Facebook forum and other online platforms such as Twitter. The government did not like it. Sir David Dalton, the Salford Royal NHS Trust chief executive appointed by Hunt to represent the government in negotiations, claimed that frenzied social-media campaigns by junior doctors were destroying any chance of the two sides reaching a deal. The 'goldfish bowl of people giving real-time commentary' was a 'huge impediment' to talks, he insisted.[54] The irony was lost on none of us that, while it was apparently acceptable for various mainstream media outlets to whip up anti-doctor sentiment through fair means or foul, when doctors sought to counter misinformation online, this was painted as destructive hysteria. Talks, yet again, ground to a halt.

In a frankly desperate effort to encourage Hunt back to the negotiating table – there was little to lose with an all-out strike fast approaching – I decided, at the unlikely age of forty-three, to organise my second ever form of direct action, the first being my junior school sit-in over swimming pool rights. Dagan and I hatched a plan to begin an indefinite peaceful protest on Hunt's doorstep, camped outside the entrance to the Department of Health, immediately in front of his famously open door. We planned to remain in place in Whitehall for twenty-four hours, sleeping rough on a pavement outside the Department. After that, we would be replaced by our colleagues for twelve hours a day, seven days a week, until we had forced a breakthrough. When news of our protest broke, we were overwhelmed by hundreds of doctors from all over the country signing up to take part, some of them travelling down to London from as far afield as Leeds and Manchester.

The aim was simple. There had to be a way of averting an all-out strike – an act of last resort that went against every grain of doctors' instincts to care for our patients – through dialogue. No dispute is so poisonous, so intractable, that words cannot in the end defuse it. It was simply not good enough for a man who claimed to value patient safety to maintain tactical silence at this critical juncture, and we intended to highlight that.

The reality was a little more complicated. First, having set up our collapsible table just outside the Department, its tablecloth emblazoned with the hashtag '#TimeToTalkJeremy', we were approached by two burly officers from the Metropolitan Police.

'Uh oh,' I whispered to Dagan. We had checked the legality of our protest meticulously, but feared we were about to be ushered away on some kind of spurious pretext.

'Hello, doctors,' one of the officers said. 'What's going on here?'

We explained who we were, what we were doing and why. There was a long pause. The two policemen glanced at each other. Then, one of them leaned in closely and said, in a low but firm voice,

'Now you listen to me. You're not doing anything wrong by being here, you're not breaking any laws whatsoever, and if anyone – I mean, anyone – tries to tell you that you can't stay here, you tell them you've spoken to the Met and we've told you that's nonsense. And, if you have any problems at all, I want you get straight in touch with us. OK?'

'Thank you so much,' we said, smiling slightly incredulously.

'No, thank *you* for taking a stand. You keep on fighting. We don't want to see what they've done to us lot being done to doctors as well.'

Again, the extraordinary solidarity from yet another profession who themselves felt equally beleaguered was astounding. It did not stop there. Throughout the day, as civil servants walked in and out of their Department, many of them came up for a chat. Some surreptitiously sneaked a BMA badge from our stash and furtively hid it in their handbags. Others were more vocal.

'I can't ever say this publicly,' said one of Hunt's own departmental employees, 'but I think what's being done to junior doctors is appalling. Well done for standing up to it.'

Hunt himself was nowhere to be seen. A Department of Health employee tipped us off that there was an underground back route into the building, one that Hunt was forced to use for the duration of the protest. As night fell, we were overwhelmed by thousands of online messages of support from fellow doctors, so many of whom bought us takeaway dinners, delivered anonymously to the Department of Health by courier bike, that we simply could not eat them all and passed them on in turn to homeless shelters in London. The sense of solidarity was truly inspirational.

That night, we crawled into our sleeping bags to try to sleep under our tablecloth, acutely conscious of the sheer absurdity of two doctors, both parents with young children at home, sleeping rough to try to persuade a Cabinet minister to talk to a trade union. It was bitterly cold. A drug addict appeared in the early hours, haranguing us for half the night. Direct action, I discovered, was not for the faint-hearted. Early in the morning, a member of the security team arrived who had been assigned to keep an eye on us when we had launched the protest the day before.

'Did you really do it? Were you really here all night?'

When we confirmed that, yes, we really had, he immediately offered to get us a coffee, as did many other early birds arriving at their Department that morning. Just before going inside, he told us, 'You know you made quite an impression, yesterday?'

Hunt, he explained, had spent a considerable time staring down at us while standing, arms crossed, at one of the Department of Health's large glass windows that look directly across onto Downing Street. Apparently, his face was thunderous and the Department of Health press office had been in meltdown. For the next few weeks, twelve hours a day, seven days a week, two doctors remained doggedly stationed outside the Department. Hunt was forced to creep unseen into the back entrance of his own Department for the duration of the protest. For a man so protective of his public image, it must have been infuriating. But it was all to no avail. The government refused to return to talks with the BMA, and NHS patients in their thousands were subjected to the first full walkout of junior doctors in its seventy-year history.

A few weeks after this bleakest point in the dispute, the BMA's credibility was decimated when a vast cache of private electronic WhatsApp messages exchanged between executive members of the BMA's Junior Doctors Committee was leaked to the *Health Service Journal*. Their impact was crushing. The committee's chair, Johann Malawana, described a secret strategy of dragging out the dispute for eighteen months in order to 'tie the Department of Health up in knots'.

'The more I think about it, the more I love our plan,' he messaged the group. 'Basically five weeks of headlines about juniors strikes through January and February . . . The best solution may actually [be] to draw this right out into the Europe debate and leadership debate.'[55]

Another member of the secret WhatsApp group claimed – contrary to everything I and so many other grassroots junior doctors had stated loudly and unequivocally for months – that weekend pay was 'the only real red line' for junior doctors.[55]

I was incandescent. This was simply not true. My red line was drawn at the threat to my patients and, frankly, to my own sanity of the government trying to eke out a seven-day service from a workforce barely fit for five. To be misrepresented by the government was one thing, but to discover that my own union had so misjudged its members' concerns was devastating. I had gone on strike in good faith – voiced my safety concerns in good faith – but now I felt undermined by my union, which had made its own members look untrustworthy. The leaks were the beginning of the end. The government and the BMA agreed on the wording of a new contract but, in spite of Malawana's personal insistence that the new deal was better for doctors and patients, BMA members did not buy it. A clear majority of junior doctors, 58 per cent, chose to reject it.

Ironically, given the government's earlier claims that the dispute was the product of a small number of BMA extremists intent on toppling the government through whipping up gullible doctors into an irrational frenzy, it turned out that the union was willing to compromise on what the majority of its members regarded as beyond the pale. A contract that exacerbated gender pay gaps, left doctors with weakened protections against excessive hours and made it cheaper for hospitals to spread us more thinly, was unacceptable to the rank and file.

The dispute swiftly degenerated into the unedifying spectacle of doctor turning on doctor, the 98 per cent mandate for strike action replaced by furious infighting and bitter disappointment. The BMA flip-flopped between various strategies for inaction, extreme industrial action and, ultimately, abandonment of any meaningful opposition to the contract. By the time the contract was imposed upon the first wave of juniors, hundreds of members had already quit the union in disgust.

Far more significant for patients were the doctors now abandoning the NHS, feeling unable to carry on any longer. In the context of an already desperately under-doctored health service, Hunt's 'victory' over the upstart juniors looked like a classic case of winning the battle but losing the war. I collated testimony from some of the individual juniors who made the painful decision, during the dispute, to quit their NHS training. One of them left the UK in June 2016 with twelve years of postgraduate medical training under his belt, a whisker away from becoming a consultant. In spite of having seven years of general training in obstetrics and gynaecology, a PhD and one year of subspeciality training in maternal and foetal medicine, he had decided to repeat all of that training from scratch in the US:

> The government shows so little respect to its junior doctors and consultant workforce . . . I'm now in my first year at NYU School of Medicine in New York, where I am treated like a fully trained professional, not a commodity to be exploited. In making this transition, I have taken a pay cut of 50%, increased my contracted hours by two thirds – from 48 to 80 hours per week – and persuaded my husband to completely give up his career to join me. As such, I hope it is abundantly clear that my motivations for making such a move are not related to finances or contractual terms and conditions *per se*. It is a response to the systematic degradation of my profession in the UK, which is being achieved through lies, misrepresented statistics and media spin.

This government's biggest mistake has been its

failure to acknowledge that doctors are not driven by money or arbitrary work schedules but rather by their desire to practise their craft and do what is best for their patients. The NHS runs largely on good will and mine has finally run out, extinguished by the considerable stress of living and working through a damaging industrial dispute that has dragged on for over a year now. Imposition is simply not the answer, and will only drive more of my colleagues to join me by relocating abroad.

Another trainee described her deep shame at now pursuing private-sector alternatives to the NHS career she no longer felt able to endure:

Last Thursday was my last shift working as a middle grade emergency department doctor for the last four years. The hospital, and by extension the NHS, have had the best of me. I've had plantar fasciitis, sciatica and I have more grey hairs than black now. As a type 1 diabetic, I come home from 10 hour shifts feeling exhausted.

I'm actively looking for a job outside medicine. I've asked my friends in the pharmaceutical industry to keep their eyes peeled and ears to the ground for me. I'll be creating a non-medical CV and LinkedIn account to get myself out there for anyone who can use my experience to better the world of medicine outside the NHS. I'm ashamed and sad that it's come to this.

In my own case, a year spent locked in unsought-for conflict with the government had come at a heavy price. Inevitably, being embroiled for so long in a spin war had tarnished the love and wonder I had felt for medicine, and I had no way of knowing if this could be revived. During the dispute, I had applied for higher training in my chosen speciality of palliative medicine – caring for patients at the end of their lives – but increasingly I had begun to fear I was too disillusioned to do my patients justice. They deserved the doctor I had always imagined being on entering my chosen specialism: brimming over with pride and enthusiasm, not despairing at the future of the NHS. I chose to withdraw my application. It felt like the abandonment of my patients, my principles and the profession I had loved. I had no idea what I would do next.

Something curious started to happen once the government had quashed junior doctors. Some of the most senior figures within the medical establishment, the ones who had so strenuously attacked us for striking, began to repeat in public precisely the concerns we had raised, unsupported, for over a year. Hot on the heels of parliament's spending watchdog, the Public Accounts Committee, condemning the government for making 'no coherent attempt' to assess how many staff would be needed for a viable seven-day NHS, Chris Hopson, the head of the organisation representing the country's hospitals, NHS Providers, suddenly decided to speak out. When asked in late 2016 by the BBC's Andrew Marr whether a seven-day NHS was deliverable, given the overstretched NHS budget, he admitted something he had steadfastly refused to concede throughout the dispute, namely,

'It's impossible to deliver it on the current level of staff and the current money we have available. If something has to give at the moment when we're trying to do what we're currently doing, it can't cover important new policies like seven-day services.'[56]

Sir Bruce Keogh, the medical director of NHS England, began writing soothing articles about junior doctors being 'an important but sometimes neglected pillar of the NHS',[57] and even the GMC, which had been so critical of striking doctors, was at pains in its annual report to emphasise its concern at the depth of anger, frustration and alienation among junior doctors, urging that this, 'should cause everyone to pause and reflect'. As it put it,

> There is a state of unease within the medical profession across the UK that risks affecting patients as well as doctors. The reasons are complex and multifactorial, and some are long standing. The signals of distress are not always easy to interpret but they are unmistakable.[58]

It felt like too little, too late. If an entire generation of doctors – the ones who should be the profession's most vivacious and keen, had become this disenchanted and cynical – then the price of the government's trouncing of the BMA was one the NHS could ill afford.

CHAPTER 12

WONDER

'Quick! I need a medical student! Someone get me a medical student.'

The head sticking out of the consulting room door had the wild-eyed zeal of a shaman in the grip of a vision. His excitement was impossible to resist.

'Me!' I yelled, happening to be walking by on my way to the hospital canteen. 'I'm a medical student!'

The consultant closed the door behind him, furtively checked the corridor for nearby patients, then bent down conspiratorially towards me. 'What I'm about to show you is absolutely incredible. You're never going to see anything like this again. This man's got a triple A so enormous I can't believe he's not dead. For Christ's sake, be gentle when you feel it.'

I could hardly believe my luck. An abdominal aortic aneurysm, or triple A, as we call them, is caused by a weakening in the wall of the aorta, the most major blood vessel in the human body, which mainlines blood straight from the heart to our extremities. Slowly but surely, the furiously pumping blood causes the damaged portion of this gigantic artery to stretch ever more thinly until, unless a doctor intervenes, the inevitable happens and its strained walls burst. Then, without emergency surgery, the patient will be dead within the hour, as five litres of blood are dumped unceremoniously into the abdominal cavity. But, these days, triple As are no longer a death sentence. Having often picked them up as an incidental finding on abdominal scans performed for unrelated reasons – or during routine screening - the surgeons then keep a careful eye on them, repeating the scans at regular intervals to monitor their size. We know that small aneurysms are unlikely to rupture but, once they approach the size of a satsuma, the odds shift dramatically against the patient. Now, they are living with a primed grenade in their belly. One in four patients with a six-centimetre triple A will be dead within a year.

The really big aneurysms – the ones that could blow at any moment – can sometimes be seen from the end of the patient's bed, pulsating visibly below the patient's ribs like a subcutaneous alien life form. Once they begin to bleed, the chances of surviving are desperately slim. This one, the surgeon told me, felt as if it was at least nine or ten centimetres in diameter. By rights, the patient should have bled out long ago. He had only come to clinic about his varicose veins but the surgeon was old-school and believed in examining everything. For me, never having seen, let alone laid hands on, a triple A, it was almost too good to be true. Gingerly – almost reverentially – I placed my palms above the umbilicus, fingertips just touching, as though offering up an impromptu prayer for the patient's survival. As blood surged into the aneurysm with every heartbeat, my hands were thrust apart, fingertips surfing the lifeblood of this middle-aged man who, thanks to one doctor's thoroughness and skill, should now escape what would have been almost certain death. My textbooks and lectures had just come to life in unforgettable Technicolor. I glanced up at the surgeon, eyes gleaming with delight and gratitude that he had taken the time to share the case with me. He grinned. 'I'm finishing clinic shortly – wait for me outside.'

The surgeon, having finished explaining the pros and cons of surgery to the patient, shared with me an anecdote from the early days of his career. While still a very junior doctor, he was working in an Emergency Department when a fairly elderly man arrived with an unusual story of pain in his abdomen. Early that morning, the septuagenarian and his wife had been climbing Helvellyn, one of the Lake District's most precipitous peaks. During the ascent, a niggling pain in the belly had gradually become impossible to ignore. He had insisted upon reaching the summit before admitting to his wife that the gnawing pain now drilled all the way back into his spine and was so intense, it was making him feel light-headed.

'Well, there's a hospital at Penrith,' she told him, 'so let's drive there, darling.'

'I'm not bloody well going to Penrith. If I absolutely must go to an A&E, then it's bloody well going to be the best, so we'll have to get back to Cambridge.'

Some thousand metres of descent on foot and two hundred miles of motorway later, Mr and Mrs Sinclair finally reached their local hospital in Cambridge. He had driven the whole way himself. Sweaty, grey and with his pulse racing, Mr Sinclair was clearly not well on arrival in hospital. But the surgeon, to his surprise on feeling the abdomen, discovered an enormous, pulsating aortic aneurysm, just like the one I had felt earlier except for the small matter that this one had been oozing blood for the past twelve hours, even as its host had summited Helvellyn. No one survives a leaking triple A for twelve hours. No one except, perhaps, a mountain-climbing seventy-something who unwittingly splints his bleeding aneurysm with his seatbelt, now successfully acting as an abdominal tourniquet.

'It was a miracle,' the surgeon told me. 'How he had walked into A&E alive I will never know. We took him straight to theatre and he survived. Went home a week or so later, perfectly well. Insane.'

—◡‿◡—

The best antidote I know to despondency and gloom is the prevailing hope of others. Wonder, like hope, is contagious and, years before I ever set foot inside a medical school, I was permanently infected by my father's. To non-medics, doctors can be mind-numbingly boring. We cannot resist obsessively discussing medicine – to us, our patients and their illnesses are endlessly enthralling. It is undeniably a little odd, for example, to have a spring in your step for an entire afternoon because you have just felt your first pulsating aneurysm. It is also frankly peculiar for a patient's life-threatening pathology to become the highlight of their doctor's week. But amazement, awe and admiration for medicine infuse many students' first encounters with their subject and, occasionally, resurface among even the most cynical and grizzled of consultants.

At the tail end of the junior doctor dispute, one of my doctor friends sent me a message that struck a chord. She was at a low ebb after what felt like a squandered year of futile campaigning, and her message was poignant: 'I'm worried I've lost the keeno lifesaver light.'

I had never heard her way of putting it before, but I knew exactly what she meant – a young doctor's insatiable urge to learn everything, to devour all the facts and the experiences in order to save patients' lives. At medical school, it was the 'keeno lifesaver light' that kept me sitting in the front row of every lecture, the infuriating one who always had her hand up, desperate to ask another question. It kept me poring over my textbooks into the early hours until I had properly mastered my biochemistry. It kept me loitering on the wards to chat with the patients because a dusty account of a disease from a library book came to life for me only when fused with someone's lived experience of their illness. Fellow keenos were everywhere: the doctors, far too busy to take time out to teach, who did so anyway, sacrificing their own time to inspire and enthuse new recruits like me, teaching us how to diagnose which valve of the heart was failing from the arcane whisperings our stethoscopes picked up, or which neurological disease a patient had inherited from the shape of their calves alone.

I discovered that not even a year of opposing the government could entirely extinguish the keeno light when, shortly after I had withdrawn my application for speciality training, one of my patients revived my curiosity of old. Dr Talbot, a retired academic, had recently returned from a trip with her husband to the Venezuelan jungle. Over the last two months, she had shed nearly two stone, and was regularly burning up with ferocious temperatures.

'I can tell you exactly what's caused this,' she said. 'I've been bitten by a tropical spider.'

An eight-legged cause seemed surprising, but, when your patient has a PhD in ecodiversity, you hesitate to dispute their diagnosis, especially when it is as exotic and tantalising as this one. What doctor would not want to treat someone felled by a rampant tarantula? I settled down in front of my patient, eager to hear the full story.

After an exhausting day's trekking, Dr Talbot and her husband had arrived back at their hotel eager to wash the dust and grime away. But, when she pulled off her hiking boot, she found her sock to be soaked in fresh blood, with what appeared to be a puncture mark on the side of her foot. She had felt unwell ever since – shivery, nauseous and unusually weary. Red spots had slowly spread over both her feet and, by the time she returned to the UK, she had required a brief admission to hospital to treat with intravenous antibiotics what had become a florid foot infection. Now, she looked too thin and exhausted, clearly not a well woman. I was transfixed.

'Once the infection was sorted,' she told me, 'I thought that was the end of the matter. But I just carried on feeling wretched. Some days I can't get out of bed. My clothes are hanging off me. And, on a bad day, the sweats are appalling.'

'Could a spider have managed to bite through a leather boot?' I mused.

'No. But it could have been hidden in the sock,' she answered.

The visual image was irresistible. Nothing renews a passion for medicine like a good old-fashioned diagnostic conundrum. That night, I scoured the Internet for information on chronic illnesses triggered by tropical spider bites, even though I knew I was clutching at straws. The fact was, we had nothing else to go on. Aside from the persistent fevers and weight loss, Dr Talbot's physical examination had yielded no clues. Her blood tests showed grumbling, chronic inflammation, but gave no indication of the underlying cause. Rogue infections, an occult cancer or some kind of autoimmune disease could all be driving her symptoms. So we hunted for hidden tumours with a top-to-toe CT scan, and ran endless blood test for weird and wonderful infections, but everything drew a blank. Meanwhile, our patient languished in her bed, becoming progressively thinner and weaker. If our medical detective work did not deliver soon, we feared for her future.

Eventually, we decided to carry out a specialised PET scan in which tiny amounts of radioactive glucose are injected into the blood, illuminating areas of the body that are particularly metabolically active due to cancer, infection or inflammation. The consensus, by this stage, was on a nasty hidden cancer, but we all hoped we were wrong. To my delight, the scan results confounded us. The great arteries of her body – the aorta, the carotids and the renal arteries – were ablaze with light, traversing the computer screen like comets. In their luminous traces, we had found our answer. The spider, in this case, was actually a red herring. Dr Talbot had a large-vessel vasculitis, a condition in which the blood vessels become inflamed and angry, often when the immune system turns upon itself, attacking healthy tissues. With a diagnosis, at last we had something to treat, and we started her immediately on powerful immunosuppressants.

This was NHS medicine at its best. A medical conundrum that piqued and intrigued even the most experienced of consultants. A patient and her family who were desperately fearful, needing all the support and sensitivity that we could muster. The expertise of three different specialist teams, all brought to bear on the case, plus state-of-the-art imaging and blood work. A diagnostic process not driven blindly, according to protocol, but using clinical acumen, lateral thinking and teamwork. A result – a diagnosis – derived as quickly as any gleaming private institution could offer, despite the dilapidation and quaint mid-century shabbiness of the ward. Too often in these straitened times, the NHS falls short of excellence, but when the system works well, as on this occasion, it can still be second to none. Not only did Dr Talbot rekindle a flicker of my old love of medicine, she restored a glimmer of my faith in the NHS as well. There were still successes, many of them, for all of us to feel proud of.

–––\/\–––

At the far end of the worktop where I stood writing in a set of notes, a telephone began to ring. The temptation to ignore it was almost irresistible. In answering a random hospital phone, you risk becoming embroiled in a complicated, lengthy conversation with someone you have no idea how to help, as your boss hovers grumpily over your shoulder, communicating through tuts and menacing stares his displeasure that you are not feverishly sorting out the patients currently swamping the A&E shop floor. It sounds profoundly selfish – these may be relatives of patients, distraught and anxious – but, when your workload means you sometimes go without eating, trying to help arbitrary callers as well as your patients is simply not always possible. This call was a case in point. A lab technician wanted to give me the result of a blood test for a patient I'd never heard of. I was already regretting picking up. Then the technician told me the result. The potassium level in the patient's blood was 10.8, over twice as high as it should be.

'It looks like someone printed out the result two hours ago, so I assume it's already been dealt with it, but I thought I should check,' she explained.

Her thoroughness was driven by awareness of the havoc a potassium of this order can wreak. The concentration of potassium in the blood is crucial in regulating the spread of electricity through the heart. Excessive potassium – hyperkalaemia – makes the heart wildly excitable, sending the electric flow haywire and potentially causing the heart to beat erratically or, in extreme cases, stop beating altogether – a cardiac arrest. I too assumed the result must have been dealt with from the simple fact that I could see on my computer screen that the patient was still alive, around the corner in resus. By rights, with potassium this high, I'd have expected her to be dead by now.

'I'm sure it's sorted, but I'll go and check myself,' I said, walking around to resus, intent on finding the patient and, crucially, on checking her cardiac monitor.

An ECG traces in graphical form the flow of electricity across the heart. Learning to interpret the meanings of its peaks and troughs, their dimensions, distortions and idiosyncrasies is a vital task to master at medical school. Elongated, oversized spikes, for example, suggest a likely diagnosis of longstanding high blood pressure. A heart attack may reveal itself through dramatic, convex bulges on the ECG trace – the 'tombstone' sign, as it is aptly known. In the case of potassium, as the level in the blood inexorably rises, so the patient's ECG warps and contorts in an ever more distinctive pattern. After a little practice interpreting ECGs, even the most junior of medics should be able to spot severe hyperkalaemia instantly.

I found Mrs Mulligan's electronic heart trace before I found the patient. It leaped out at me from her bedside monitor, screaming full-scale hyperkalaemic emergency. The chaotic trace was so bizarre it looked moments away from a cardiac arrest. Jarringly, the patient herself was in fine fettle, chatting away with the three or four family members assembled at her bedside, a piece of half-eaten toast in her hand. Often, hyperkalaemia is a silent killer. The patient is entirely symptom-free until their heart, without warning, suddenly stops beating. In this case, a nurse or doctor was nowhere to be seen and, worse, given how urgently I needed to protect the patient's heart, there was no cannula in her arm for intravenous medication. I quickly found a nurse and furtively, out of earshot of the family, explained the situation.

'Yes, it really is 10.8. No, no cannula. I'm going to get access now. Can you grab the calcium gluconate and we'll get it into her as quickly as possible?'

Then, with what I hoped was soothing chitchat with the patient – that last thing I wanted was any adrenaline surges – I stuck a needle into her vein as swiftly as possible, to enable us to give the drugs that would help protect her heart. Mercifully, we were just in time. Shortly after that, Mrs Mulligan was rushed to Intensive Care for haemodialysis, the quickest way to remove the excess potassium from her blood. A random phone call, reluctantly answered, might just have saved her life.

Some months later, I was reminded of this case when one

of the hospital's haematology consultants stayed late into the evening – unpaid, unrewarded – to give a few of us, his juniors, some impromptu bedside teaching. A phone rang at the nurses' station. No one else was there to answer it. While everyone in the group shifted uncomfortably and pretended to ignore it, Dr Fraser – Mark to patients and colleagues alike – leaned forward and picked up the receiver. 'This is Mark Fraser speaking, how can I help?' Afterwards, someone made a joke of it. 'Never, ever pick up a random phone – first rule of ward work.' Mark looked up, quietly unamused. 'Whose job is it to answer the phone on the ward?' he asked, his question met with awkward silence. 'It is everybody's job. I always imagine how I would feel if there were a member of my family somewhere in a hospital, and I was calling to try to find someone who knew about them.'

This act, so small, spoke volumes. Almost never, in all my seven years of practice, have I seen another consultant pick up a randomly ringing telephone. They are invariably left for a more lowly staff member to deal with, as if, with seniority, you earn the right to ignore the low-grade irritations of the ward. But Mark, quite rightly, regarded each ringing phone as a potential relative in distress, needing our support and kindness. Since that evening, I have never left a phone unanswered.

Senior doctors infect their juniors with more than a wonder for medicine. They provide, through their example, a model of doctoring, be it good, indifferent or downright bad. Whether they realise it or not, their every move – a conversation with a patient, a tendency to disparage their colleagues, the particular way they lay their hands on an abdomen – is scrutinised and stored away by their students and juniors alike. The more inexperienced, the more like newly hatched goslings we are, latching onto whichever living creatures larger than ourselves we first encounter on the wards, imprinting our behaviours on theirs. If callous, consultants give senior permission for heartlessness, effectively handing out a licence to be cold. If kind, they teach their juniors that kindness is valuable – a trait to take seriously and nurture.

The first consultant who ever taught me at a patient's bedside, a professor so erudite he is tipped for a Nobel prize one day, combined medical rigour with remarkable gentleness. I would watch, entranced, as, on meeting a patient on the ward, he enfolded their hands in both of his, seemingly in order to comfort and connect with them as he looked them in the eye and discussed their illness. In fact, with that simple human touch, he was simultaneously taking their pulse, assessing their hydration status, scanning their hands for clues of illness, and appraising whether they were sick or well. The patients, I suspect, thought he was just being kind. Actually, he was covertly diagnosing them. Hard, effective medicine cloaked in gentle humanity. I saw in him a model to emulate, something I have endeavoured to do ever since.

Mark Fraser, the only consultant willing to answer random phone calls to the ward, once broke all the rules at the bedside when he saw in an instant that his patient needed an approach that transcended rigid Trust protocol. We were almost at the end of our morning ward round, having deliberately saved seeing Alice Fitzpatrick until last. Mrs Fitzpatrick had been recently diagnosed with a particularly aggressive form of acute leukaemia that had not responded to chemotherapy. In an effort to tame her virulently multiplying cancerous blood cells, she had just undergone a bone-marrow transplant. After almighty doses of cancer-killing drugs, two things needed to happen. First, the cancer needed to be gone – obliterated by the chemical onslaught – second, the bone marrow from her unknown donor needed to have successfully engrafted within her bones. But our daily blood tests suggested otherwise. The marrow was empty, a factory that had ground to a halt.

Severely anaemic, and vulnerable to overwhelming infection and bleeding, she was propped up with blood transfusions day after day, waiting for the time when she would start, or so we hoped, producing her own blood cells. Eventually, with no sign of that happening, a haematologist took a sample of her bone marrow to scrutinise under a microscope in an attempt to deduce what the problem was. That morning, we had discovered the answer. The cancerous cells of old were back, still present, still multiplying in defiance of the strongest poisons we had hurled their way. Her future was bleak and it was Mark's unenviable task to tell her this.

I remember every moment. His voice, combining compassion with quiet authority, stating the facts clearly and calmly, with no ambiguity. Her face, folding in on itself with the weight of grief and fear, thin shoulders heaving beneath a wall of pinned cards from her friends and children, talismans against an unknown future. Her head bowed down to her chest, its baldness defiantly wrapped in an expensive, primary-coloured scarf. She knew, at that moment, that the hope she had nursed and coaxed through every twist of her journey was now at the point of being snuffed out. Words were not going to touch her. She needed something more primal for comfort. Ignoring the diktats of 'infection control' and, no doubt, further regulations about appropriate behaviour with the opposite sex, Mark sat himself down beside his patient, both of them perched on the edge of her bed. Tenderly, he placed his arm around her shoulders and she laid her brow on his chest. Her tears dripped onto his shirt as he quietly rested his head upon hers. They sat that way for some time, saying nothing. I was struck by how sometimes, the interaction between a patient and their doctor – each thrown together only briefly and by chance – looks less like a job than an act of love. This was one such occasion. Later, I wondered how much of himself Dr Fraser had needed to give – how much, in the end, providing solace of this kind ends up taking from a person.

Like the hundreds of doctors who have taught me on the job – usually at their own expense, working longer, later or harder for nothing but the reward of freely imparting their knowledge and skills – I was eager to teach as soon as I knew anything worth teaching. I always smile ruefully when the Department of Health press office pushes outlandish figures that purport to show the cost of training an NHS doctor from scratch. An eye-watering figure of £230,000 for medical school alone is their current favourite.[59] Yet, for the vast majority of our time as doctors-in-training, we are not being trained: we are 'delivering the service' – churning through job after job, patient after patient, with our 'training needs' hovering somewhere between an inconvenience and an afterthought. It is individual doctors who have taught me what I know – and at zero cost to the taxpayer, since they have done so in their own time, as impromptu pedagogues, invariably unsupported by their employer.

Just before medical school finals, hospitals turn into stalking grounds for paranoid students desperate to find patients with the unusual clinical signs that might floor them in their looming exams. As doctors, we have to strike a balance between protecting our patients from the unwelcome intrusions of too many exam-crazed students and trying to help them learn. Each disease has its own constellation of physical signs – lumps to feel, heart murmurs to hear, rashes to spot and other oddities – provided the student is sufficiently skilled to elicit them. The rarer the signs, the more alluring the patient. If word gets out that a patient is lurking with exceptionally unusual examination findings, students may flock to their ward in hordes, sometimes requiring us to ban them from the bedside if that is what the patient would prefer.

Once, a friend gave me a precious tip-off. 'Promise you won't pass this on to anyone else, Rach, but I have a patient with situs inversus in bed 10. He's happy for one group of students to examine him.' As soon as I could escape the ward, I ran upstairs to find the patient. He was, indeed, willing to meet my small group of students. Before leaving, I could not resist asking permission to listen quickly to his chest myself. Like every medical rarity until the moment you first encounter it, situs inversus was mythical to me, about as plausible as a unicorn strolling down my ward. A rare idiosyncrasy of embryonic development, it arises when all the major organs develop on the opposite side of the body to the usual. In a mirror image of normal, the heart sits on the right-hand side of the chest, a condition known as dextrocardia.

I placed my stethoscope over where I would expect to find the loudest heartbeat and heard . . . precisely nothing at all. No hint of a heart on the left side of the chest. It was the most delicious silence I have ever heard. And then – on the right – a healthy, normal, beating heart ringing loud and clear through my stethoscope. So wrong – like a violation of nature – and so miraculous that this was just a variant of natural, one that one in ten thousand people happened to possess. I messaged my students to join me on the ward at the end of the day to meet a patient they would never forget.

Mr Hodges, the patient, grinned magnanimously as each student listened to his heart and tried to describe their findings. None of them could quite bring themselves to confess they had heard nothing at all. 'Very quiet heart sounds,' commented one of them. 'But – um – I think there may have been a quiet murmur of aortic regurgitation present too.' Alas, he had fallen at the first hurdle of bedside teaching: never make up your findings. Eventually, Mr Hodges waded in to help. 'Why would my heart sounds be so quiet?' he asked them. Suddenly, a light flickered across one student's face. 'Please may I listen to your heart again?' she asked him. This time, her stethoscope went straight to the far side of his chest and, as she placed it over the apex of his heart, just below his right nipple, she gasped with audible delight and astonishment. Now the rest of the students were twitching with excitement. The diagnosis had dawned upon all of them and sheer wonder lit up the group. Mr Hodges must have seen it a hundred times before but still he smiled effusively.

'Thank you so much,' I said to him as we left. 'You've just made their term – and mine.'

At the heart of good medical training are the thousands of everyday encounters with senior doctors that cumulatively shape a junior's practice. Formal training, the scant hour

a week in which I am officially permitted to surrender my
bleep to enable my attendance, may sometimes be useful
but it is not a patch on the real, lived apprenticeship
in doctoring I receive on the job thanks to my senior
colleagues' goodwill and their indefatigable impulse to pass
on what they have learned. It is these relationships that are
the bedrock of everything important that I know – and they
rely upon sufficient time spent working together as a team
that we inspire, encourage and motivate each other.

Huge numbers of doctors love nothing more than to teach.
Some of the senior ranks of the NHS, wringing their hands at
what to do about all-pervasive despair among frontline staff,
are missing a trick, because there is nothing quite like seeing
our subject through a student's eyes, aglow with enthusiasm,
for reigniting our own passion for medicine. To lift the spirits
and boost flagging morale, giving one good tutorial is worth
more than a thousand Zumba classes. But time is the crux
of the matter. Without time, with workloads so punitive that
doctors struggle to claw their way through them, a luxury
such as teaching others – no matter how personally fulfilling
and how vitally important for the future of the NHS at large
– becomes impossible to sustain.

There is, in short, much that is endangered in the complex,
fragile, extraordinary ecosystem of kinship, affection, respect
and goodwill that inspires individual doctors to teach and
train each other. Without the time and continuity to build
relationships with fellow doctors, these qualities – so important
and sustaining within the profession – face extinction. I am
reminded of Hector, Alan Bennett's brilliantly idiosyncratic
teacher from his play *The History Boys*, who captures the
essence of teaching so beautifully:

'Pass the parcel. That's sometimes all you can do. Take it, feel it, and pass it on. Not for me, not for you, but for someone, somewhere, one day. Pass it on, boys. That's the game I want you to learn. Pass it on.'[60]

The word 'doctor' originates from the Latin '*docere*' – to teach – and in my experience there is no better way of keeping the wonder and love of medicine alive than the endeavour to pass it on. But in an era of austerity, where every pound of Treasury expenditure must be rigorously justified, perhaps concepts as fluffy as wonder and goodwill are – just like kindness – entirely superfluous. After all, none can be counted. We cannot price up any of them. Yet the truth is, though these values cannot be bought and sold, they inspire the staff who drive the NHS more than any profit motive. And that – in an era of haemorrhaging staff, dwindling motivation, burnout and sickness at record highs – makes them priceless. If we wish to maintain a first-class health service, we squander them at our peril.

CHAPTER 13

CHEER

H er eyes don't leave mine as I walk towards her bedside. I have a horrible feeling she already knows.

Tree lights twinkle in the corner, muffled laughter from the staff room escapes onto the ward.

'Margaret,' I smile, with as much warmth as I can muster. On this day of all days, I want to do this well but, as an inexperienced doctor, I haven't done it many times before.

'Hello,' she smiles back, with a composure I lack. 'You have something to tell me, don't you?'

No moment is good for breaking the news to a patient that their scan shows terminal cancer, but Christmas Eve, of all days, is stunningly bad.

Even while draped in a hospital gown, hooked up to a drip to stop the vomiting and pain, Margaret Hamilton, a recently retired intensive care nurse, retains all the poise and self-possession her former role demands. My team and I have just looked at her images. Our Christmas cheer had vanished in an instant as, starting grimly at the screen, our faces fell. Cancer isn't just present, it's everywhere. Liver, pancreas, bowels, pelvis – too many tumours to count.

Sitting now beside Margaret, who has insisted on no sugar-coating, I gently explain the extent, the spread. This dignified woman – who herself has spent so many Christmases past tending to the most desperately unwell NHS patients – manages a faint and rueful smile.

'We were planning to go trekking in the Himalayas next year,' she tells me. 'Saving up for big adventures after we retired.'

We chat. Her main concern – as so often among NHS patients – is not for herself, but for somebody else. She's kept her husband blissfully unaware of her suspicions, and he's going to be broken-hearted. Only when I offer to return that afternoon to help her tell him, does her composure briefly slip. 'Thank you,' she mutters, eyes glinting. 'I don't think I could do this by myself.'

Sometimes, the wonder I feel as a doctor stretches beyond the feats of the human body to those of the NHS itself. Last year, on Christmas Day, for example, the NHS delivered nearly 400,000 Christmas lunches – and 1,800 Christmas babies. From Penrith to Penzance, London to Tobermory, an army of staff came together to try and give those of us unlucky enough to spend Christmas in hospital the very best chance of some seasonal cheer. 100,000 nurses were at work in our hospitals, while in care homes across England some 200,000 care workers supported the vulnerable and elderly.

There were 40,000 cleaners and more than 12,000 porters on duty, with 1.5 million pieces of linen such as bedsheets used during the day.

The sheer scale of the NHS's Christmas statistics is staggering. So much activity, so many teams up and down the country doing their best for their patients, because disease does not respect Bank Holidays and illness or accidents can strike you down at any time. But what fills me with awe as an NHS doctor at Christmas is not the eye-watering numbers, but the fierce humanity showed by patients and staff alike.

Everyone, deep down, would rather be somewhere else. My language is never bluer than when I curse the rota coordinator on finding out that, yet again, I'm on duty at Christmas, another year the kids won't see their mother. I kiss them goodbye, still tucked up in reindeer pyjamas, and step out into the cold, feeling hard done by. But it only takes a few moments at work before I'm asking myself why the idea of working an NHS Christmas is so galling, when the reality is often so uplifting.

Last time, I walked into my hospital wearing my hair in tinsel-wrapped Princess Leia braids. A porter in a Santa hat immediately high-fived me. A couple of the nurses skipped past, at the end of their night shifts, winking as they stuffed Quality Street into their mouths. The doctors' mess was decorated with cardboard hospital bedpans: it's a little known fact that there is nothing better shaped for bedecking walls with seasonal reindeers. My consultant fully embraced the Star Wars theme, and brought my son's plastic light sabre onto the ward. Doctors may use defibrillators to shock their patients' hearts but, on this occasion, we had a festive Force as well.

One of the patients, a good eighty years old and not long this side of a major heart attack, insisted on us eating his chocolates – we were forbidden from leaving his room until we'd each consumed at least two or three Celebrations apiece. A family I'd never met before thrust a Christmas card into my hands, filled with thanks and gratitude for their loved one's care. It wasn't long before the smell of Brussels sprouts and NHS gravy began to permeate the ward. I've yet to see anyone crack the secret of making appetising hospital meals, even when adorned with Christmas crackers. The patients didn't care though. They grinned in their paper hats as a local church choir came to the ward and sang carols.

As lunch was being served to the patients, my consultant summoned the doctors and nurses into the mess. I laughed. There was a feast of treats piled high upon the table and, at his insistence, thimblefuls of Champagne with which we all, as a team, toasted Christmas. My ward felt more profoundly infused with Christmas spirit than anywhere else I could have been that day. I hugged tight these members of my other family – the ones with whom the blood ties aren't genetic but literal, as we go through the haemorrhages, crises and deaths on the job – together, sustaining a collective cheer.

The NHS runs on camaraderie, and never more so than at Christmas. My father, himself a young doctor in the swinging sixties, remembers a medics' revue traipsing from ward to ward on Christmas Day in his hospital, rallying the spirits of patients, nurses and other doctors alike. Later, as a small child, I'd clutch nervously at his hand as, every year on Christmas morning, he'd whisk me and my siblings off to meet his patients, disconcertingly wizened and gnarled to a wide-eyed six-year-old, on a ward that smelt of iodine and cabbage. I'd watch their faces light up with delight as their doctor arrived at their bedsides. Sometime, he was their only visitor all day long.

But it's not all goodwill and affection. Christmas offers no protection again the perils of modern NHS winter crises. In 2017, with conditions of gridlock so severe in our hospitals that the British Red Cross dubbed them a 'humanitarian crisis', patients queued for so long on trolleys in corridors that some of them ended up dying there. We make superhuman efforts to get vulnerable patients home to their loved ones in time for Christmas, but the carers they need simply aren't always there. Every year, we have patients who, though medically fit to go home, are marooned in hospital for no other reason than that Britain has woefully underfunded social care services.

Nor do dying and distress pause for Christmas festivities. Once, in A&E, having dealt with the young man who had accidentally 'sat' upon a bauble, I encountered a middle-aged woman who – weeks after first noticing weakness in her arms and legs – finally panicked when she could no longer lift the gravy granules out of her high kitchen cupboard, let alone a turkey into the oven. Her family joked that she was bonkers. 'You just want to get out of watching the Queen, don't you, Mum?' In fact, examination of her limbs revealed dramatically distorted neurological signs that fitted, almost certainly, with a dread diagnosis, that of motor neurone disease. She was swiftly whisked from A&E to the neurology ward, and I later learned she had died before Easter.

Perhaps most poignant of all are the patients we

occasionally encounter who are dispatched by their families into NHS hands for the holiday. Once, on Christmas Eve, paramedics rushed to the home of an elderly lady, Ethel Campbell, whose son had called 999, describing a fall down the stairs, a broken hip, a possible serious head injury. They were surprised on ringing the doorbell to find Ethel herself answered the door, frail and forgetful, but adamant she had not fallen, and eager to offer them a cup of tea in her kitchen. As the son was nowhere to be seen, they took the safe precaution of delivering Ethel to A&E.

From top to toe, I checked Ethel meticulously. No tender bones, no new aches and pains, just an elderly woman with possible dementia who seemed tickled pink with all the attention, and refused to relinquish my hand.

Eventually, I managed to speak to her son on his mobile phone – at Heathrow airport.

'No, I don't have time to discuss my mother, our flights leave in a minute. No, I didn't actually see it myself but she may have had a fall and there's no food in her flat. You'll just have to have her over Christmas because we're not back until New Year.'

I hung up the phone, and wondered what I was going to say. No-one ever completely understands from the outside what a family faces within, and it is certainly not a medic's place to judge. All I knew was that Ethel was about to discover she'd be sharing Christmas with an NHS family, and I was the one who had to tell her. Her face lit up when I returned to her bedside, then quivered as she clutched my hand and began to cry.

The real reward of working in a hospital at Christmas is, of course, the privilege of caring for others, less fortunate, who would do anything to be elsewhere. If the staff are longing, on one level, to be with their loved ones, imagine how much the patients yearn to flee. But no matter how frail, or unwell, or cut off from those they love, patients invariably face Christmas Day in hospital with an uncomplaining dignity that can take your breath away.

When I returned to Margaret Hamilton's bedside that Christmas Eve, some eight years ago, my shift – on paper – was meant to have ended. I'd worked flat-out all day, racing through my jobs, hoping in vain to make a rare exit on time so that I might share in the children's all-important bedtime, the hanging of stockings on bedposts, the careful arranging of carrots and mince pies on the hearth. Part of me ached to rush away. But when I saw from a distance the husband and wife holding hands, their shoulders slumped and faces drawn, there was nowhere else I could have contemplated being.

After a long and difficult conversation, Margaret's husband sat silently sobbing, his face buried in his hands, as she asked me a crucial question.

'The children and the grandchildren are all arriving tomorrow. Do I tell them, or do I let them enjoy the holiday?'

We talked further. There were no easy answers. As I stood up to leave, Margaret asked me to move closer. I leant across the bed towards her. She kissed me on the cheek, saying: 'Thank you. You were very brave today. This has been my Christmas present.'

Here was a woman receiving the worst news a person can hear, yet her concern was for everyone around her, even her doctor. At the time, I couldn't imagine a more potent example of humanity at its dignified best than her quiet strength and selflessness. The truth is, in my years as an NHS doctor, I've seen similar over and over – and it never fails to floor me.

—\/\—

Once, at an age when the question of whether Father Christmas was real was a matter of burning importance, my son asked me: 'Mummy, how is he able to visit all the boys and girls in the hospital? How does he get in? Are there any chimneys?'

Around this time, his understanding of my job was tenuous at best (when someone asked him what I actually did in the hospital, he answered, with the utmost solemnity, 'Mummy kisses other doctors to make them feel better'), and he saw the presence of children in hospital as worrying evidence against the existence of Santa.

This was a good question. One day, I looked forward to telling him that events inside a hospital at Christmas can occasionally be sufficiently remarkable to make even among the hardest-bitten of medics believe, for one day only, in magic.

One Christmas, my friend Gemma, a paediatric intensive care doctor, was called to A&E to tend to an emergency.

'You always steel yourself a little bit,' she told me, 'but this time was worst than most. The dad had a reindeer jumper on. You never want a parent in resus at Christmas.'

Before his parents had been able to stop him, Tommy, a boy aged five or six, had run out onto some ice and, as it snapped into shards around him, plunged beneath the water. Eventually, bystanders had managed to retrieve the child, but not before he had stopped breathing and his heart had ceased to beat. Paramedics had given chest compressions all the way to the hospital, but the child's hypothermia was so severe that, on arrival, he remained as white as ice himself, eyes closed, lips blue, looking more statue than human.

'We didn't stop,' Gemma said. 'You never know with children. They can survive cardiac downtime that would destroy an adult brain.'

Slowly, gently, the trauma team began to warm the boy. At some point, despite everyone's worst fears, his heart defied its extended submersion and resumed a rhythm, against all odds, faltering at first, little more than a flicker, but gaining in strength with each passing second.

'The parents were crying with joy, but I still felt sick inside,' Gemma said. Though his body had come back from the brink, at this stage nobody knew if Tommy himself, the child he had been, was intact or had been obliterated. It was entirely possible that Tommy had endured catastrophic brain damage. Gemma followed his progress daily in the paediatric ICU. At first, strong anaesthetics kept him intentionally unconscious to give his traumatised brain a chance to heal. After several days, the team had dared, gingerly, to lift the sedation. To everyone's delight and astonishment, an ordinary, lively, inquisitive boy emerged with no obvious signs of brain damage. Tommy, it seemed, was back.

'I know I'm obsessed with scientific evidence,' Gemma told me afterwards, 'but this was enough to make you believe in anything. It felt like a bloody miracle, a Christmas miracle.'

—⁣\/⁣—

If you are unlucky enough to face us at Christmas – and, at its worst, a hospital admission can feel frightening, humiliating, hopeless – you'll meet doctors and nurses whose sense of team spirit rivals that of the military. We might look grotesque in our novelty Christmas jumpers, straining over bulges caused by too many Celebrations, but we'll do our best to reach out and help you. We may be unable to fix you, but we will not leave you alone.

In turn, we'll be lucky enough to meet you. The newborn Christmas infant, howling her entrance to the world beneath hospital strip lights. The teenager with bone cancer who wants to be left alone, but can't help but grin at the consultant's discomfort in his under-sized, straining Santa suit. The ninety-six-year-old man delivered by ambulance to A&E who, it turns out, needs nothing so much as someone – anyone in the world – to talk to. The newly-retired ITU nurse who presents a brave face to her family after her dreams of travelling the wide world have been dashed into a small, sharp, shrunken future of palliative chemotherapy before her symptoms overwhelm her.

In all my forty-four Christmases, I've never seen anything as remarkable as the indomitable spirit shown by the NHS patients for whom it's been my privilege to care. This year, I will arrive on my specialist palliative care ward on Boxing Day with a spring in my step and a smile on my face. There may be grief of an unimaginable order as families are wrenched from their loved ones. But in the messy, ugly, calamitous times there will also be love, and compassion, and kindness. Patient, doctor, nurse, family member. Just human beings trying their best at Christmas, when the NHS does all of us proud.

CHAPTER 14

CANDOUR

'Hey. Any chance I could come round on my way home from work?'

It was not like Sam, an old friend from medical school, to call me early one morning out of the blue. I had just dropped the children off at school and he had completed a night shift as a surgical registrar in his hospital. For all the feigned nonchalance in his voice, I could tell he needed to talk. An hour or so later, after a long, fraught motorway drive in which he struggled to keep his eyes open, Sam arrived at my house. I took one look at him and started brewing strong coffee.

'What's up? Was it a shift from hell?'

It was the tail end of 2016. For months, the papers had been full of NHS horror stories. Maternity, paediatrics and A&E departments folding up and down the country due to lack of doctors. Patients stacked up for hours on trolleys in corridors

217

since there was no space in A&E. Desperately sick babies being transported hundreds of miles to the only intensive-care beds available anywhere in the country, potentially endangering their lives. And then, a week before Christmas, the unprecedented news, leaked to the press, that a letter had been sent to every NHS Trust in England ordering it to suspend virtually all elective surgery for an entire month in an attempt to reduce dangerously high hospital bed occupancy rates. A month's worth of surgery cancelled at a stroke – the misery for the hundreds of thousands of patients denied their operations did not bear thinking about.

As the surgical registrar on call in his local hospital, Sam was responsible for all the surgical inpatients who became unwell overnight, plus any new patients arriving in A&E needing review by a surgeon. Not to mention the small matter of actually performing the emergency operations when required. Even at the best of times, emergency surgical nights are brutal. But this one was in a league of its own.

'Do I blow the whistle, Rach? I mean, how bad do things have to be before you can't stop yourself going to the GMC or the press?'

'You can't make any sensible decisions now,' I counselled. 'You're too tired to think straight. You have to get some sleep first.'

'You know exactly what happens to whistleblowers. You know I'd be destroyed.'

The NHS has a long and grubby history of treating individuals who have tried to blow the whistle on unsafe practice with ruthless brutality, ruining careers and lives.

'I know. I know what they'd do to you, Sam. But you have to get some rest, please.'

The experience that had so traumatised my friend involved a young child. A&E had been in full-blown, early-hours meltdown. Patients and relatives occupied every available chair. Most had been waiting six hours just to see a doctor, let alone be treated or admitted into hospital. The drunks and the bigots were hurling abuse at the staff. Someone could not be stopped from screeching 'Away in a Manger' at a volume that could shatter glass. Many members of the public, seething with rage at the delays, were not holding back at the nurses. Amid all the ugliness and chaos of the Emergency Department, Sam had been asked to see an eight-year-old girl with abdominal pain. When he found her, Ayesha was flushed and whimpering, clutching her mother's hand. Her pulse was racing, she was hot to touch and the pain in her abdomen was making her cry. She looked, in a word, 'toxic' – likely to be suffering a serious infection. Sam's money was on appendicitis. The very high number of while cells in her blood also seemed to fit with infection.

But something was not quite right. Her abdomen, when Sam had felt it, was completely soft to the touch. Ordinarily, when the abdominal cavity is severely infected, the overlying muscles of the abdominal wall are held completely rigid, clenched in an involuntary spasm. The unusual softness of Ayesha's belly had held Sam back from taking her to theatre. Nobody wants to be the slash-happy surgeon who unnecessarily cuts open a child. But nor was a CT scan an option to aid the diagnosis since the radiation dose was too high for a young child, unless absolutely necessary. Sam decided to observe Ayesha for a short period, having started intravenous antibiotics, while teeing up the emergency theatre staff for a likely imminent surgery.

All of this was routine stuff for a junior surgeon on call. What happened next was not. A besuited manager suddenly materialised to inform Sam that he was banned from taking the child to theatre since there were no beds into which she could be admitted afterwards. Not only that, he should never have admitted the child for fluids and antibiotics, given the lack of beds.

'I'm sorry but I don't think you appreciate the gravity of the situation,' he explained calmly. 'If she doesn't pick up over the next hour with antibiotics, then I'm going to have to take her to theatre because there's a good chance she will die if I don't.'

'No, you don't understand,' pressed the bed manager. 'There are no beds, and I'm telling you that you will not be taking this patient to theatre. If you think they need surgery then it's up to you to find a hospital somewhere else that will take them.'

'But if there are no paediatric beds anywhere in the hospital,' Sam pressed back, 'then why on earth are you still allowing ambulances to bring sick children to A&E? That's not safe. Why are you not on divert?'

Hospitals that put out a 'divert' – effectively closing their doors to ambulances since they have run out of beds into which to admit patients – face large fines for doing so. Diverts are consequently loathed by the management, costing a Trust that is invariably in financial deficit from the outset even more money that it simply does not possess. In spite of all the other patients requiring his attention, Sam was forced to spend the next two hours frantically phoning every hospital in the vicinity trying to find one that would agree to admit his patient. But to no avail. Nowhere was willing to admit Ayesha because, like his own hospital, they too had no beds.

'At this point,' Sam told me, slumped on the sofa with his head in his hands, 'it was all I could do not to burst into the A&E waiting room and yell to all the parents to get the hell out of the place and go somewhere that might actually be safe.'

Increasingly concerned by the state of his patient, who by now had started to become delirious, he called his sleeping consultant at home.

'I'm sorry for disturbing you, but I really need your expertise,' he explained. 'I don't know what the right thing is to do.'

Less than half an hour later, Sam's consultant was present in A&E, assessing Ayesha alongside his registrar. He had never seen a presentation of appendicitis quite like this one, he said, and agreed with Sam that, given how unwell the child now appeared, an exploratory operation was essential. 'If we leave her much longer and she gets any sicker, she won't survive the night.'

At this point, the bed manager resurfaced. He repeated – to one of the most senior consultant surgeons in the hospital – that under no circumstances would Ayesha be permitted to go to theatre. 'There isn't a bed for her and that means no operation, end of story.'

'But look,' said the surgeon. 'She's in a bed now. A bed in a side room in A&E. She can come straight back here after theatre, can't she?'

'No, she can't,' insisted the bed manager. 'This is an assessment bed, not an admission bed. It's for assessing paediatric cases in A&E.'

The surgeon paused before answering, working hard, one imagines, to frame a response that did not involve expletives. 'If there are no paediatric beds in the hospital, then why are we still assessing paediatric patients in A&E? What exactly happens when the conclusion of the assessment is that we need to admit the child?'

The bed manager had no answer. But even a senior doctor's explicit concerns that the child might die without surgery were not enough to persuade him to relent. Enough was enough.

'I see,' said the consultant, curtly. 'Well. Let me make this crystal clear for you. This child is going to theatre. Now, if you wish to call the chief executive of this hospital, wake him up at home and get him here in his pyjamas to tell me to my face that I am not allowed to save my patient's life, then – and only then – will I not operate on this child. Otherwise, please get out of my way.'

With that, Sam and his consultant physically wheeled Ayesha themselves down to theatre, where they surgically explored her abdomen. At the scalpel's first touch, thick yellow liquid burst under pressure from the abdominal cavity. All four quadrants of her belly were swimming with pus from a horrendously inflamed appendix, the worst the consultant had ever seen. 'It smelled,' Sam told me, 'of rotten fish. The anaesthetist had to leave briefly in order to retch.' Later, the consultant told Sam that, had they not operated when they did, the child almost certainly would have died.

As I listened, aghast, to Sam's tale, the what-ifs made me hold my head in my hands. What if Sam had not been sufficiently resolute and conscientious to call his boss at 2 a.m.? What if the consultant had been less senior, less confident, more easily cowed by a dogmatic bed manager? What if a little girl had indeed languished in her A&E bed until sepsis overwhelmed her and she died? Perhaps most fundamentally – given that Ayesha had survived only by the skin of her teeth, because two surgeons had stood up to an asinine system in which a man in a suit, not a doctor, dictated whether life-or-death surgeries may occur – what if elsewhere, in other parts of the country, children were slipping through the net? Might other Ayeshas, in short, have already died because hospitals without a single available paediatric bed would rather allow ambulances to keep bringing sick children to their swamped A&Es than be fined for diverting them elsewhere? How would we even know this?

No one could pretend that this is good healthcare. It is not; it is utter madness. Hearing the tale made me want to cry. To a doctor, let alone a mother, the notion that anonymous suits could be stalking hospitals at night, flexing their muscles in this manner with clinicians, was frankly terrifying. It is doctors, not bureaucrats, who know what their patients need, particularly when those patients are *in extremis*. And if financial pressures are distorting care in this manner – right now, under the radar, in our NHS hospitals – then something has gone horribly wrong with the health service we long to believe is the very best of Britain.

—/\/—

The tragedy for doctors, nurses and managers alike – not to mention the patients we strive so hard to look after – is that we operate within a system that makes fools of us all. When nearly every hospital Trust in the country is running up multi-million-pound debts, as they are, because their income is vastly outstripped by the needs of their patients, Trusts do not stand a chance. Of course, a Trust will fight tooth and nail to avoid the fines that accompany diverts when it is already, financially, on its knees, already facing punitive measures set from on high to address its alleged fiscal irresponsibility. The system – above all the government's £22 billion of 'efficiency savings' that no one in the NHS thinks we can possibly achieve – is set up to pressure Trusts to shave costs wherever possible, let alone incur avoidable ones.

Yet even this misses the most important point – the inescapable, on-the-ground reality – that on this particular night there were no beds. Not in Sam's hospital, not in any of the local hospitals. There was literally nowhere for Ayesha to go. Even if ambulances had been diverted from Sam's hospital, how many miles would they have had to drive to find a hospital that could actually admit children safely? What might the potential risks of those long journeys have been for unwell, unstable children? Ultimately, we all know that words – no matter how fine – in the end come up against reality. In the case of the NHS, reality is the actual care that patients receive and that frontline staff both deliver and bear witness to. Reality, on occasion, is nights like Sam's, when a child nearly dies because there is no capacity in the system to give her the care she needs. And if, as a doctor, my duty of candour – of being honest and open with my patients about mistakes or failings of care – means anything at all, then it behoves me and all of us who work within the NHS to speak out, uncowed, about this reality. How else can we stand up and look our patients in the eye?

'If you admit you are a doctor in distress, then this will all go away.'

'This' was the threat of formal disciplinary action against me, made by a manager in one of my previous hospitals. Candour, I had discovered to my peril, costs. I had had the temerity to break an internal Trust rule I was not aware existed and now I was reaping the consequences. It is difficult to convey how frightening it is, in a profession as rigidly hierarchical as medicine – and as notoriously hostile to perceived troublemakers – to be threatened with disciplinary proceedings. On discovering via email that I might be formally disciplined, I burst into tears on the spot. In medicine, a disciplinary incident dogs you for the rest of your career, its recording a requirement on every subsequent annual appraisal and every future job application. For a junior as junior as I was then, with most of my career still stretching ahead of me, that was a distressing prospect. Which, of course, is precisely why, for a Trust, even a whisper of a threat to take formal action against you is such a powerful means of achieving silence and conformity.

'What am I going to do?' I cried to my husband plaintively, temporarily immersed in fear and panic. The answer was provided for me. I received an email summoning me to report to the senior manager to explain my subversive act in person. The prospect of being hauled over the coals by someone fully cognisant of his power to damage my future in medicine was not one that I relished. That night I slept little and fitfully.

Often, doctors who face discipline do so because their desire to protect their patients has forced them into the role of reluctant whistleblower. They know the risks of speaking out, yet the duty they feel to put their patients' interests first compels them to be candid. Having failed to persuade their hospital management to take seriously their safety concerns, in the end they resort to going above them – perhaps to the doctors' regulator, the General Medical Council, or to the institution that safeguards NHS standards for patients, the Care Quality Commission. Then, if not beforehand, the full force of their employer descends on them like the wrath of God. Money – supplied courtesy of the taxpayer – is no object as a stellar Trust legal team is lined up against the whistleblower. The NHS is littered with former doctors who, after attempting to raise concerns, have lost their jobs, homes, marriages and health after bitter legal battles with their Trusts. Whistleblowers are meant to have legal protections that enable them to raise concerns about the organisation in which they work in good faith. But, in truth, whistleblowing often destroys doctors, nurses and anyone else who tries to speak out. In standing up for their patients, clinicians can end up sacrificing themselves.

Nowhere was a culture of denial and cover-up more pervasive than in Mid Staffs. When individuals attempted to flag concerns through 'incident forms', online reports about issues threatening patient safety, these never appeared to be acted upon. When concerns were reported at Trust board level, these too were invariably ignored. Complaints from patients and their families were swept under the carpet. Sir Robert Francis, in analysing why so few staff members spoke out in Mid Staffs, describes professionals trying their best to raise issues but who, when that failed to have any effect, became disillusioned and in the end gave up. Fear of reprisals also deterred them. Dr Pradip Singh, a consultant at Mid Staffs who tried, if belatedly, to raised concerns about patient safety, was asked why he had not gone further. He explained, in essence, that, though he was brave, he was not brave enough:

> Q. How do you answer the criticisms that I suppose might be made that if you'd cared more you would have gone outside the hospital and raised, as one might put it, merry hell?

> A. I would have then ended up becoming either a stroke or a heart attack, and being on the road.

> Q. You mean out of a job?

> A. Yes. Clear and simple. And I am brave – I mean, what I did takes a lot of guts to do. But I'm not Nelson Mandela . . . You're always watching your back. At the end of the day, I'm a human being. I might make a mistake and that could be the end of my career, because it will be used against me. Because the kind of job we're in, things will occasionally go wrong. It doesn't matter how good you are, and then that will become the excuse for destroying your career.[9]

Francis identified frontline clinicians' fear of speaking out as one of the most important factors that permitted the cruelties of Mid Staffs to flourish unchecked for so long. So detrimental did he regard this culture of fear to the overall aim of ensuring patient safety that he went on to investigate more broadly the experiences of NHS staff who attempted to raise concerns. His 'Freedom to Speak Up' review found that the barriers deterring individuals from speaking out about their concerns were ongoing and relentless:

> The NHS is blessed with staff who want to do the best for their patients. They want to be able to raise their concerns free of fear that they may be badly treated when they do so and confident that effective action will be taken . . . Unfortunately I heard shocking accounts from distressed NHS staff who did not have this experience when they spoke up.[61]

My own transgression was by comparison minimal. I was not even a whistleblower. In expressing my concerns to the press about an unfunded seven-day NHS policy several years before the junior doctor dispute began, I had merely committed the sin – albeit a cardinal one, as I would go on discover – of naming the Trust at which I then worked. This, with hindsight, was exceptionally naïve. Unbeknown to me, a draconian Trust media policy required all employees to liaise with the press office before making any reference to the Trust in the media. That my comment referred to a national government policy, neither criticising nor attacking my Trust in any way, was no defence; I was nonetheless in breach of a formal Trust policy.

I sat before the manager with a churning stomach, yet what I hoped was an implacable exterior. I was told again that if I admitted I was a doctor in distress, 'this' would all go away. This is a well-documented tactic used by NHS employers against staff who speak out, an attempt to tar them with the stigma of mental instability, neatly delegitimising their concerns from that moment onwards. It needed confronting head on.

'I can't do that,' I stated, 'because it isn't true. If you look through my online portfolio, which I'm sure you have done, you will see that my feedback from my colleagues and from patients is superlative. I am not a doctor in distress. I am someone who saw it as her professional duty to speak out against a government policy I believe will be to the detriment of my patients, because it is unfunded.'

It is fair to say this was not well received. Contrition and admission of mental frailty were expected, not unrepentant idealism. An hour later, the meeting concluded with a curt statement that, no, this was not the end of the matter and, yes, I may yet face formal disciplinary proceedings. Eventually, after nearly two months of worry, I was informed that the matter had been closed. The Trust CEO actually took me aside for a quiet coffee during which he apologised for the whole incident. Alongside my feelings of immense relief, I was left with the uncomfortable conclusion that, if this was how an NHS doctor was treated when they had not actually blown the whistle at all, how much more oppressive must the treatment be of someone brave enough to speak out about local Trust practices they believe are putting patients at risk. It is a wonder anyone puts themselves in the firing line in a culture so authoritarian and closed.

—∿—

Some months after this unpleasant experience, I was chatting with a fellow parent on the sidelines of our sons' Saturday morning football match. He was a barrister, specialising in medical negligence, and he took a keen interest as I described my head-to-head with my Trust.

'Something you might not be aware of, Rachel, is that I actually work in Sir Robert Francis's chambers. I suspect he may well be keen to hear your story.'

I'd had no idea. But the thought of assisting Francis, however trivially, in his efforts to make the NHS safer for patients was an honour. Several weeks later, I received an invitation to attend an evidence-gathering session as part of the 'Freedom to Speak Up' review. Francis had previously described junior doctors as the 'eyes and ears' of the NHS whose testimony and fearlessness in speaking out had been integral to exposing the horrors of Mid Staffs. He was keen to hear in person from juniors from across the country with experience of whistleblowing. We convened at an informal meeting chaired by Francis himself in a hall in central London. My story was inconsequential compared with what others had endured. Young doctor after doctor described harrowing treatment at the hands of their Trusts, simply for endeavouring to raise genuine concerns about their patients' safety being jeopardised. Some had been bullied, smeared and denigrated. Frequently, according to the juniors' testimony, the mental-health card was played by Trusts who attempted to paint the whistleblowers as unreliable or incompetent due to emotional instability.

I remember looking around the room feeling pride and anger in equal measure. Junior doctors reside near the bottom of the NHS food chain. They have nothing like a consultant's clout. That these juniors were standing up for their patients, sometimes enduring ferocious workplace bullying as a result, was something I found deeply humbling. That Sir Robert

Francis had proactively sought out their testimony gave me hope in a more transparent and open future for NHS clinicians and patients alike.

Ironically, the Trust that took issue with my accidental insubordination behaved impeccably towards one junior doctor whistleblower. Conditions in the hospital's Surgical Emergency Unit (SEU), where I had once experienced such understaffing, did not improve after I left. So overstretched had the juniors become that one of them took matters into his own hands. Barely a year into his career as a doctor, he wrote a letter to the most senior member of the Trust, its chief executive officer, detailing the dangers to patients of the unit's understaffing. Every SEU house officer had signed it, a collective *cri de coeur* from the most junior doctors manning the front line. Their concerns had been roundly dismissed by their consultants and immediate managers and so, *en masse*, they had decided to go straight to the top. And – to his enormous credit – the CEO not only listened, he insisted that the understaffing must be dealt with. Thus, thanks to one gusty house officer, a whole department was changed for the better. It was a model of exactly how a Trust could do it right.

Nor did it not stop there. For a few years, several other doctors and I had run an annual teaching session for final-year students who were about to embark on their lives as new doctors. In it, we invited current house officers to share with the students their real-life stories of how things had gone wrong when they began to practise medicine. The aims were simple but important. To show that mistakes happen to everyone, that they are nothing to feel ashamed of, that every mistake is an opportunity to learn and to make the wards safer for patients, that doctors are as fallible as anyone – and that this is OK, this is human. Sometimes, the stories were harrowing. One or two doctors cried in describing what had happened. The Trust, keen to embrace a culture of transparency and candour, invited us to extend the sessions to an audience of junior doctors as well. It felt progressive – a small step towards a less adversarial future in which learning from mistakes, not apportioning blame, took priority for our patients' sakes.

Candour is no longer an optional extra for doctors, and rightly so. For too long, patients and their relatives have been kept in the dark about individual and systemic failings that have led to loved ones' harm. As a direct result of the brutality of Mid Staffs, in 2015 the General Medical Council and Nursing and Midwifery Council introduced a new professional duty of candour upon all individual doctors and nurses working in the UK. A clear attempt to circumvent the cover-ups of old, it required us to be honest with patients and apologise when mistakes were made, something that can only be for the good of our patients.

There remains, however, a tension between the new duty of candour and enduring conditions that discourage speaking out. Bullying and a blame culture are still rife within the NHS, but there is also something more insidious driving individual doctors and nurses away from frank disclosure, namely, the example we are set by our ultimate bosses, the politicians to whom we are in some ways accountable. The government purports to champion candour within the NHS.

In the foreword to the government's formal response to the 'Freedom to Speak Up' report, Jeremy Hunt declared:

> I want to pay tribute to those members of staff, patients and their loved ones who stood up for a culture of truthfulness and compassion, and who would not give in to those who put what they thought were the interests of the system before what was right. The only way to honour their courage is to stand with them by continuing to build a culture that listens, learns and speaks the truth.[62]

These are fine words. They inspire hope and optimism. But are they sincere? The report itself went on:

> In an organisation as large and as complex as the NHS – operating under pressure, under intense scrutiny and in which life or death decisions are made every day – no matter how strong the professional instinct to do the right thing, no matter how powerful the impulse to care, there are inevitably times when it might feel easier to conceal mistakes, to deny that things have gone wrong and to slide into postures of institutional defensiveness.[62]

That temptation – to conceal, to deny, to shrink into kneejerk defensiveness – is well recognised not only at hospital and individual levels, but also above them, at the level of the government itself. We are all familiar with – some might say sick of – political spin, the legions of governmental press officers whose sole purpose is to package and polish reality into the least unpalatable form in order to persuade voters of an administration's effectiveness. But, for health workers, this process is uniquely discomforting, given that everyone within the NHS now has a professional obligation to be candid, except, it seems, its highest echelons, the political masters who apparently cannot bear to leave the facts unvarnished and unspun. From the perspective of a lowly member of the NHS front line, candour, like gravity, seems only ever to tug downwards. Politicians float freely, immune from its grasp.

Nowhere is this more apparent than in the thorny matter of ensuring our hospitals are safely staffed. Having identified draconian cuts in staff numbers – the result of a deliberate Trust policy to save money – as one of the fundamental causes of the horrors of Mid Staffs, Sir Robert Francis rightly made safe staffing a key imperative for the NHS. To ensure that patients were never again subjected to such abject failures of care, he explicitly recommended that NICE (the National Institute for Health and Care Excellence, formerly the National Institute for Health and Clinical Excellence) should be commissioned to develop evidence-based guidelines for minimum staff numbers. Francis chose NICE for a reason. Unlike most of the quangos that proliferate in the NHS, NICE has a reputation for strict independence from political control, basing its guidance on objective, evidence-based analyses of clinical and cost-effectiveness.

But staff, as we know, cost money. And though NICE set to work appraising the evidence – concluding that at least one nurse to every eight acute medical patients was necessary to ensure patient safety – after the Conservative Party's 2015 general election win, something unexpected happened:

NICE abruptly announced it was abandoning its safe-staffing programme at the behest of NHS England, which would now oversee the work instead.[63]

Sir Robert Francis was unimpressed. 'I am surprised and concerned by this news,' he told the *Health Service Journal*, adding,

> I specifically recommended the work which NICE has been undertaking for a reason, namely they have an evidence-based and analytical approach which I believed would be very helpful in filling what appeared to be a gap in the discussions on this topic. NICE also has an advantage not enjoyed by NHS England of being independent.[63]

Fears abounded that NHS England, a politicised body that shares an intimate relationship with the government of the day, would prioritise the political imperative of cutting costs above the patient-safety imperative of introducing sufficiently robust staffing standards to prevent another Mid Staffs. Nursing leaders and patient-safety campaigners condemned the announcement, including, most embarrassingly for Jeremy Hunt, relatives of patients who had died at Mid Staffs. One leading local campaigner, Julie Bailey, who had fought tirelessly for a public inquiry, condemned the move as an 'absolute disgrace', warning Hunt that he would lose all credibility with patients and the public by backing it:

> We are so disappointed. Jeremy Hunt has championed patients and their safety. This will be a huge step backwards. We're not prepared to go back to those

dark days. We fought too hard for the Francis Report
and now we must ensure that his recommendations
matter and are implemented to ensure it never
happens again.[63]

An unpalatable truth had been exposed. For all the
government's lofty rhetoric, when it came to the crunch – and
Francis's recommendations came at too high a price for the
Treasury – curbing NHS spending, not protecting patients,
was the first priority. Jeremy Hunt's unequivocal response
to Francis looked increasingly hollow. On the matter of safe
staffing, it seemed, he was willing to settle for obfuscation
above candour.

CHAPTER 15

HAEMOSTASIS

The most underrated heroes of the human body are surely its humble scabs. No adults, only children, truly appreciate the visceral joys of a well-formed scab. As a small girl, I could lose myself for hours painstakingly picking at the crusts on my knees, the pleasures of a decent de-scabbing topped only by an occasional nibble to see if dried blood tasted the same as fresh. Both my children, I note with approval, are often similarly engrossed, demonstrating the enduring appeal – in a world of Wi-Fi and tablets – of the good, old-fashioned scab.

Almost as extraordinary as the pleasures of scab-picking are the processes underlying their formation in the first place. Haemostasis – the opposite of haemorrhage – is the body's way of preventing bleeding by forming clots that contain blood within damaged blood vessels. The lowly scab is the final product of some of the most intricate chemical

237

reactions that occur anywhere within the human body. So bewildering is the infamous 'clotting cascade' – the chain of events that causes liquid blood to solidify into a clot or scab – that generations of medical students have given up ever truly understanding it. Only a rare breed of doctor, an erudite subtype of haematologist nicknamed a 'clotter', properly grasps the processes by which we staunch our bodies' bleeding.

In real life, stopping a haemorrhage – achieving haemostasis in a patient – can make you want to whoop with relief. Unchecked blood fills doctors with dread. We know we must act fast or lose the patient. It takes a while to discover as a junior doctor that a little blood goes a very long way. Once, on the cardiology ward, I was called to see a man who had recently returned from a procedure to implant within his chest a cardiac pacemaker, a small metal box that would from this point onwards do the job of triggering his heartbeat. Stealthily, unbeknown to anyone, ever since the cardiologist had inserted the device, blood had been leaking from a tiny nick in one of the vessels close to the heart. By the time I was summoned, the pressure of leaking blood had built up to such a degree that it was now pouring out of his chest wall through the gaps between his stitches. Three or four nurses stood at the bedside, aghast. The patient, ashen-faced, stared in horror at the bloodbath in the centre of his chest while I wrestled with myself to appear confident and calm. Very junior, very out of my depth, the most constructive thing I could do at this point was call for urgent senior help. When the cardiologist arrived – suave, aloof and devilishly handsome – everyone at the bedside was practically swooning. For the patient, admittedly, this was due to blood loss, but the rest of us were romantically swept off our feet. Deftly, the cardiologist snipped open all the stitches, extracting from the gaping wound a large bloody clot – which he briefly held aloft in the manner of a big-game hunter posing with the head of his felled impala – before whisking the patient away to theatre to repair the leaking vessel. 'Hmph! That wasn't a big bleed,' he said nonchalantly, as he disappeared round the corner. Never had haemostasis looked cooler.

The haemorrhage of staff from the NHS threatens its survival just as surely as unstaunched blood around a human heart. If we want the NHS to endure, achieving haemostasis is essential. At my lowest ebb last year, like so many more of my junior doctor friends and colleagues, I decided I had to quit medicine. Withdrawing my application for speciality training was not enough. I reached the point of knowing I had to walk away completely, whether temporarily or permanently I simply could not tell.

The moment my own keeno lifesaver light went out was around ten o'clock one summer evening. A long shift on call was nearly over. There had been a couple of crash calls, one or two sick patients, nothing too arduous at all. But because we were a doctor down on our ward – and had been for many months now – I'd been fighting fire since nine that morning just to keep on top of all the ward jobs. Now, I felt hungry, tired and angry with everyone. The management for ignoring the excessive unpaid hours I was being forced to work daily, the BMA for dithering and failing to define what they were fighting for, the press for accusing me of naked avarice, the Health Secretary for launching a wholly avoidable media war against doctors. I'm sure there was also a hefty whack of self-pity.

That morning, one of my favourite patients, a softly spoken Scot in his seventies, was desperate for a chat. I promised him I would come and find him later. Callum's case had touched us all. A virulent skin infection had spread into his bloodstream, causing his kidneys to fail permanently. In a matter of days, he had gone from being fearsomely active, with not a single health problem, to requiring renal dialysis three times a week, each time being hooked up for most of the day to the machine that did the work of his kidneys. Though he was sometimes tearful at being plunged so abruptly from the finest health into immobility, he worked so hard at being stoical. No matter how overstretched I was on the ward, I always eked out a few minutes to chat with him. He loved to discuss the merits of different single malts, insisting I was to go home and try out various obscure new whiskies.

That night, though, my ability to give had run dry. All day, I'd been too busy to sit down with Callum, as I had promised him I would. Every time I scuttled past the open door to his room, dashing to the next patient requiring my attention, he called out, eager to chat.

'Come on, Doc, we've got whiskies to discuss. When are you going to sit down?'

Each time, I sheepishly muttered my apologies, inwardly cursing the workload. Eventually, head down, too embarrassed to meet his eye, I felt the anger that had been brewing inside me all day finding a new and wholly undeserving target. 'Can't you see, Callum?' I wanted to cry at him. 'Can't you see that I'm always running past your room? I haven't even eaten a proper meal today. I can't stand still, let alone chat for hours about whisky.' Though I said none of this out loud, my thoughts appalled me all the same. It felt as though the beginnings of callousness – that first twisted step towards the cruelties of Mid Staffs – might be perverting the doctor I had always aspired to be.

Finally, every last job done, an hour or so late for the babysitter, I hovered uncertainly in the empty doctor's mess, torn between letting down a patient who needed my support and having the chat I had promised him I would. I knew I could just about summon the energy to listen and be kind, but I was paranoid that, if I arrived home that night even later than I was already, my children's much-loved babysitter might be pushed by my erratic hours that bit closer towards quitting. So I slunk away, avoiding Callum's room, dragging my heels with shame.

When I began life as an NHS doctor, in the mornings I would freewheel down the hill towards the hospital with a grin on my face. I would lock up my bike and trot towards the doctors' mess, itching to get started. I brimmed with pride. Not merely at being a doctor but being, even better, an NHS doctor – a public servant whose graft served not to enrich corporate shareholders but simply to help my patients. Now, it seemed that the dehumanising system in which I worked had finally soured the love I felt for medicine, for the NHS and – above all – for my patients. I knew that when my contract ended that summer, I could not continue as an NHS doctor.

$$\wedge\!\!\!\wedge$$

As 2016 drew to a close, the BBC questioned whether the NHS would 'break' in 2017. Nick Triggle, a senior BBC •

health correspondent, painted an ominous picture of what might lie in store. 'Seasoned observers have started talking about a return to the 1990s when images of overcrowded hospitals and stories of patients waiting years for treatment dogged John Major's Tory government at almost every turn,' he wrote in the final week of 2016. 'Could the same happen to Theresa May?'[64]

His prediction was horribly prescient. In the first week of January 2017, the inhumanity and jeopardy into which a desperately under-resourced health service will at some point inevitably descend erupted into the national press. Reports described one hospital, the Worcestershire Royal, where a woman died of a heart attack after waiting for thirty-five hours on a trolley in a corridor, while a man, also lying on a trolley, suffered torrential bleeding from a burst aneurysm and could not be saved. The husband of a third patient, left in a corridor for a staggering fifty-four hours after suffering a stroke, said, 'It was horrendous. The nurses did all they could but the place was in meltdown. It was manic. There were at least twenty people on trolleys. It was very difficult to manoeuvre around them. A porter told me they were putting some patients in a decontamination room – basically a big shower room – to cram in more beds. They ran out of pillows and blankets.'[65] Other relatives described the hospital as looking like a 'war zone', echoing testimony given to Sir Robert Francis by nurses working at Mid Staffs.

The hospital was by no means unique. British Red Cross volunteers and Land Rovers were drafted in to help transport patients between their homes and many other beleaguered NHS hospitals. While this was by no means the first year that the British Red Cross had assisted the NHS, this time the charity's CEO, Mike Adamson, condemned the situation as a 'humanitarian crisis', stating, 'We've seen people sent home without clothes, some suffer falls and are not found for days, while others are not washed because there is no carer there to help them.'[66]

With overwhelmed hospital Trusts up and down the country being put on 'black alert' due to overstretch – too few beds and too few doctors and nurses to cope with the number of patients – the president of the Royal College of Emergency Medicine, Dr Taj Hassan, said, 'Figures cannot account for untold patient misery. Overcrowded departments, overflowing with patients, can result in avoidable deaths. The emergency care system is on its knees, despite the huge efforts of staff who are struggling to cope with the intense demands being put upon them.'[66]

Story upon story began to fill the media of misery, indignity and dangerously substandard care – seriously unwell patients being dumped in hospital gyms with no oxygen, alarm bells or even sufficient food for patients; adults being placed on children's wards; an NHS maternity unit being closed to pregnant women in order to house the flood of patients from A&E; patients' lifesaving cancer operations being postponed. The defining image of the crisis became that of a baby boy with possible meningitis forced to wait for five hours in an A&E on a makeshift bed of blankets on a pair of plastic NHS chairs.[67] Even Simon Stevens, the CEO of NHS England, told MPs at the House of Commons Public Accounts Committee that the Prime Minister, Theresa May, was 'stretching it' to pretend she had given the NHS the budget it had asked for. Stevens left no one in any doubt that, if the public's expectations on health were to be met, more money was required. He effectively challenged the government either to find more money for the NHS and social care or to be honest with the public about the consequences of failing to do so.

In terms of the government's credibility on the NHS, it felt like crunch time. For the first few days of the crisis, the Health Secretary went to ground. Unseen, unheard and unavailable for comment, he infuriated frontline staff by his absence. In the hiatus before Hunt re-emerged I knew, with utter clarity, how our morale could be restored. What we needed at that moment, more than ever before, was candour. A government that confronted the crisis instead of trying to deny it. One that entered into an honest dialogue with the public about the unsustainability of safe, world-class healthcare in the face of shrinking resources. By openly acknowledging the risks of continuing to try to do too much with too little money, the government would make NHS doctors and nurses feel as though their warnings on behalf of patients were finally being heard.

I had a glimmer of hope Jeremy Hunt might surprise us. My optimism stemmed from the surprising discovery, during the junior doctor dispute, that he was willing to converse face to face with one of his most vocal junior doctor critics.

We were at what was probably the most fraught point in the entire dispute, September 2016, and the BMA had just announced its longest strike yet, five consecutive days of complete withdrawal of junior doctor labour, in only twelve days' time. Many rank-and-file junior doctors were uneasy about the impact on their patients' safety of such a long strike called at such short notice. Some of them openly expressed their unwillingness to take part in the action. My concern was the lack of clarity from the BMA about what, precisely, the aims of the strike were beyond 'do not impose this contract'. The union, I believed, had backed themselves into a strategic cul-de-sac, having threatened their own version of Hunt's 'nuclear option' without actually spelling out why.

I asked via an intermediary whether Hunt would be willing to meet me in private. Really, I was clutching at straws. I had no power or inside knowledge with which to break the impasse between the government and the BMA – nor, crucially, any mandate with which to attempt to do so – but I hoped that articulating one grassroots doctor's concerns might at least help convey why we were so angry and determined.

Given the number of times I had called Jeremy Hunt dishonest in print and on television, I was astounded he agreed to meet me. But he did. In a tiny parliamentary office, perched on shabby old sofas, we surveyed each other awkwardly. I felt mildly nauseous. He wore the pained expression the Queen might adopt on being trapped in a small lift with Johnny Rotten. Inexplicably, my opening attempt at ice-breaking small talk involved decapitation. I described how my daughter, aged five, had recently spotted a tall man entering my hospital and shrieked, 'Mummy! That's Jeremy Hunt going into your hospital. Go after him and chop off his head.'

After this inauspicious start there was, as expected, much we disagreed on: that the government's seven-day pledge was unfunded and unstaffed; that the evidence for a weekend effect in hospital deaths was contentious; that there were no data demonstrating how the new contract would improve patient safety, and strong reasons for fearing it would do the opposite. Far more surprising though were our areas of agreement. 'I have totally failed to communicate with junior doctors and I have torn my hair out trying to think of how I could have done it differently and better,' he admitted – and I appreciated the honesty. He also stated unequivocally something I had never heard him say in public: that he knew Britain did not have enough doctors. The most striking common ground, however, was what he described as his 'context to the dispute' – a commitment to improving patient safety born out of the appalling events of Mid Staffs. He even joked that Sir Robert Francis could be blamed for the junior doctor dispute, since it was Francis who had made him care so deeply about safety that he would do whatever it took to keep patients safe, even if that meant being hated by doctors.

For a frontline clinician, there is clearly something concerning about a Health Secretary who seems to regard doctors' hostility to his plans as the cross he must bear for putting patients first. It suggests profound mistrust of our motives – as though, unlike him, we doctors are somehow too self-interested to prioritise our patients' safety. I could have chosen to bristle with fury at this subtext, or simply dismissed as bogus his claims to champion patient safety, as if they must be insincere when uttered by a Health Secretary. Yet, on safety, he spoke with disarming, almost messianic zeal. What disconcerted me was not his lack of conviction, but its surfeit. In short, if I suspended my scepticism, I could accept that we shared some common ground. And, if he and I, who disagreed on so much, could meet, talk and agree upon the absolute pre-eminence of patient safety, then a less adversarial future in which frontline staff were not permanently pitted against the Department of Health was, at least theoretically, possible.

I had to believe in this possibility because the alternative, I was certain, was no NHS. Haemostasis – arresting the haemorrhage of belief, joy, meaning and enthusiasm from the working lives of frontline doctors and nurses, not to mention those staff themselves from the institution to which they were once so committed – entails first and foremost conditions of work that cease, for so many NHS staff, to be unendurable. But it also requires a rekindling of faith. Right now, in spite of everything, the vast majority of the NHS's 1.4 million employees still passionately believe in the institution in which we work. It inspires us, matters to us, embodies many of the ideals we hold dear. Most corporations could only dream of a connection of this kind between their brand and their employees. How much would a Google or a McDonald's pay for that kind of devotion from their staff? Abusing, taking advantage of and ultimately squandering this enormous reservoir of goodwill no longer seems merely profligate, but fatal. With the political custodians of the NHS apparently knowing the price of everything and the value of nothing, its lifeblood – its staff – continues to ebb away.

Faith can be rebuilt, however. Some simple straight talking at a ministerial level about how the NHS is really performing – and, crucially, how much funding the NHS really receives – would do wonders for revitalising a workforce at breaking point. Is this kind of political candour really so outlandish? Would it be political suicide to talk honestly and openly about the fact that, one way or another, a world-class health service requires more money and that, as a nation, we need to decide how much we are willing to pay for it, whether through taxation, insurance or other means? Are the British public that immature? I think not. No one really believes you can fund exemplary healthcare on a shoestring, even if politicians like to pretend otherwise.

My glimmer of hope was short-lived. In response to the unfolding crisis, the government launched into its most audacious effort yet to spin away NHS frontline reality. Prime Minister Theresa May rubbished the British Red Cross's claim.[68] Jeremy Hunt took to the airwaves to deny the crisis, claiming that only 'one or two' hospitals were in trouble, with the 'vast majority' actually coping better this winter.[69] A leaked memo sent to hospital managers by senior officials from NHS England revealed feverish attempts from above to downplay the scale of the unfolding disaster. It instructed hospitals on the 'lines' to take if questioned by the press about the pressures they faced, urging avoidance of language such as 'black alert' and issuing a bland form of words to use with the media.[70] And, in one of the more surreal moments of the winter, I entered into a bizarre exchange on Twitter with one senior medical establishment figure, Chris Hopson, the CEO of NHS Providers, who also took umbrage at the Red Cross's use of 'humanitarian crisis', listing the Syrian refugee crisis, the Nepal earthquake, the West Africa Ebola outbreak and the drought in Somalia and Central America as examples of real, *bona fide* crises.

Is this really how bad things have become, I wondered, that the best we can actually say of our ailing health service is, well, at least it is not as bad as Aleppo?[71] An old surgical friend, on call during the week of the 'non'-humanitarian crisis, told me how he was forced to carry out a surgical procedure on a screaming patient on the floor in A&E, pinned down by another doctor in full view of the other patients and relatives, since all the trollies in the corridors were full. 'An elderly couple who had been stationed in India for much of their working life came up to me afterwards,' my friend told me, 'to say that they couldn't believe what they had witnessed. They said the patient would have received better care if they'd been in a state hospital in Delhi. And they were right. That week they would have.'

As a doctor, it was painful to discover that, even with people literally dying on trolleys in hospital corridors – and even after everything Sir Robert Francis had advocated – the government's first instinct remained, as ever, to downplay and deny a bad-news story that might reflect badly upon them.

The problem for Hunt and May was, in the days immediately following their denial of the crisis, statistics emerged that flatly contradicted the claim that only one or two hospitals were in trouble. Evidence leaked to the BBC showed that vast numbers of NHS patients – over 18,000 of them in the preceding week alone – had endured trolley waits of over four hours; 485 patients had waited over 12 hours – treble the number seen during the whole month of January in the preceding year.[72] Newly released Department of Health statistics then showed that a shocking 40 per cent of England's 153 acute-hospital Trusts had issued alerts in the week leading up to Hunt's claim because they were experiencing major problems with too few beds and too many patients.[73] Even Sir Robert Francis himself felt the need to reference the government's lack of candour, describing in the *Health Service Journal* an 'increasing disconnect' between what people on the ground saw going on in the NHS and what was said nationally:

Let's make no bones about it, the NHS is facing an existential crisis. The service is running faster and faster to try to keep up and is failing, manifestly failing.

The danger is that we reach a tipping point; we haven't reached it yet, but there will come a point where public confidence in the service dissipates.[74]

I was not willing to stand by as the government tried once again to silence doctors' efforts at raising patient-safety concerns. As far as I was concerned, my duty of candour required me not to. So, using my contacts and doctor networks on social media, I gathered testimony from doctors working in Emergency Departments across the country and passed it, with their agreement, to the *Guardian* newspaper. The tone of some of the comments was desperate. One doctor wrote,

It's been like an absolute war zone recently. The government at the moment, not to mention my regulatory bodies, are ignoring the worst hospital conditions in my memory. The London ambulance service is similarly overwhelmed. They couldn't provide me with a transfer ambulance for an emergency case, an 11-year-old with a sight-threatening infection, in less than 70 minutes. The target is eight minutes. It is a miracle the child didn't lose an eye.'[7]

Another junior stated,

Our hospital is crumbling and is unsafe on a daily basis. Medical professionals are talking of quitting as they believe someone will soon die on our watch. It is completely out of control . . . I am so angry that it is being ignored and swept under the carpet. I am angry that we are left to pick up the pieces and apologise for a system we've put our hearts and souls into, but now have no control over.[75]

The crescendo of concern in the NHS, as well as among MPs of all parties, became impossible for the government to ignore. But, in a surprise move that took me straight back to the beginning of the dispute that had originally turned me into a doctor-activist, Theresa May decided to blame a new group of doctors – not juniors, this time, but general practitioners – for the problems now engulfing NHS Emergency Departments. The reason A&Es were overwhelmed, a Downing Street source briefed the press, was the failure of GP surgeries to offer proper seven-day services, putting pressure on hospitals across the country. Using the same *modus operandi* they had previously deployed against juniors, Number 10 invited the public to blame GPs for the NHS's ills by insinuating that certain GPs did not put patients first: 'Most GPs do a fantastic job, and have their patients interests firmly at heart,' said the Downing Street source. 'However, it is increasingly clear that a large number of surgeries are not providing proper out of hours care – and that patients are suffering as a result because they are then forced to go to A&E to seek care.'[76] May ordered all GPs to be open seven days a week, from 8 a.m. to 8 p.m., or lose some of their funding.

A predictable flurry of negative headlines followed in which irresponsible GPs who, it was claimed, took three-hour lunch breaks or 'shut up shop' all afternoon were named and shamed for the A&E crisis whose existence May had denied only days earlier.[77] As with the junior doctor dispute, any statistics and evidence that contradicted May's blame narrative were conveniently ignored, not least the fact that the government's previous pilot of seven-day GP services had cost a whopping £45 million pounds yet saved the NHS only £3 million in reduced A&E attendances.[78] Moreover, according to every health expert and think tank, the key driver of the A&E crisis was not GP failings at the front door but the lack of staff, hospital beds and social care at the back, all precipitated by government cuts. Doctors, academics and MPs from all parties, including Sarah Wollaston, the Conservative MP who sits on the Commons Health Select Committee, united in condemning May's attempt to divert attention away from the crisis by scapegoating GPs for lack of seven-day care.

We had come full circle. The potency of the seven-day soundbite for engineering the right kind of headlines had proved once again to be irresistible for Downing Street. No matter that May's rhetoric was deeply offensive and undermining for GPs already facing intolerable workloads. No matter that it was factually misleading. So long as it took the heat off the government, seven-day spin was back, blaming frontline staff for the shortcomings of a health service set up, by underfunding, to fail. The chorus of outrage from GPs everywhere mirrored the fury of junior doctors a year earlier, when Jeremy Hunt had portrayed us as indirectly causing thousands of avoidable deaths at weekends.

Nothing, it seemed, had changed. With the same tired blame narratives being reeled out to deflect attention way from the evidence of an NHS is crisis, the future of the health service looked hopeless.

CHAPTER 16

HOPE

Once, I believed my job could require of me no greater act of callousness than that of taking away a patient's hope. I have observed the faces as other doctors do just that, how they fold and crumple beneath the blow of those words. And I have been that doctor myself, many times. You cannot be cured. You are going to die. He will never wake up. There is nothing more we can do.

Increasingly, though, I am unsure. It is misplaced hope, I suspect, that is the least kind thing we can give a patient. Yet almost as tenacious as hope itself is the doctor's desire not to have to strip it away, to be the bearer of despair and hopelessness, even when we know the time for honesty is now.

Familiar as I am in my working life with both building and destroying the hopes of others, for myself – as perhaps for most of us – hope, like health, was something I largely took for granted. Its absence, however, was crushing. By the summer of 2016, there was so much I had lost faith in. My capacity to continue as the doctor I wished to be, the ability of the NHS to keep safe the patients entrusted to its care, the very survival of a health service so starved of funds and optimism. As my training post came to an end, a sense of hopelessness initially pervaded my newly emptied days.

On my stepping away from the NHS, life was by no means bad. To begin with, escaping the pressures of the hospital felt like liberation. I started to write. The daily rhythm of the writing and the school run, all my newfound time with Dave and the children, were exotic and unfamiliar. The time out – temporary respite from the burden of doing two doctors' jobs or living with the fear that someone, inevitably, was going to slip through the net on my watch – was as restorative as any doctor's prescription. I would stand on the sidelines of a school football match, watching my son and his friends being spattered in mud, feeling as though I could breathe again.

And then, in the space away from the hospital, something happened that was as uplifting as it was unexpected. I could not, it turned out, leave medicine. I missed my patients too much. Just as I had hung on the tales of medicine my father and grandfather told, I found that, whenever I ran into one of my doctor friends, I lived vicariously through their stories from work, relishing every detail. Sure enough, as the weeks went by, I hankered more and more after the hospital. I began to feel as though what mattered to me most, despite lying dormant and defeated, was still alive and capable of renewal. I remained, at heart, a doctor. I wanted to be back there, amid my friends and colleagues but, most of all, surrounded by patients. Hearing on the grapevine about a job in palliative care, the speciality I had been set on pursuing, I decided to apply.

Hospices are often understandably feared, seen as sinister citadels of death and dying behind whose doors lurk our most primal taboos. They are, for many, the embodiment of hopelessness. But, to me, the hospice is often filled with more of what matters in life than almost any other part of the hospital. Families who cherish their loved ones, whose shared grief is a testament to their love and longing. Patients who face what we all, at times, pretend not to know is coming, with such dignity and strength it can floor you. Staff who strive their utmost to give those at the end of their time the best possible life they can live. Humanity, compassion, complicated medicine, simple human touch or time – precious time spent listening and bearing witness. Even in an NHS at the end of its tether, the hospice, still, is a space in which you can be every bit as much of a healer you imagined all doctors to be, but which our overstretched, understaffed hospitals and general practices threaten to strip from the heart of the health service. On learning I had been given the job, it seemed so right, so natural, it felt like returning home.

On my first day back at work as an NHS doctor, the bike ride was a journey back in time. The wind lashed my face but the sky was blue. I freewheeled down the hill into the hospital grounds, as keen and eager as the house officer I had started out as eight years before. No one was more surprised than I was.

Tucked away on the most peaceful part of the site, the hospice sits within immaculate gardens, devotedly tended by volunteers. Inside, there is a calm rarely encountered in the frenetic activity of an acute hospital Trust in action. Artwork, natural light, discreet nooks and crannies containing semi-hidden armchairs, a merciful absence of hospital posters ordering people to wash their hands, eat more fruit, take part in the lunchtime Zumba.

We squeezed into a room slightly too small for purpose, ready to be briefed by the outgoing night team. I took my place among the other doctors, nurses, a child psychiatrist, social workers, occupational therapists, a music therapist, a psychologist and the hospice chaplain. The day's ward list – each patient, their room number and their reason for admission – read like a litany of medical nightmares. Lung cancer, heart failure, breast cancer, sarcoma, motor neurone disease, glioblastoma, bowel cancer, ovarian cancer, end-stage renal failure. But, as we focused in turn upon the needs of each patient, the diseases were scarcely mentioned. What could we do to help Grace feel sufficiently confident to spend a few hours at home with her husband this week? Had the new medications in the syringe driver successfully tackled Bob's pain? Would it be OK for Jim's old jazz band to join him and play in the hospice chapel? Was Simon's daughter less distressed now? Had Anna's wedding dress arrived and were we all aware the wedding was this Saturday? Life, as much as death, was everywhere and our job was to ensure it was the best life possible, no matter how fleeting.

One of the most humane aspects of the hospice are the sofas that double up as beds in each room, enabling a loved one, should they wish, to stay night and day beside a patient who is dying. When I started work, Sarah had already spent forty-eight hours at her husband's side. They had made a pact, she told me, that, when the time was right, Stuart would like to come here, but only if she were there too. In the confines of their room, dimly lit, curtains half drawn, a collection of cards arranged at the bedside, it seemed that their fifty years of marriage – a lifetime entwined – had more weight and substance than Stuart himself, who by now was so diminished by cancer he seemed more spirit than man.

'It's as though I've already said goodbye,' Sarah told me. 'He has one foot here but one foot over there, and, although he knows I'm here, I think in his own mind he has already departed.'

She stroked her husband's sunken cheek, knelt down and kissed his brow. In the lightest touch, the greatest intimacy. Even as life ebbed away, love had never seemed stronger. We had managed, through painstaking management of the drugs in his syringe driver, to successfully keep his symptoms at bay. I withdrew, satisfied both husband and wife were as comfortable as possible, humbled by the tenderness I had witnessed.

Death, of course, can be the farthest thing from peaceful, even in a hospice setting. Theresa, a patient in her forties with ovarian cancer, was tormented by the prospect of no longer being there for her teenage children. Though she worried terribly about the impact of their visiting their mother in a hospice, with her grossly swollen limbs and pain on manoeuvring, the prospect of attempting a visit back home filled her with even greater anxiety. It took coaxing, reassurance and meticulous attention to her symptoms to persuade her that a visit was possible. The whole team – nurses, doctors, occupational therapists – rallied all week to help build her confidence.

'All I want is to lie on my bed with Jasmine like I used to and chat and hold her hand,' said Theresa.

At the end of my first week at work, Theresa attempted her visit. I held her hand and calmed her nerves before she departed, and on her return I went to her room to find out how she had managed. Her face was unrecognisable. The drawn, grey, defeated mask had been replaced by exhausted radiance.

'We lay on the bed together and we chatted, just like we used to,' she said, tears brightening her eyes. 'I didn't think that was possible. I never believed I'd get home again.'

I smiled. How could I not? With the support of the entire team of staff at the hospice, a mother had shared at home with her daughter time she never thought she would have. The overarching frame of her cancer remained every bit as bleak and brutal, but within that we had enabled Theresa to experience more of what mattered than she knew was possible, and her joy at the realisation shone out of her.

$$-\wedge\!\!\wedge-$$

In a parallel universe, the intensely personal care of the hospice would be everywhere in the NHS. Finite resources, of course, preclude that. Nor, in acute or emergency settings, would I wish too many of them to be diverted away from the fundamentals of addressing patients' urgent, life-threatening needs. Nonetheless, it is perfectly clear that, as resources are squeezed ever tighter, compassion, kindness and attention to patients as individuals are being rationed as surely as the cataract surgeries, hip operations and the latest expensive cancer drugs. Staff may continue to remove themselves from brutalising conditions of work – as I did temporarily – or, with their compassion and commitment to the NHS fatally worn down, they may morph into burned-out clock-watchers.

Either way, the health service is compromised, moving a step away from what it should – and still could – be.

Like the other great schisms in British politics in 2016 and 2017 – over Brexit, Nigel Farage, the price of Marmite, the shape of a Toblerone – the National Health Service is one of the great polarising forces of national life. In polls, the NHS consistently tops the list of things that make us most proud to be British, beating our history, the royal family, our system of democracy and our culture and arts. A cradle-to-grave health service, free to all in need, irrespective of their bank balance, clearly chimes with something deep within us, our sense of kinship, perhaps, with our fellow citizens – or a more basic human response to pain and suffering, a primal instinct to look after each other and be kind. Yet, though we love the NHS, we cannot escape the evidence that the health service is increasingly struggling to deliver good care.

In his final piece of writing, produced in the days before his death from inoperable lung cancer, the *Times* newspaper columnist A. A. Gill captured beautifully the strengths, ambitions, paradoxes and failings of our sacred, yet threadbare, NHS:

> It seems unlikely, uncharacteristic, so un-'us' to have settled on sickness and bed rest as the votive altar and cornerstone of national politics. But there it is: every election, the National Health Service is the thermometer and the crutch of governments. The NHS represents everything we think is best about us . . . You can't walk into an NHS hospital and be a racist. That condition is cured instantly . . . You can't be sexist on the NHS, nor patronising, and the care

and the humour, the togetherness ranged against the teetering, chronic system by both the caring and the careworn is the Blitz, 'back against the wall', stern and sentimental best of us — and so we tell lies about it.[79]

The lies, or at least exaggerations – that the NHS is uniquely brilliant, second to none, simply the best in the world – were painfully brought home to Gill when he discovered he was ineligible on the NHS for an expensive, novel cancer drug, which, though unable to cure him, might have given him more time with his loved ones. Had he lived in other European countries, the new agent nivolumab might have been available to him immediately, but in England, he explained, in order to access it without delay, he would have to pay for it himself. In the context of the NHS having such poor outcomes for cancer survival, one can only imagine Gill's distress at being denied, as he saw it, the prospect of precious weeks' and months' more life on the grounds that nivolumab failed to offer the NHS sufficient value for taxpayers' money.

In spite of this, Gill seemed to intuit precisely why so many of us cling so fiercely to the NHS – because of the story it tells us about ourselves. If we did not have the NHS to believe in, then how pinched and diminished might our collective self-image become? We want to convince ourselves we are decent, humane and generous, a society of individuals ever willing to reach out towards each other. But, if we are unwilling to pay sufficient tax for a system that ensures everyone receives the medical care they need, regardless of their ability to pay, then where does that leave us? Forced to confront the fact that we are too mean, ultimately, to fund the NHS's future?

This is highly charged, emotive stuff. NHS detractors often dismiss these sentiments as nothing more than obfuscatory fluff. For them, the cold, hard, unpalatable truth is that the NHS is a monolithic dinosaur, a clunky, plodding relic of old that underperforms, overspends and should, by rights, have been extinct long ago were it not for the mawkishness of those who ignore the benefits of the free market's invisible hand. As political strategist John McTernan claims, writing for the right-wing think tank the Institute of Economic Affairs,

> Facts and arguments don't matter when it comes to the NHS – only emotion and sentiment register. Commentators often talk about us living in a 'post-fact' world. If that is so the NHS led the way – debate about its future has been conducted in post-factual terms for quite some time.[80]

This, of course, is a glib overstatement. It is perfectly possible to believe passionately in the political principles underpinning the NHS, while taking a cool, level-headed look at the evidence for how well and cost-effectively our health service is performing. Indeed, it would be odd for doctors, steeped as we are from university onwards in the science of practising evidence-based medicine, to exclude from our efforts a rational appraisal the overall efficacy of the NHS. Politically, I may cherish an equitable, income-tax-funded health service but, as a doctor, I want the best for my patients, so the NHS had better deliver.

Undeniably, some of the international data make grim reading. They show the NHS lagging behind other European and Western countries on many important performance indicators, with cancer being a striking example. For example, mortality data compiled by the OECD show the UK languishing in the bottom third of the thirty-five OECD countries for five-year survival for colorectal, breast and cervical cancer.[81]

Is this any surprise, however, given how little of our gross domestic product we choose to spend on health? At the time of writing – and despite Britain being the world's sixth richest economy – the most recent OECD data show that in 2013 (the latest year for which full figures have been published) the UK spent only 8.5 per cent of its GDP on healthcare, placing the UK thirteenth out of the original fifteen countries of the EU.[82] The EU average spend was 10.1 per cent of GDP. For health economists such as John Appleby, the chief economist of the independent health think tank the Nuffield Trust, the key question, therefore:

> is increasingly not so much whether it is sustainable to spend more – after all, many countries already manage that and have done for decades. Rather, it is whether it is sustainable for our spending to remain so comparatively low, given the improvements in the quality of care and outcomes we want and expect from our health services.[83]

To put it another way, do we wish to cut NHS services to fit the current budget, or to provide the budget to fit the healthcare we want? Money, of course, is not the whole story. The NHS can still at times be infuriatingly lumbering. But, while there are, no doubt, ingenious ways of driving up NHS efficiency, merely shrinking the workforce and rationing the care the NHS provides is the opposite of clever. Less is not the new more. Shoestring budgets are not the route to international excellence. In health politics, just as in medicine, there is no place for false hope, disingenuousness or wishful thinking.

Transparency, if it means anything at all within the NHS, begins with candour about the costs of a world-class health service. If we want the best, we cannot avoid paying for it. Yet politicians' fear of conducting this debate openly with the public ensures the continued denial, for political ends, of the facts about the crumbling state of the health service the government professes to cherish.

—∿—

Discovering I was unable to walk away from caring for patients stirred in me a renewed sense of optimism. It suggested there was something stubborn and tenacious keeping the NHS afloat. At work, I see this everywhere. My nursing and doctor colleagues may be harried and exhausted but, for so many of them, as for me, the rewards of caring for others still outstrip the costs. And we cling, I suppose, to the glimmer of hope that one day things will change – a political sea change towards the NHS, new investment into services in terminal decline, another doctor or nurse on the rota.

The swiftest way to snuff out that hope is to deny the existence of the problems. This, at root, is the most corrosive consequence of the government's weakness for spin because it takes away from NHS staff our right to speak, to be heard, to be believed, to have a voice. If no one listens when you try to say that patients are imperilled, if no one believes you when you say the NHS is at breaking point, if you are smeared and undermined by the government for trying to speak out, then in the end you cannot be blamed for hanging your head in mute despair. You have successfully been silenced.

Junior doctors screamed for a year about the dangers of overstretch and understaffing – and the misery of the 2016-17 winter crisis confirmed much of what we warned about – yet the Department of Health continues to maintain its elastic approach to evidence. You might therefore conclude, as I did temporarily, that junior doctors achieved nothing – our efforts were futile – and indeed that in today's 'post-truth' era I am naïve to hope for more. After all, 2016 was the year in which a Cabinet minister claimed that the British people had 'had enough of experts' and, across the Atlantic, a proven serial liar went on to win the US presidential election. Facts and expertise have never looked more vulnerable.

For me, the lowest point in the junior doctor dispute came when, after a year of deploying contentious mortality statistics with devastating aplomb, Jeremy Hunt used his speech at the 2016 Conservative Party autumn conference to utter the extraordinary statement, 'I say to the BMA and all junior doctors let's not argue about statistics.'[84] In almost the same breath, he used statistics – again contentiously – to add rhetorical ballast to his seven-day NHS policy. This time, he implied that weekend care was inadequate by claiming that, 'when we checked', only in one in ten hospitals were patients being reviewed by a consultant within fourteen hours of being admitted. In fact, independent statisticians had shown that at least 80 per cent of patients are reviewed within that timeframe.[85] It was another statistical sleight of hand.

Statistics – facts – are the bedrock of good medicine.

Doctors are scientists, not quacks, and health policy should be as evidence-based as our practice. It takes a special kind of chutzpah both to misuse statistics and to tell doctors to stop arguing about statistics all in the same twenty-minute speech. What could be more 'alt-fact' than that? Particularly when you have just positioned yourself – again – as the champion of NHS candour, avowing, as Hunt did in the very same speech, that patients 'want to know that in our democracy no citizen will ever be rendered voiceless or powerless by a mighty state or a mighty bureaucracy, even one as loved as the NHS'.[84]

Throughout the year of bitter wrangling, if ever a phrase captured how junior doctors felt, it is that we were 'rendered voiceless or powerless' by the government. And, as patients and their families learned the hard way from Mid Staffs, when concerns are ignored for long enough, staff in the end give up trying to raise them. Their silence does not mean things are better, but that fatalistic resignation has taken root.

Yet it does not have to be this way. Giving up is a choice. As the American author and activist Rebecca Solnit writes:

> Your opponents would love you to believe that it's hopeless, that you have no power, that there's no reason to act, that you can't win. Hope is a gift you don't have to surrender, a power you don't have to throw away. And though hope can be an act of defiance, defiance isn't enough reason to hope. But there are good reasons.[86]

Perhaps the best reason for maintaining hope is that, though Hunt achieved his desired 'win' over junior doctors, he inadvertently gave us both a voice and the confidence to use it. There is a pleasing irony to the fact that, for all the attempts to paint junior doctors as BMA-duped 'militants', no single individual has done more to inspire confidence, determination and the will to speak out among junior doctors than Jeremy Hunt himself.

Nor has anyone united so successfully a previously disparate bunch of doctors into one cohesive whole, 54,000 juniors with a shared sense of identity and a newfound taste for disruptive candour. We are, after all, our patients' advocates every day at work – now we have extended that sense of advocacy into the political sphere, pushed by the disingenuousness of the current government's stance towards facts and evidence in the NHS.

Once so subservient, heads tucked below the parapet, my generation of doctors has learned the hard way how to speak out and be heard. We are certainly not going to stop now. Whether the government likes it or not, there will be continued transparency and the facts will out, if not from the Department of Health or the powerbrokers of the medical establishment then from the grassroots up.

—∿—

'Rach! Can you believe it? Can you believe what's happened to Sally? It's a miracle!'

It was 8 a.m. I'd arrived early for my Sunday morning shift in the cancer centre, hoping quietly to nurse a double-strength latte while preparing for the morning ward round. Being immediately accosted by a nurse on arrival was far from usual, but then Sally Morley was no ordinary patient.

'What? What's happened?' I asked, immediately concerned. 'Is Sally OK?'

'OK?' the nurse laughed. 'I told you, it's a miracle. Just go and see for yourself.'

Some two months earlier, my first ever week as a junior doctor in the cancer centre, Sally had been the ward's success story. A vivacious former care-home worker in her early sixties, she had been diagnosed with a particularly virulent form of leukaemia upon which standard chemotherapy had not landed a blow. Her last chance was a bone marrow transplant that had involved gruelling arsenals of drugs. The transplant had gone exceptionally well. She had weathered the side effects of her chemotherapy with remarkable robustness and unflagging good humour, and her donor bone marrow had engrafted beautifully. With normal blood counts that now showed no trace of leukaemia, she was poised at last to leave the hospital and renew life at home with her devoted husband.

Ron had barely left her side throughout her six-week stay in the cancer centre. When the drugs left her skin intolerably dry and itchy, he tenderly rubbed rose-scented lotion into her limbs to sooth them. When chemo put her off eating, he delivered lemon sorbet to her bedside, the only food she could contemplate. 'Why can't I meet a Ron?' lamented the single nurses. 'Why do I never date the good guys?'

On the Tuesday, I had carefully written her discharge summary, packed with information for her general practitioner. She had been set to go home the next day. But, on the Wednesday morning ward round, something had changed. Sally, ordinarily so irreverent and full of cheek, was subdued, almost vacant, when we arrived at her bedside. Nothing too alarming, only subtle alterations, but the Sally of old was not quite there. Blood tests revealed possible causes.

Her sodium was too low; her heart rate, in addition, was far too high, rattling along at an inexplicably ferocious pace. By the Thursday, her deterioration was striking. She smiled only half-heartedly in response to our questions, unable even to vocalise a response. Worse, she seemed distressed at her confusion, picking in agitation at her hospital bedsheets, clawing at the cannula in her arm.

'What's happened?' Ron begged my consultant. 'What's gone wrong? Why is she like this?'

The truth was, none of us knew.

'Sally!' he would say, gripping her hands. 'Sally, it's me, Ron. It's Ron, your husband. Sally, are you there?'

She would turn blankly towards the sound of her husband's pleas, gently touching his cheek with the back of her hand as though driven by innate compassion for her fellow man, despite no recognition of this one. Too often the effort would cause her to lapse into a twilight state of befuddled doziness, lost in a world of her own. Ron's anguish was terrible to witness.

Weeks passed. Despite the endless bloods, brain scans and lumbar punctures, no cause of her decline could be found. Nevertheless, Ron insisted Sally would recover. 'She's a fighter,' he would tell me. 'I know she's there, and she's going to beat this.' Gently at first, we tried to counsel caution, instil the idea that, with no diagnosis and no improvement in her function, the chances of recovery were slowly ebbing away. Ron would not hear a word of it. 'Sally's going to get better,' he repeated, sitting doggedly at her bedside.

Eventually, one day, we made a diagnosis. The drops of cerebrospinal fluid I had eked from her spine in yet another painful diagnostic lumbar puncture were packed with a virus known as HHV-6. Ordinarily a mild and self-limiting infection, HHV-6 tends to colonise us all in early childhood, without our even noticing. Typically, it then lies dormant in the bloodstream, silently accompanying us into adulthood. But later in life, should someone require strong immunosuppression such as the chemotherapy drugs we had given Sally, the virus can sometimes reactivate, running rampant through the brain and occasionally causing severe disability or even death.

We treated Sally with the most aggressive antiviral drugs on the market, but all, apparently, to no avail. If anything, she continued to deteriorate, lurching between distressed, vacant and virtually comatose, sometimes all in the space of a day. The Sally we had come to love sank further and further away from us, leaving behind a husband who continued to dote upon her smallest need while refusing to mourn the loss of the wife who seemed submerged for ever.

'There's a chance she'll get better, isn't there, Rachel?' Ron would ask me, eyes wide and beseeching. I ached to keep his hope alive, to give him reasons to believe, but in truth the wisest consultants in my team were by now profoundly pessimistic. 'The longer she stays like this, the more likely the brain damage is permanent,' my boss had said in the early days. Now we were many weeks down the line and none of us believed Sally would recover. Hope existed only in Ron, and even in him it was rapidly dwindling.

Then, early in the morning of my Sunday on-call shift, everything changed. When a healthcare assistant had arrived to check the patients' observations, Sally had asked her with perfect lucidity what day of the week it was. Astonished, the nurses rushed straight to Sally's bedside. She dumbfounded them all by asking, quite clearly, for breakfast. They hastily called Ron at home and urged him to come straight to the hospital.

And so it was that when I entered Sally's room some hours later, feeling giddy myself with hope and intrigue, this quiet, unassuming, devoted husband almost fell into my arms, beaming and crying and scarcely making sense of the miracle of his wife being back.

'Oh, Ron,' chided his wife affectionately. 'You are a silly one, aren't you? Pull yourself together.'

'Hello, Sally,' I said, smiling incredulously. 'How are you feeling this morning?'

'Well, *I'm* all right,' she said. 'I just don't know what's wrong with this husband of mine.' The virus had obliterated several months of memory. She had no recollection of being in hospital or even of receiving a diagnosis of leukaemia, but Sally the person was intact.

None of us could explain it. Medicine drew a blank. Every once in a while, a patient confounds all their doctors' worst fears while fulfilling their loved ones' greatest hopes. 'It was like someone had switched on a light switch,' Ron said to me later, still shaking his head in disbelief. '*Flick* and there she was again. It's a miracle, just a miracle.'

—∿—

Early on at medical school, I was taught to take a sceptical attitude towards misplaced certainty. 'Never' and 'always' are two words that doctors use at their peril. Exceptions, I swiftly learned, are everywhere, with patients and their diseases rarely conforming to the textbook descriptions I committed so carefully to memory. Yet, in the muddy, uncertain, imperfect, unpredictable world of my hospital, its activity revolves around certain fixed axes.

Pivotal to our health service are the instincts driving its staff. By and large, most of my colleagues have been propelled towards the NHS by a keenness to improve the lives of those of us unlucky enough to experience sickness. We try our best to help our patients through their journeys with illness, even if sometimes we do not get it right. Our primary motivation is helping others, not our own enrichment. Our patients inspire us every day. We have the privilege of routinely observing in those patients and their families more of what is good in people – strength, dignity, love, compassion – than I ever fully appreciated before becoming a doctor. We bear witness to the best and the worst of life, the cruellest blows, the unlikeliest recoveries. We do our bit to assist, if we possibly can. And there is always, even when medicine is exhausted, our touch or voice or smile. It can hurt. It can thrill. It can take your breath away. Painful, bittersweet, overwhelming, magnificent medicine. For me, no other job could come close.

EPILOGUE

Shortly after my temporary departure from medicine, my father rang me one afternoon as I set out on the school run. He had just been told he had cancer. The nasty, aggressive sort. The news you hope never to have to break to your patients. The air felt punched from my lungs and my hands began to tremble. I pulled over. As we talked data, statistics, doctor to doctor, I was dimly aware of the daughter, the father, hovering on the outskirts of our brief, professional, calm conversation. They remained there, disconnected, but afterwards, on the roadside, phone flung in the footwell, like anyone who learns the life of someone they love is in jeopardy, I crouched over the steering wheel in tears, unable to move for the force of the refrain, 'Don't die. Don't die. Dad, don't have cancer. Please don't die.'

For years I have looked after patients with cancer. Spent innumerable hours talking with them and their families, believing I had sufficient insight and empathy to understand the cataclysm through which they were living. As so often, it turns out I was wrong. Until it is felt, I am not sure cancer is truly understood, even by the most seasoned oncologist. The world of scans, procedures, surgeries, chemotherapies is saturated with more hope and fear than I ever knew possible, even after years of medicine. Every nuance of every conversation with the doctors is scrutinised feverishly – the exhausting, endless vigilance. You try logic, research, blind faith, cold reason, every mental power you possess to stave off the worst-case scenarios. You ache with longing to take away the diagnosis, to protect your dad from the hand fate has dealt him. Your medical degree is bloody useless.

Throughout it all, this impotence and anguish as your loved one submits to the indignities of major illness, there has been one overwhelming positive. Thank God, I have thought, so many times over, thank God we do not have to worry about how we will ever pay for Dad's treatment. No demands for his credit card on arrival in hospital, no bills for eye-watering sums landing later on the doormat, no agonising over whether to remortgage the house to fund the next round of chemo.

That I live in a country that chooses, through our taxes, to provide healthcare without charge to those in need has never made me more proud or grateful. And the thanks and tubs of chocolates my family shower effusively on the staff dispensing the toxic treatments, compassion and kindness to my dad should really be flung wide. For right now, in a sense, like that of every NHS patient, his life is in the hands not of one doctor but of the nation – all of us who pay the taxes without which the NHS would crumble. His oncologists, his nurses, his hospital bed, it is ultimately thanks to the British people that they exist at all.

Reading headlines about the latest winter crisis in the NHS – patients dying in hospital corridors, life-saving cancer operations being cancelled – is not easy when someone you love requires hospital treatment. What if Dad takes ill? What if there are no beds? How will we make sure he is safe, not abandoned on a trolley for hours on end? But the hardest thing for me – both as a doctor and as a daughter – has been the Prime Minister's denial of the problems.

For the stark truth, one of which she simply cannot be unaware, is that after six years of shrinking the share of GDP it spends on health, the government's shoestring has snapped. The NHS no longer has the funds to keep up with rising demand. Hospitals have run out of beds. GPs are rationing appointments. There are not enough nurses. There are not enough doctors. Babies with suspected meningitis are lying on makeshift beds on plastic chairs in A&E. The NHS is falling apart before our eyes and staff are screaming that patients are unsafe. Another Mid Staffs – the scandal David Cameron vowed would never be repeated – is not looming: it is already here. Yet the government is choosing to turn a blind eye.

As winter unfurled into spring, the NHS crisis only deepened. In late March, the CEO of NHS England, Simon Stevens, announced the grim news that, in order to try to balance the books, he was effectively dumping the commitment – enshrined in the NHS constitution no less – to treat at least 92 per cent of patients in England needing non-urgent surgery within eighteen weeks.[87] The move was necessary, he claimed, so that hospitals could concentrate on more urgent priorities such as A&E overstretch and improved cancer care. But the ten-year-old 92 per cent target had been introduced to prevent the misery of patients enduring agonising waits for seemingly humdrum yet potentially life-transforming operations such as hip and knee replacements and cataract surgeries. Its abandonment spelled potential misery for tens of thousands of patients, particularly the elderly.

Barely weeks after Stevens's announcement, news broke that areas of London were banning cataract surgery in all but 'exceptional' circumstances.[88] The Royal National Institute of Blind People (RNIB) immediately condemned the move, with Fazilet Hadi, director of engagement at RNIB, stating, 'All patients should be given access to cataract treatment without delay and based on their clinical need. When a cataract begins to affect a person's sight their vision will continue to deteriorate until it's removed. Patients with severe cataracts are at risk of social isolation, depression and fall-related injuries such as hip fractures.'

I thought once more of my father, whose own cataract operations a few years earlier had turned a bleak future of disablement and blindness into one of radiant Technicolor. The simplest, speediest surgeries. The most radical, life-affirming results. Were we really willing to condemn our elderly to a fate of entirely avoidable blindness, I asked myself, unless they were rich enough to pay?

The NHS is not perfect and could undoubtedly benefit from innovation and reform. Money is not everything. But, unless it is adequately funded, our health service is clearly destined to fail. And, if that happens, presumably the NHS would be replaced or augmented by a non-tax-funded, privately delivered alternative. That might, I suppose, be what the public want (though the polls uniformly say otherwise) but at the moment we are not being given the unspun facts and information upon which to make an informed opinion. It is Theresa May's right as Prime Minister to decide that the country cannot afford the additional public spending required to maintain our current standards of healthcare. But, if she does, she owes it to the public to be honest about the reduced level of healthcare we can expect from now on – to come clean on what the NHS will no longer provide – and face the political consequences of doing so.

In the end, I fear that the greatest threat to the longevity of the NHS may not be the current incumbent in Downing Street but, paradoxically, one of the things that make all of us so resilient: the boundless capacity of the human spirit to live life in denial of suffering and death. Cancer, heart attacks, car crashes, brain damage – we know the bolts from the blue are out there, we just never believe it is us they will strike. Perhaps it is only when you or your family are smitten that you fully appreciate – with relief and gratitude – that the NHS is there, ready and waiting to scoop up your loved one and put them back together again, without a punitive bill attached.

But, as a hospital doctor, I see lives ripped apart by illness every day. Catastrophes are my daily bread. It could be me, my children, or you tomorrow. Yet, if it is, the NHS will be there, holding, helping, comforting, soothing. For me, there is nothing in Britain that better represents the decency, humanity and generosity of spirit of the country to which I belong. The patient whose status gives me the greatest concern today is the NHS itself, and ultimately its fate rests not in my hands but in yours.

ACKNOWLEDGEMENTS

I never believed I could really write a book until receiving a tweet, of all things, from Lauren Gardner at Bell Lomax Moreton, from which this book began. Thank you so much, Lauren, for being the most supportive, encouraging and inspiring agent a new author could ever hope for. You have expertly guided me every step of the way, and it was your faith in me that made me believe in myself.

Huge thanks to James Hodgkinson, my fantastic editor at John Blake Books, who was willing to take a risk with a junior doctor activist, and whose unwavering belief in the importance of the book kept me going. All your wise observations on the writing (not to mention your emergency GIFs, when required!) helped me no end. Thanks too to Emma Stokes at John Blake, and Lizzie Dorney-Kingdom, September Withers and everyone else at Bonnier Publishing for your help and expertise.

Thanks to Taryn Youngstein, Denis Campbell, Tim Littlewood, John Reynolds, David Oliver, Jane Grundy and Rebecca Inglis for your incredibly helpful comments on the manuscript. I really appreciated you taking the time to read it and help shape its finished form.

The government's dispute with junior doctors galvanised not only us juniors but also our consultant, GP, nursing and other NHS colleagues. Thank you so much to all those NHS staff who stood by us. It meant so much to us that you showed us solidarity. Thank you, Johann Malawana, for bringing juniors together, inspiring us to take a stand. Thanks to Neena Modi, Jane Dacre, Simon Wessely, Taj Hassan, Philippa Whitford, Partha Kar, Stella Vig, Rob Galloway, Trish Greenhalgh and Alistair Hall for your particular support of juniors. Phil Hammond, you were so kind and supportive throughout. Most of all, thanks to all those members of the public who backed us in person, in the media and out on the picket lines. It wasn't easy reading anti-doctor spin most weeks in the press – and your support genuinely helped us keep going.

One of the great positives of what was, at root, a profoundly demoralising and destructive dispute was forming new and enduring friendships with so many other impromptu junior doctor activists. Marie, Nadia M, Ben W, Amar and Fran – the five indefatigable junior doctors who organised the most successful crowd-funded case in UK legal history, taking on Jeremy Hunt in the High Court – and Paola, Lolly, Amrita, Ruhe, Aislinn, Azra, Mei, Reena, Aoife, Ben D, Nadia R, Matteo, Roshana, Zoe, Hoong-Wei, Jeeves and Matt: it has been my privilege to campaign with you and come to call you friends. In particular, Taryn and Dagan, the intelligence, passion and commitment with which you fought for what you believed in has been a constant source of inspiration. Dagan, special thanks for those two memorable nights we shared – on the Department of Health's doorstep.

Huge thanks to my Mum, an NHS nurse and health visitor, and my Dad, an NHS doctor, who raised me to believe that working hard, trying your best, being kind and looking out for others were the things that really mattered. Every day, I see your qualities writ large across the NHS – they are both commonplace and priceless. Dad, I have always tried to emulate the doctor you were to your patients – I hope I've managed to come close.

Finn and Abbey, I am sorry your mum spent two years so distracted by something as baffling and dull as domestic politics. One day, I like to believe you too will stand up for what you believe is right, but for now, my sincere apologies.

Above all, Dave, my heartfelt thanks. Your love, support, patience and encouragement have meant so much to me, every step of the way. Thank you for always believing in me.

REFERENCES

1 *Health at a Glance 2015*. OECD, 2015 (Paris: OECD
Publishing), available at http://dx.doi.org/10.1787/health_glance-
2015-en.

2 'Making healthcare more human-centred and not system-
centred', Jeremy Hunt, 16.07.15, available at https://www.gov.uk/
government/speeches/making-healthcare-more-human-centred-and-
not-system-centred.

3 'Jeremy Hunt: "We have 6,000 avoidable deaths every year"',
BBC News, 16.07.15, available at http://www.bbc.co.uk/news/
health-33546800

4 '"I'm in work Jeremy... are you?": Angry doctors take to
Twitter to post pictures of themselves on duty after Jeremy
Hunt claimed medics weren't doing enough weekend shifts',
Lydia Willgress, Mail Online, 18.07.15, available at http://www.
dailymail.co.uk/news/article-3166330/ImInWorkJeremy-Doctors-
Twitter-post-pictures-work-Jeremy-Hunt-claimed-medics-weren-
t-doing-weekend-shifts.html#ixzz4f5I8KrEG.

5 Jeremy Hunt, Twitter account, 18.05.15, available at https://twitter.com/jeremy_hunt/status/622398974478155776

6 Lauren Nicole Jones, Twitter account, 18.07.15, available at https://twitter.com/Lauren_SLT/status/622402426843340800?ref_src=twsrc%5Etfw&ref_url=https%3A%2F%2Fwww.theguardian.com%2Fpolitics%2F2015%2Fjul%2F18%2Fjeremy-hunt-provokes-anger-on-twitter-for-breaking-patient-confidentiality.

7 'These four words that may offend you… may also just save you', Louis Profeta, Linkedin, 01.11.16, available at https://www.linkedin.com/pulse/those-four-words-may-offend-you-also-just-save-louis-m-profeta-md.

8 Press statement. Robert Francis, The Mid Staffordshire NHS Foundation Trust Public Inquiry, 06.02.13, available at http://webarchive.nationalarchives.gov.uk/20150407084003/http://www.midstaffspublicinquiry.com/sites/default/files/report/Chairman%27s%20statement.pdf.

9 'Independent Inquiry into care provided by Mid Staffordshire NHS Foundation Trust, January 2005 – March 2009, Volume I', The Mid Staffordshire NHS Foundation Trust Public Inquiry, 24.02.10, available at http://webarchive.nationalarchives.gov.uk/20150407084003/http://www.midstaffspublicinquiry.com/sites/default/files/First_Inquiry_report_volume_1_0.pdf

10 'Report of the Mid Staffordshire NHS Foundation Trust Public Inquiry. Executive Summary', Sir Robert Francis, The Mid Staffordshire NHS Foundation Trust Public Inquiry, 05.02.13, available at http://webarchive.nationalarchives.gov.uk/20150407084003/http://www.midstaffspublicinquiry.com/sites/default/files/report/Executive%20summary.pdf.

REFERENCES

11 'Thousands of NHS nursing and doctor posts lie vacant', Dominic Hughes and Vanessa Clarke, BBC News, 29.02.16, available at http://www.bbc.co.uk/news/health-35667939

12 'Rapid Response Re: Government's own documents question "seven day NHS" feasibility', Tom Hines and Rachel Clarke, *British Medical Journal*, 24.08.16, available at http://www.bmj.com/rapid-responses?sort_by=field_highwire_a_epubdate_value_1&sort_order=ASC&items_per_page=5&page=21697

13 'Almost half of junior doctors reject NHS career after foundation training', Denis Campbell, *The Guardian*, 05.12.15, available at https://www.theguardian.com/society/2015/dec/04/almost-half-of-junior-doctors-left-nhs-after-foundation-training.

14 'Shocking letter reveals the stress of being a midwife', Paddy Shennan, *The Liverpool Echo*, 22.10.16, available at http://www.liverpoolecho.co.uk/news/health/shocking-letter-reveals-stress-being-12062284.

15 'NHS hospitals now so overwhelmed patients could die, says top doctor', Denis Campbell, *The Guardian*, 10.03.16, available at https://www.theguardian.com/society/2016/mar/10/nhs-hospitals-overwhelmed-patients-could-die-top-doctor.

16 'Hard Truths. The Journey to Putting Patients First. Volume One of the Government Response to the Mid Staffordshire NHS Foundation Trust Public Inquiry', Department of Health, January 2014, available at https://www.gov.uk/government/uploads/system/uploads/attachment_data/file/270368/34658_Cm_8777_Vol_1_accessible.pdf

17 'Five Year Forward View', Department of Health, October 2014, available at https://www.england.nhs.uk/wp-content/uploads/2014/10/5yfv-web.pdf.

18 'Jeremy Hunt: Junior doctors have been misled by the BMA', Jeremy Hunt, *The Telegraph*, 31.10.15, available at http://www.telegraph.co.uk/news/health/11968014/Jeremy-Hunt-Junior-doctors-have-been-misled-by-the-BMA.html.

19 'Jeremy Hunt angers junior doctors by saying some are paid "danger money"', Rowena Mason, *The Guardian*, 30.10.15, available at https://www.theguardian.com/society/2015/oct/30/jeremy-hunt-angers-junior-doctors-by-saying-some-are-paid-danger-money.

20 'Moderate doctors must defeat the militants', Daniel Finkelstein, *The Times*, 11.11.15, available (behind paywall) at http://www.thetimes.co.uk/tto/opinion/columnists/article4610596.ece.

21 'Jeremy Hunt offers junior doctors pay rise in bid to end dispute', Denis Campbell, *The Guardian*, 03.11.15, available at https://www.theguardian.com/society/2015/nov/03/jeremy-hunt-offer-junior-doctors-pay-rise.

22 'The Conservative Party Manifesto 2015', p. 38, March 2015, available at https://www.conservatives.com/manifesto.

23 'Nuffield Trust responds to "seven-day NHS"', Nigel Edwards, The Nuffield Trust, 28.03.15, available at http://www.nuffieldtrust.org.uk/media-centre/press-releases/nuffield-trust-responds-seven-day-nhs.

REFERENCES

24 'No coherent attempt to assess headcount implications of 7-day NHS', Public Accounts Committee, 11.05.16, available at https://www.parliament.uk/business/committees/committees-a-z/commons-select/public-accounts-committee/news-parliament-2015/nhs-staff-numbers-report-published-15-16/.

25 'The tragic naivety of immature junior doctors and their strike', James Kirkup, *The Telegraph*, 25.04.16, available at http://www.telegraph.co.uk/news/2016/04/25/the-tragic-naivety-of-immature-junior-doctors-and-their-strike/.

26 'Junior doctors are making a critical mistake', Hugo Rifkind, *The Times*, 26.04.17, available (behind paywall) at http://www.thetimes.co.uk/article/junior-doctors-are-making-a-critical-mistake-grp3cv9zl.

27 'BMA has marched doctors into a dead end', Daniel Finkelstein, *The Times*, 07.09.16, available (behind paywall) at http://www.thetimes.co.uk/edition/comment/incompetent-bma-has-led-doctors-astray-wjlhnstcq.

28 'Women Surgeon Statistics', The Royal College of Surgeons, available at https://www.rcseng.ac.uk/careers-in-surgery/women-in-surgery/mission-and-goals/women-surgeon-statistics/.

29 'The one sex change available on the NHS that nobody has been talking about', Dominic Lawson, *The Sunday Times*, 17.01.17, available (behind paywall) at http://www.thesundaytimes.co.uk/sto/comment/columns/dominiclawson/article1656813.ece.

30 'Always #LikeAGirl'. Always, 26.06.14, available at https://www.youtube.com/watch?v=XjJQBjWYDTs

31 'Like a lady doc', British Medical Association, January 2016, available at https://storify.com/TheBMA/like-a-lady-doc

32 'Junior doctors hit out at column blaming the feminisation of NHS for causing out of hours crisis', Caroline Mortimer, *The Independent*, 18.01.16, available at https://www.independent.co.uk/life-style/health-and-families/health-news/junior-doctors-hit-out-at-column-blaming-the-feminisation-of-nhs-for-causing-out-of-hours-crisis-a6817991.html.

33 Dagan Lonsdale, Twitter account, 17.01.16, available at https://twitter.com/daganlonsdale/status/688863469874077696.

34 'Prime Minister: My one nation government will close the gender pay gap', Press release, Prime Minister's Office, Number 10 Downing Street, 14.07.15, available at https://www.gov.uk/government/news/prime-minister-my-one-nation-government-will-close-the-gender-pay-gap.

35 'Junior doctors' contract causes outrage as official report highlights "indirect adverse effect on women"', Serina Sandhu, *The Independent*, 01.01.16, available at http://www.independent.co.uk/news/uk/home-news/junior-doctors-contract-causes-outrage-as-official-report-highlights-indirect-adverse-effect-on-a6963146.html.

36 'RCS & RCP joint statement on publication of junior doctors' contract and equality analysis', The Royal College of Surgeons, 01.01.16, available at https://www.rcseng.ac.uk/news-and-events/media-centre/press-releases/rcs-and-rcp-joint-statement-on-publication-of-junior-doctors-contract/

REFERENCES

37 'Chair's Update', Maureen Baker, The Royal College of
General Practitioners, April 2016, available at
http://e.rcgp.org.uk/linkapp/cmaview.
aspx?LinkID=pageid100264520znfrz-njrffjjt-xnrft-nqnrx9-z-x-f-f-n

38 'Junior doctors outraged over new contract that "discriminates
against single women"', Charlie Cooper, *The Independent*,
01.01.16, available at http://www.independent.co.uk/news/
uk/politics/junior-doctors-outraged-over-new-contract-that-
discriminates-against-single-women-a6963356.html.

39 'Jeremy Hunt's junior doctors' contract will "contradict UN
women's rights", says WHO director', Alexandra Sims, *The
Independent*, 03.01.16, available at http://www.independent.co.uk/
news/uk/politics/jeremy-hunt-s-junior-doctors-contract-will-
contradict-the-un-status-of-women-says-who-director-a6966756.
html

40 'Doctors need "emotional resilience" training like soldiers in
Afghanistan', Laura Donnelly, *The Telegraph*, 29.08.15, available
at http://www.telegraph.co.uk/news/health/news/11787678/
Doctors-need-emotional-resilience-training-like-soldiers-in-
Afghanistan.html.

41 'NHS staff health & wellbeing: CQUIN supplementary
guidance', NHS England, 2016, available at www.england.nhs.uk/
wp-content/uploads/2016/03/HWB-CQUIN-Guidance.pdf .

42 '£5million plan to improve the health of NHS staff', NHS
England, 02.09.15, available at www.england.nhs.uk/2015/09/
improving-staff-health/

43 'The night shift in A&E: a hellish blur where my best is never enough', Anonymous junior doctor, *The Guardian*, 20.10.16, available at https://www.theguardian.com/healthcare-network/2016/oct/20/night-shift-ae-hellish-hospital-beds-patients.

44 *Is Tomorrow Hitler's? 200 Questions on the Battle of Mankind*, H. R. Knickerbocker, 1941 (New York: Reynal & Hitchcock), p. 96.

45 'In memory of Rose who we miss every day', Heather Polge, JustGiving, available at https://www.justgiving.com/fundraising/HeatherPolge.

46 'Christmas No1 campaign for NHS choir wins nearly 100,000 fans in a week in rebuke to Jeremy Hunt', Dan Bloom, *The Mirror*, 27.10.16, available at http://www.mirror.co.uk/news/uk-news/christmas-no1-campaign-nhs-choir-6715925.

47 'NHS choir: "I want to show how proud I am of the health service by getting our song to No 1"', Sarah Johnson, *The Guardian*, 23.12.15, available at https://www.theguardian.com/healthcare-network/2015/dec/23/nhs-choir-no-1-bridge-over-you.

48 'Justin Bieber backs NHS Choir for Christmas number one.' BBC News, 23.12.15, available at http://www.bbc.co.uk/newsbeat/article/35167996/justin-bieber-backs-nhs-choir-for-christmas-number-one.

49 'Jeremy Hunt pressures junior doctors to end strike', Nicholas Watt and Denis Campbell, *The Guardian*, 12.01.16, available at https://www.theguardian.com/society/2016/jan/12/jeremy-hunt-pressures-junior-doctors-to-end-strike.

REFERENCES

50 "Video shows moment Jeremy Hunt refuses to talk to junior doctor outraged at new contract', Adam Withnall, *The Independent*, 11.02.16, available at http://www.independent.co.uk/news/uk/politics/jeremy-hunt-literally-ignores-the-concerns-of-a-junior-doctor-confronting-him-in-westminster-a6867381.html.

51 "'I made Jeremy Hunt look like a rogue trader", says TV ambush doctor', Ross Lydall, *The Evening Standard*, 12.02.16, available at http://www.standard.co.uk/news/health/i-made-jeremy-hunt-look-like-a-rogue-trader-says-tv-ambush-doctor-a3179146.html.

52 'Jeremy Hunt squirms as Andrew Marr reads letters from junior doctors', Adam Withnall, *The Independent*, 07.02.16, available at http://www.independent.co.uk/life-style/health-and-families/health-news/jeremy-hunt-squirms-as-andrew-marr-reads-out-letters-from-junior-doctors-a6858921.html.

53 'Jeremy Hunt called "a liar and manipulator" by junior doctor Rachel Clarke during live BBC interview', Chris York, The Huffington Post UK, 08.02.16, available at http://www.huffingtonpost.co.uk/2016/02/08/jeremy-hunt-junior-doctor_n_9185024.html.

54 'Junior doctors' Facebook and Twitter campaigns "were partly to blame for talks on a new contracts breaking down", according to Government negotiator', James Dunn, *Daily Mail*, 13.02.16, available at http://www.dailymail.co.uk/news/article-3445458/Junior-doctors-Facebook-Twitter-campaign-blame-talks-new-contracts-breaking-according-Government-negotiator.html

55 'Leak reveals junior doctors' plot to "draw out" contract dispute for 18 months and "tie government in knots"', Henry Bodkin and Laura Donnelly, *The Telegraph*, 26.05.16, available at http://www.telegraph.co.uk/news/2016/05/26/leak-reveals-junior-doctors-plot-to-draw-out-bitter-contract-dis/.

56 'Seven-day NHS "impossible under current funding levels"', BBC News, 11.09.16, available at http://www.bbc.co.uk/news/health-37331350

57 'Five ways to improve support for junior doctors', Sir Bruce Keogh, Health Service Journal, 29.07.16, available (behind paywall) at https://www.hsj.co.uk/sectors/acute-care/five-ways-to-improve-support-for-junior-doctors/7009576.article.

58 'GMC concerned about "state of unease" in medical profession', General Medical Council, 27.10.16, available at http://www.gmc-uk.org/news/27482.asp.

59 https://fullfact.org/health/cost-training-doctor/

60 *The History Boys,* Alan Bennett, 2004 (Faber & Faber, London)

61 Sir Robert Francis publishes his report on whistleblowing in the NHS', Freedom To Speak Up, 11.02.15, available at http://webarchive.nationalarchives.gov.uk/20150218150343/https://freedomtospeakup.org.uk/wp-content/uploads/2014/07/Press_release.pdf.

62 'Learning Not Blaming', Department of Health, July 2015, available at https://www.gov.uk/government/uploads/system/uploads/attachment_data/file/445640/Learning_not_blaming_acc.pdf.

63 'NHS patient safety fears as health watchdog scraps staffing guidelines', Denis Campbell, *The Guardian*, 04.06.15, available at https://www.theguardian.com/society/2015/jun/04/nhs-patient-safety-fears-nice-scrap-staffing-level-guidelines-mid-staffs-scandal.

64 'Is the NHS going to break in 2017?' Nick Triggle, BBC News, 29.12.16,
available at http://www.bbc.co.uk/news/health-38323184.

65 '"It was manic": patients describe meltdown at Worcestershire hospital', Steven Morris, *The Guardian*, 06.01.17, available at https://www.theguardian.com/society/2017/jan/06/it-was-manic-patients-describe-meltdown-at-worcestershire-hospital.

66 'NHS faces "humanitarian crisis" as demand rises, British Red Cross warns', Denis Campbell, Steven Morris and Sarah Marsh, *The Guardian*, 06.01.16, available at https://www.theguardian.com/society/2017/jan/06/nhs-faces-humanitarian-crisis-rising-demand-british-red-cross.

67 'Baby boy forced to spend FIVE HOURS in A&E without a bed - THIS is what you're doing to the NHS, Prime Minister.' Ben Rossignton, The Mirror, 13.01.17, available at http://www.mirror.co.uk/news/uk-news/heartbreaking-picture-poorly-boy-2-9612899.

68 'Theresa May rejects claims of "humanitarian crisis" in NHS hospitals', Katie Forster, *The Independent*, 08.01.17, available at http://www.independent.co.uk/news/uk/politics/theresa-may-nhs-humanitarian-crisis-sky-interview-hospitals-red-cross-justine-greening-jeremy-hunt-a7515801.html.

69 'Jeremy Hunt states only "one or two hospitals" are in trouble despite claims of humanitarian crisis', Joe Watts, *The Independent*, 09.01.17, available at http://www.independent.co.uk/news/uk/politics/jeremy-hunt-nhs-one-or-two-hospitals-trouble-halth-secretary-red-cross-humanitarian-crisis-a-and-e-a7516926.html.

70 'NHS accused of trying to spin its way out of trouble', Laura Donnelly, *The Telegraph*, 10.01.17, available at http://www.telegraph.co.uk/news/2017/01/06/crisis-crisis-nhs-accused-trying-spin-way-trouble/.

71 Chris Hopson, Twitter account, 06.01.17, available at https://twitter.com/ChrisCEOHopson/status/817486459968114689.

72 'Leak shows full extent of NHS winter crisis', Faye Kirkland and Nick Triggle, BBC News, 10.01.17, available at http://www.bbc.co.uk/news/health-38570960.

73 'NHS crisis: 40% of hospitals issue alert in first week of new year', Denis Campbell, *The Guardian*, 13.01.17, available at https://www.theguardian.com/society/2017/jan/13/nhs-crisis-hospitals-issue-alert-first-week-january.

74 'Jeremy Hunt: NHS problems completely unacceptable', Matthew Weaver, *The Guardian*, 10.02.17, available at https://www.theguardian.com/politics/2017/feb/10/jeremy-hunt-nhs-problems-completely-unacceptable.

75 '"The worst conditions in memory": NHS doctors describe a week in A&E', Denis Campbell, *The Guardian*, 08.01.17, available at https://www.theguardian.com/society/2017/jan/08/an-absolute-warzone-nhs-doctors-describe-their-week-in-ae.

76 'Theresa May to tell GP surgeries to give patients appointments when they want them or face funding cuts', Peter Dominiczak and Laura Donnelly, *The Telegraph*, 13.01.17, available at http://www.telegraph.co.uk/news/2017/01/13/theresa-may-tell-gp-surgeries-give-patients-appointments-want/.

77 'The doctor WON'T see you now: Mail names and shames some of the thousands of GP surgeries shutting up shop in the afternoon', Sophie Borland and Ben Wilkinson, *Daily Mail*, 11.01.17, available at http://www.dailymail.co.uk/news/article-4111188/The-doctor-WON-T-Mail-names-shames-thousands-GP-surgeries-shutting-shop-afternoon.html.

78 'Prime Minister's Challenge Fund: Improving Access to General Practice First Evaluation Report: October 2015', NHS England, October 2015, available at https://www.england.nhs.uk/wp-content/uploads/2015/10/pmcf-wv-one-eval-report.pdf.

79 'AA Gill: "More life with your kids, more life with your friends, more life spent on earth – but only if you pay"', A.A. Gill, *The Sunday Times*, 11.12.16, available at http://www.thetimes.co.uk/article/more-life-with-your-kids-more-life-with-your-friends-more-life-spent-on-earth-but-only-if-you-pay-d7lwpht3j.

80 'Universal Healthcare without the NHS', Kristian Niemietz, Institute of Economic Affairs, 2016, available at https://iea.org.uk/wp-content/uploads/2016/12/Niemietz-NHS-Interactive.pdf.

81 'NHS: UK now has one of worst healthcare systems in the developed world, according to OECD report', Paul Gallagher, *The Independent*, 04.11.15, available at http://www.independent.co.uk/life-style/health-and-families/health-news/nhs-uk-now-has-one-of-the-worst-healthcare-systems-in-the-developed-world-according-to-oecd-report-a6721401.html.

82 'How does health spending in the UNITED KINGDOM compare?' OECD, 07.07.15, available at https://www.oecd.org/unitedkingdom/Country-Note-UNITED%20KINGDOM-OECD-Health-Statistics-2015.pdf.

83 'How does NHS spending compare with health spending internationally?' John Appleby, The King's Fund, 20.01.16, available at https://www.kingsfund.org.uk/blog/2016/01/how-does-nhs-spending-compare-health-spending-internationally.

84 Jeremy Hunt's speech to Conservative Party Conference 2016, available at http://press.conservatives.com/post/151337276050/hunt-speech-to-conservative-party-conference-2016

85 'Let's argue about statistics', David Oliver, *British Medical Journal*, 21.10.16, available at http://www.bmj.com/content/355/bmj.i5649.full.print

86 *Hope in the Dark,* Rebecca Solnit, 2016 (Canongate, London)

87 'NHS "waving white flag" as it axes 18-week waiting time operation target', Denis Campbell, *The Guardian*, 31.03.17, available at https://www.theguardian.com/society/2017/mar/31/nhs-surgery-target-operations-cancelled-simon-stevens.

88 'Patients fear NHS group may axe cataract surgery', Sarah-Kate Templeton, *The Times*, 09.04.27, available at https://www.thetimes.co.uk/article/patients-fear-nhs-group-may-axe-cataract-surgery-95d8vsj26.